Economic Development in Ceylon

H. N. S. Karunatilake

Economic Development in Ceylon

PRAEGER SPECIAL STUDIES IN INTERNATIONAL ECONOMICS AND DEVELOPMENT

Praeger Publishers New York Washington London

PRAEGER PUBLISHERS
111 Fourth Avenue, New York, N.Y. 10003, U.S.A.
5, Cromwell Place, London S.W.7, England

Published in the United States of America in 1971
by Praeger Publishers, Inc.

Library of Congress Catalog Card Number: 76-156474

Printed in the United States of America

CONTENTS

Chapter | Page

Chapter | Page

Chapter | Page

Chapter | Page

LIST OF TABLES

Table | Page

Table		Page

LIST OF ABBREVIATIONS

CISIR	Ceylon Institute for Scientific and Industrial Research
EPU	European Payments Union
FAO	Food and Agricultural Organization
FEEC	Foreign Exchange Entitlement Certificate
GNP	Gross National Product
GPS	Guaranteed Price Scheme
IBRD	International Bank for Reconstruction and Development
ILO	International Labor Organization
IMF	International Monetary Fund
MEP	Mahajana Eksath Peramuna (The United People's Party)
OGL	Open General License
PL	Public Law
TRI	Tea Research Institute
UNCTAD	United Nations Conference on Trade and Development
UNP	United National Party
UNTAA	United Nations Technical Assistance Administration

INTRODUCTION

Ceylon has a long recorded history which probably extends over two thousand years. Available historical records show that the economy was able to sustain a comparatively large population,* and the mainstay of the system was agriculture with paddy as the predominant crop. The ruins of extensive irrigation works scattered over one-third of the island bear evidence to this fact. The emphasis was on subsistence with little or no external trade.

More recent records of the economy extend over a period of approximately 400 years, when the emphasis was on commercial crops. The Portuguese and Dutch secured an economic foothold in the island in order to procure commercial crops such as cinnamon and other spices. The strategic location of the island appeared to be a secondary consideration.

Economic advancement in the modern sense started some forty years after the British occupation of the island in 1802. From around 1840 onward, there is evidence of fairly sustained economic growth in the plantation sector of the economy. The subsistence sector, or the rural economy, which was primarily concerned with the production of paddy and a few other domestic agricultural crops, continued to co-exist with the plantations. But with the rapid development of the plantations the domestic agricultural economy declined rapidly. This trend appears to have begun even before 1802. Some sixty years after the arrival of the British, attempts were made on a limited scale to rehabilitate the rural economy by restoring ancient irrigation works.

---

*Estimates in the historical chronicles vary from five million to more than 20 million. After the 10th century, repeated wars and malaria are said to have destroyed the greater part of the population.

The impact of this was marginal because rural rehabilitation required much more than mere attention to the basic infrastructure. The social repercussions of the growth of the plantation economy were significant. But despite this, the rural peasant, even with his limited means, was able to provide for his daily sustenance. Through exports, the country was able to earn sufficient foreign exchange to procure all essential imports, even rice, in which the country had been self-sufficient before 1800.

Since the monetary mechanism prevailing before 1950--the Currency Board system--automatically insured equilibrium in the balance of payments, the administration found it relatively easy to maintain a satisfactory level of imports of consumer goods for the rapidly expanding population. There was no shortage of foreign exchange because the Currency Board system insured that import capacity did not exceed available foreign exchange reserves.

A fundamental characteristic of the economic structure of Ceylon is the existence of a typical dual economy. This was created by the rapid progress of the plantations. The traditional and modern sectors that constitute the dual economy have co-existed for more than 100 years in virtual isolation. The rate of advancement evidenced in the plantation economy was totally lacking in the rural economy. One reason for this was the virtual isolation of the plantations from the villages. The organization of the plantation economy was such that the two sectors continued to function independently. In fact, there was a fundamental cleavage between them. The plantations were motivated by commercial profit and maximizing productivity in terms of investment. The rural sector was based on subsistence agriculture with self-sustenance as the prime motivation. The only relationship that would have developed in time between the two sectors would have been the employment of domestic labor; but because of the traditional dislike for manual work, the local population was unwilling to work on plantations and labor had to be imported from India.

The development of the plantations, at least in

the period 1850 to 1940, worsened the condition of the peasantry. World War II helped to some extent to open up new avenues of temporary employment for the peasantry and provided essential foodstuffs on subsidy. The first efforts to bridge the cleavage between the traditional and modern sectors were made in the late 1940's with the introduction of the social service schemes, beginning with education and free medical aid. These free services, for which the government incurred progressively increasing expenditure, has helped to improve considerably the well-being of the rural population. Despite this, until the early 1960's, differences in income levels between the urban rural sectors were reduced only to a limited extent because of low agricultural productivity and the lack of adequate employment opportunities. At the same time, education and free services extended to the villager has stimulated an influx into urban areas, bringing with it pressure on housing and other amenities. This trend is due to the fact that employment opportunities are available mostly in the towns. In rural areas, there is a considerable amount of self-employment, but much of it is seasonal.

Economic development today is heavily weighted towards modernizing the traditional sector, not only because there is an economic gap but also a social one. For social barriers to disappear, the older peasant class with traditional ideas must give way to the younger generation who have profited by free education and welfare schemes. The technological differences are being eliminated gradually because agricultural policies during the last ten years have been directed at improving the techniques of cultivation and have encouraged the use of better inputs. Although progress has not been spectacular, an appreciable impact has been made.

This study helps to highlight the difficulties that a country committed to a high level of consumption expenditure has to face in its efforts to achieve a higher rate of economic growth. An important issue is to what extent a relatively poor country could, in the initial stages of economic development, afford to allocate resources for consumption and social services in preference to a high rate of capital formation. Although a high level of expenditure on consumption and social services in countries with a very low level of savings and capital formation cannot be justified economically, in the long run investment in education could provide dividends. In this respect Ceylon is better equipped than most other developing countries. There is no dearth of educated people, and a variety of skills is freely available. Furthermore, because of improved standards of nutrition and better health services, the population as a whole, given the opportunity, could function far more effectively as productive units than those in other developing countries.

Since the end of the Korean War boom, a factor that has tended to retard economic growth has been the comparatively high level of consumption expenditure by government and the private sector. The Korean boom in fact brought about a false sense of security, and it gave hopes that further favorable price increases for raw materials could be expected in the future. Other than the tea boom of 1955, no such favorable price movements occured during the two decades under review. The successive plans that were prepared could not be implemented because of balance of payments difficulties after 1958. Furthermore, it was felt that the rest of the economy, excluding the plantation sector, could wait until plan documents were ready. No attempts were made in the meantime to have a coordinated project by project program until the plans were ready. Thus Ceylon's attempts to plan long-term economic development ended in dismal failure.

Despite all this, considerable progress was made in the 1960's in industrialization. This was achieved by restrictions applied on imports of manufactured goods when the balance of payments situation in the early 1960's was acute. The program of industrialization in the country began around 1960; and substantial results were observed within five years, but not without heavy social and economic costs, which have now turned out to be problems of some magnitude. These aspects include the heavy dependence on imported raw materials, the use of appropriate technologies, and the location of industries. The policies after 1964 to step up agricultural output and the attendant results have been one of the most noteworhty features in the country's economic development. The increase in production, particularly of paddy, the decrease in rice imports, and the ability to reach self-sufficiency in a few subsidiary products have had far reaching social consequences. This is reflected in progressively better standards-of-living conditions in the rural areas. It has also been one of the most effective means of redistributing wealth in the country.

Economic Development in Ceylon

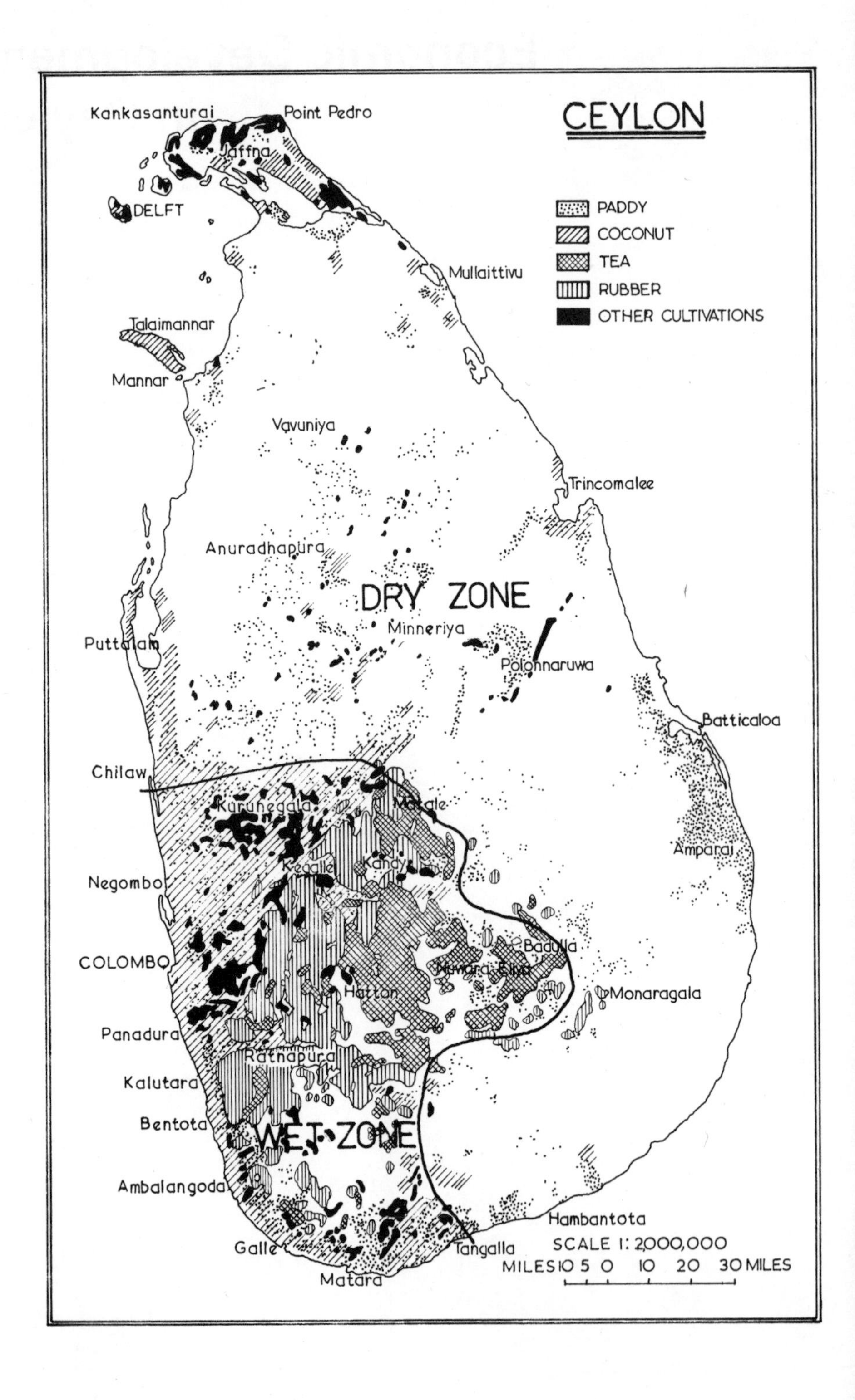

CEYLON
PADDY
COCONUT
TEA
RUBBER
OTHER CULTIVATIONS
Kankasanturai
Point Pedro
Jaffna
DELFT
Mullaittivu
Talaimannar
Mannar
Vavuniya
Trincomalee
Anuradhapura
DRY ZONE
Minneriya
Puttalam
Polonnaruwa
Batticaloa
Chilaw
Kurunegala
Matale
Amparai
Negombo
Kegalle
Kandy
Badulla
COLOMBO
Nuwara Eliya
Hatton
Monaragala
Panadura
Ratnapura
Kalutara
Bentota
WET ZONE
Ambalangoda
Hambantota
SCALE 1: 2,000,000
Galle
Tangalla
MILES 10 5 0 10 20 30 MILES
Matara

CHAPTER 1

THE ECONOMY BEFORE INDEPENDENCE

Structurally the economy of Ceylon at the time of its independence in 1948 hardly differed from that of 1925 or 1930. In fact, during the first five decades of this century, the principal source of economic activity was the plantations and to a lesser extent subsistence agriculture. For the economic community as a whole, agriculture, both plantation and subsistence, were the main sources of livelihood. However, national income estimates show that even though there was little or no diversification before 1950, there were appreciable gains in productivity. The World Bank Mission in 1952 reviewed the progress achieved in the following terms, "In the past 75 years the population of Ceylon has trebled. Yet typical living standards, while low in comparison with the West, have been maintained and almost certainly improved; at present they are among the highest in Southern Asia. This advancement of levels of national well-being has been achieved by a virtual revolution in Ceylon's agriculture over the past century, accompanied by limited industrialization. The revolution has lain in organized large-scale production and processing of agricultural commodities for export--specifically tea, rubber and coconut products."[1]

The occupational grouping of gainfully occupied workers at the 1946 census showed that Ceylon's population was predominantly rural and agriculture was the main occupation (51.3 per cent). The services sector before 1945 was largely associated with the plantations.

NATIONAL INCOME

Before 1940, official estimates of Ceylon's gross national product were inexact because reliable statistical information was not readily available. Most of these earlier calculations were made on rough estimates, only slightly better than intelligent guesses. The first attempt to prepare a systematic statement of national income was made in 1947 by Dr. Das Gupta, who published a set of estimates for the years 1937, 1938, 1942, and 1944 in an appendix to the report of the Commission on Social Services.[2] In 1949, the Director of Census and Statistics published for the first time a set of official estimates of national income in Ceylon.[3]

Between 1937 and 1947, national income nearly trebled, from $101.5 million to $291.8 million. Tea was the biggest crop and increasingly the largest contributor to national income, accounting for nearly 30 per cent in 1947. The second important crop was coconut, which contributed about 20 per cent to national income, of which domestic consumption represented about 35 to 40 per cent of total production. Rubber, as an export crop, was next in importance, and the increase in output in this ten-year period was almost 90 percent. Rice, which is the predominant crop of the rural economy, fluctuated more markedly than the three main commercial crops. Total production in 1937 was estimated at $5.2 million, whereas in 1943 there was a very sharp increase, more than threefold, to $16.1 million. In 1944, there was a slight decline and in 1947 there was an increase when the crop was estimated at $14.3 million. (These estimates of rice production are not very accurate because attempts were not made in these years to estimate production scientifically.) This increase was due partly to the inducements to step up domestic production during the war period when rationing and shortages emerged.

National income estimates give some indication of the relative importance of other sectors in the economy. The total output of other food crops rose from $1.8 million in 1937 to $5.9 million in 1947. These consist mostly of fruits, vegetables, and other minor cereals like gingelly, sorghum, and condiments used in the preparation of food. Ceylon has traditionally consumed a considerable amount of subsidiary foodstuffs such as onions, chillies, potatoes; and the very small level of domestic production of these commodities shows that the country has had to depend to a very large extent on imports. The other products mentioned in the estimates are tobacco, livestock, and fish that were produced purely for domestic consumption. But other than for fresh milk and beef, the country continued to depend on imports of good tobacco, a very large quantity of fish both in dried and canned form, and milk products.

Particularly after 1942, there was a fair increase in the contribution of industry to the national product. Total output from industry in 1937 was $8.9 million, $18.3 million in 1942, and $19.5 million in 1947. This increase resulted from the establishment of a series of factories by government to produce a few basic consumer goods which could not be imported in the war years.

In 1937, income arising from trade, which is the principal service industry, was about one-third the total income from the production of tea and about one-fourth in 1947. Fluctuations in income have been closely associated with price movements of the main exports and levels of productivity in these industries. In relation to trade, professional earnings have not shown significant increases. The latter was $2.2 million in 1937, and at $3.7 million in 1947 it was less than double. This is largely because the professional services were not directly influenced by the level of activity in the export sector. There was also greater stability because incomes were derived more or less on a fixed basis, other than in a few professions like law, where remuneration was determined independently. In the other major professions, such as medicine, engineering, and the technical services, the principal source of employment was government service where fixed salaries were paid.

The other items in the national income estimates were domestic services, land and buildings, central and local government, and military expenditure. The only significant increase here was in military expenditure, from $21.8 million in 1942 to $44.4 million in 1943 to $73.1 million in 1944, decreasing to $4.2 million in 1947. In 1944 alone, military expenditure represented more than 30 per cent of the income derived.

The first attempt to produce a set of statistically correct national income estimates was made by the Central Bank. The bank prepared figures for the years 1949 and 1950, and the gross national product was estimated at $748.2 million and $759.7 million, respectively.[4] These estimates have shown that Das Gupta's estimates were not very reliable because they were based on income derived from productive activity. For instance, whereas Das Gupta stated that income derived from production of rice was $14.3 million in 1947, the Central Bank estimated the total value of rice produced and consumed at $25.9 million, reflecting a difference of almost 70 per cent. Also under estimated by Das Gupta is the total value of personal services amounting to $3.4 million for 1947 whereas in the Central Bank estimates the figure was $41.3 million.

THE PLANTATIONS

In this chapter, the principal sectors of the economy will be outlined, beginning with the plantations and followed by the rural sector. The plantations were owned mostly by overseas investors or by large companies that were either registered in Ceylon as rupee companies or abroad as sterling companies. Before 1950, economic activity was confined largely to the private sector. Apart from the few wartime factories producing consumer goods and a few colonization schemes, there was little or no state participation in industry or agriculture. About 70 per cent of the tea estates were owned by expatriates, while the Ceylonese ownership of rubber was very much greater. Of the three major crops, the largest Ceylonese ownership was in coconut, where about 90 per cent of coconut lands was owned by citizens of the country.

A considerable amount of literature has appeared over the years on the plantation economy, particularly on the tea industry. Most of it has been descriptive travelogues; very few writers have attempted to examine the economic aspects of planatation agriculture. Data on the rubber industry are contained in official documents, and in the bulletins of the Rubber Research Institute. There is even less information on the coconut industry, other than those publications put out periodically by the Coconut Research Institute that deal mainly with methods of cultivation and control of disease. A discussion of these three major crops would naturally emphasize their contributions to GNP, increase in productivity over the years, volume of employment generated, and the extent to which their interdependence with the other sectors of the economy have provided income and employment in transport, finance, and banking.

The developed sector of economy, the plantations, was fairly closely linked to the urban economy. The urban economy was mostly concerned with services and included the general administrative system of the country, the banking and financial institutions, the agency houses, retail and wholesale houses, and the transport organization. The services sector provided employment to as many if not more than the number of people who were employed in the plantations in the 1930's and 1940's. There were some 800,000 employees in the plantations and about 1 million associated with services in the urban and rural areas. The development of the service industries in the period before 1948 has been due almost entirely to the progressive expansion of plantations.

Similarly, the development of roads and railways has been due entirely to the opening up of land under tea and rubber at mid and at higher elevations. Ceylon has all along had an excellent network of roads, and these roads were constructed with a view to developing the new lands earmarked for tea and rubber in the hill country and to establish a sound system of communications between the interior and the principal towns, notably Colombo and Kandy. In the same way, the development of the postal and telegraph systems was also associated with the need to ensure better communications with the plantation economy and for the speedy transaction of business and trade.

THE MAIN EXPORT CROPS

With the end of the coffee era in the 1870's, tea gradually assumed importance as the main hill country crop. Although tea has covered an area which is only slightly less than that under rubber, it has always been the largest and the most productive commercial crop. The acreage under tea has not increased substantially over the last thirty years. The Census Report of 1946 gave the extent as 456,398 acres, and two-thirds of this acreage was in the Kandy, Nuwara Eliya, and Badulla districts. The location of the crop is determined purely by elevation and climatic conditions to which the crop displays a remarkable sensitivity. Because to some extent elevation affects quality, the distinction is always made between low grown, mid-grown, and high-grown tea; this last category is usually grown at elevations above 4,000 feet.

Tea was pioneered by foreign capital and foreign private enterprise. Before 1950, about 60 per cent or one-fourth of the total acreage under tea was owned by Rupee companies, or companies registered under the Company Law in Ceylon. Sterling companies or companies registered in the United Kingdom, controlled the largest number of estates of over 500 acres, which produced the very best tea. These estates have been the most economically productive units and may be classified as among the best run agricultural properties in the world.

From the beginning, tea has been a labor intensive crop. Cultivation of tea lands has been done by hired labor, mainly of Indian origin, except in the case of small holdings of less than 10 acres, where the work is undertaken by the families of the proprietors. The management of the bulk of the estates was in the hands of expatriate superintendents and other senior staff while the field staff was almost wholly of Ceylonese or Indian origin. Tea is relatively a more capital intensive product than rubber or coconut because of the heavy overheads in factory equipment and the high cost of maintenance.

Until the late 1950's, no government assistance was necessary because of the excellent management of estates, particularly those owned by companies which were able to produce an adequate surplus not only to pay attractive dividends but also to look after and maintain the industry. It was mostly the small estates owned by individual proprietors that required government assistance because of their relatively lower profitability; hence, the tea subsidy scheme was introduced in 1959.

The Tea Research Institute has played a major part in the remarkable progress achieved by the industry in the 1930's and 1940's. In matters relating to the control of disease and pests, and in producing high yielding planting material, its work has been invaluable. This institute has been maintained and financially supported by the industry itself.

Rubber was introduced in the 1880's, and the first exports were made in 1900 when a pound brought $0.26. The acreage under rubber at this time was only 1,750. With increasing demand, the price of rubber rose to $0.86 in 1901, and the acreage under cultivation also rose progressively to 659,909 by 1946. The largest rubber-growing area forms a triangle bounded by Kalutara, Ratnapura, and Colombo; and the crop is confined to elevations of 200 to 1500 feet. Exports had risen from 50,000 tons in 1932 to 100,000 tons in 1946. The most interesting economic aspect of rubber has been the remarkable variation in price both before 1950 and thereafter. The price of rubber fell sharply during the great depression. In 1932, the average price was $0.02, whereas in the Korean boom in 1951 the average price was $0.36.

The Ceylon Rubber Commission of 1947 reported that more than 70 per cent of the rubber trees were well over thirty-five years-old; and that during the war years many trees had been slaughter-tapped, reducing their life span considerably. Trees were also stricken with disease, so that yields dropped from an average of 350 pounds to 150 pounds per acre.*

The replanting program was urged by D. S. Senanayake, Minister of Agriculture and Lands, as early as 1938, but very little was done thereafter. By the end of 1940, the replanting program had progressed far in several other countries. Malaya had replanted 12 per cent and French Indochina 40 per cent, whereas Ceylon by 1946 had replanted only 10 per cent. The Rubber Commission also reported that rubber replanted in the period 1940-46 had not been properly done and was in their opinion "utterly useless and many areas have reverted to jungle." The commission, furthermore, studied the problems of the industry in the early post-war period when prices had fallen to low levels; and in addition to recommending a very high rate of replanting, it also examined the possibilities of growing alternative crops on rubber lands.

Coconut occupies the largest land area (920,942 acres in 1946, excluding town and village gardens) of the three major plantation crops, covering almost the combined acreages of tea and rubber. Today the acreage has not changed substantially. Most plantations are along the western seaboard stretching from

---

*For an account of the rubber industry before 1950, see Report of the Commission on the Rubber Industry in Ceylon. Sessional Paper. No. 18 of 1947 (Colombo: Ceylon Government Press).

Puttalam in the northwest to Matara in the south and a few small tracts are in the Trincomalee and Batticaloa districts. The heart of the coconut industry is in Kurunegala, which is the eastern corner of the triangle extending from Colombo to Puttalam. About 70 per cent of the holdings are very small, being less than 20 acres in extent. About 90 per cent of the estates belonged to Ceylonese, and only a very few of these were public companies. The coconut industry is not as well organized as the tea and rubber industries and requires relatively less labor, other than seasonally when the nuts are picked. To the Ceylonese investor, coconut has traditionally been a sound investment because it guarantees a more stable income; and the products of the palm could be put to multifarious uses, each with its own economic value.[5]

As mentioned earlier, coconut plantations have given rise to many other industries. Prior to 1948, more than 50 per cent of all manufacturing and processing industry in Ceylon depended on raw materials from the coconut palm. Coconut oil and desiccated mills use copra or the dried kernel of the nut while fiber mills have depended on the fiber from protective covering of the nut. Further processing of fiber resulted in industries making coir yarn, rope, mats, brooms, and brushes. These have provided a livelihood to more persons than those directly employed on the estates.

ESTATE LABOR AND MANAGEMENT

Since tea and rubber were labor intensive products, the plantations depended heavily on labor. Table 1 gives the estate population by race.

The bulk of the working population on the plantations consisted of expatriate workers of whom Indian Tamils predominated while Ceylonese labor averaged about 10 to 12 per cent in the pre-war years. The table includes the village population resident in the immediate vicinity of the estates. It probably also includes the relatively small nonresident Sinhalese population. In most instances the Sinhalese villager worked only part time on the plantations because agriculture, which was his main source of income, was highly seasonal.

TABLE 1

Estate Population by Race

	1921	1931	1946
Low country Sinhalese	37,111	50,490	79,946
Kandyan Sinhalese	17,468	25,296	53,060
Ceylon Tamils	2,716	5,541	33,339
Ceylon Moors	2,300	2,831	5,824
Malays	1,483	1,988	1,451
Burghers and Eurasians	2,039	2,031	1,861
Total Ceylonese	63,117	88,177	175,435
Indian Tamils	493,944	692,540	655,854
Indian Moors	4,214	4,665	4,258
Europeans	2,670	2,814	1,027
Others	-	1,738	4,782
Total Non-Ceylonese	500,828	701,757	675,920
Grand Total	563,945	789,934	851,359

Source: Census Report of Ceylon, 1946

The viability of the plantation economy depended mainly on the availability of plenty of cheap labor from South India, and in 1870 immigrant labor started arriving in the island. The bulk of the immigrant labor came from the poorest and desert-like regions of South India. They were used to hard living and were able to subsist on a very small income. Sinhalese labor was unaccustomed to the type of work entrusted to Indian labor. Work on a tea plantation normally begins around 6 A.M. and goes on uninterrupted despite rain or spells of chilly weather, until late afternoon. It also involved working on steep and rocky inclines, where the tea plant flourished. The ability to get labor on low wages helped the industry to advance rapidly and to cushion it when there were sharp fluctuations in world market prices.

The overall management of the tea and rubber estates was in the hands of specialized firms managed by Englishmen who had gradually secured extensive economic interests in the island. Even to this day, the organization of plantation enterprise in Ceylon rests very largely on the managing agency system. The initial popularity of the agency system in many colonial territories may be attributed to the unfamiliar conditions surrounding most colonial ventures and the tendency for the overseas investor to be separated from the actual location of the enterprise. The latter fact gave opportunities for mismanagement and fraud, and to overcome this a reputable institution, operating locally, overlooked the enterprise on behalf of the proprietors living abroad.

The operational expenses of most new plantations, at first in coffee and later on in tea, formed a significant charge on the funds of managing agency houses; they in turn obtained money from the banks in the form of block advances. In financing these ventures, the banks presumably went beyond the strict areas of banking business, but the sound knowledge of management that the agency houses enjoyed helped to overcome attendant risks. The policy of giving advances to estates was attractive for its own sake as well as for the business of the agency houses as a price for the financial support it gave the estates. The managing agencies have played a crucial role in meeting the working expenses of estates. But with the further development of land under tea and rubber, this tended to decline, because tea and rubber companies were able to amass substantial internal resources from which they were able to meet their regular working expenditure and also to finance extensions, renewals, and repairs.

Estate management also ensured for agency houses

a regular import business in a wide range of plantation requirements such as fertilizers, tea chests, tea packing accessories, agricultural tools, and building materials. Some of their import business resulted from activities that were not connected directly with the management of plantations, such as ships, stores, and equipment for the steamers that called at the ports. Then again, the general import of consumer goods was undertaken by them on behalf of local dealers in return for commissions based on the value of requisitions.

The plantations have always remained excellent examples of successful large-scale capitalist enterprise in Ceylon. Even staunch critics of free enterprise have admitted that this form of organization has promoted uninterrupted progress in the plantation economy. The bulk of the capital for the development of the plantations was found locally. Mainly for tea and to a lesser extent for rubber, land was available on long lease from government or bought outright at a very nominal cost. Plenty of immigrant labor was available on low wages, and only minimum requirements of clothing and foodstuffs had to be imported. Planting material was easily procured from estates already established, and recurring costs were incurred in maintaining the plantations in good condition. Recurrent costs were highest in tea, where the estates had to be maintained with meticulous care. The land had to be regularly weeded and ridged to prevent erosion, and new plantations involved regular picking to encourage a maximum flush of tender shoots and periodic pruning to keep tree growth under control. All this attention required only domestic inputs. Before the 1940's, much of the manure used in tea estates was organic, and limited quantities of pesticides were used. However, the construction of factory buildings for processing or manufacturing tea required a capital investment with a relatively high import content.

Funds for investment were raised partly by issuing shares and partly obtained from commercial banks, where agency houses acted as the intermediaries. The Sterling companies issued shares in the London market, and the bulk of these were purchased by investors abroad. A few of the tea companies were registered as rupee companies where shares were offered in the local share market. Further development was possible by utilizing reserves for capital work. The working capital procured from the banking system, through the agency houses, was used mainly to buy stores, foodstuffs, and to pay wages.

The tea industry has enjoyed a considerably greater amount of self-financing than the rubber and coconut industries because the potential for larger estates to build up reserves has always been present on account of profitability resulting from excellent management and the relatively low incidence of taxation in the pre-1950 period.

TRADE

Ninety per cent of Ceylon's exports were plantation products, and the most important were tea, rubber, and coconut. Cocoa was fourth in importance. (There were only a few large cocoa estates; the bulk was in small holdings. This crop was normally cultivated with either tea or rubber.) Next came cinnamon, cardamoms, and citronella, which consisted primarily of small holdings; the largest single extent did not exceed fifty acres. The only mineral that was exported in quantity was graphite. The values and quantities of exports in the years 1938 and 1948 are given in the Tables 2 and 3.

Between 1936 and 1948, although export values had increased, there was no great variation in the quantities produced and exported, except in the case of rubber. The amount exported could be taken as a satisfactory index of what was produced in the country because home consumption of even tea and coconut was only a fraction of what was produced.

The main imports consisted of three major groups--food, drink, and tobacco; raw materials; and manufactured articles. Import values of these items are given in Table 4.

TABLE 2

Value of Exports of Estate Products
(In millions of dollars)

	1938	1948
Tea	29.0	99.2
Rubber	7.6	24.1
Coconut Products	5.8	27.9
Cocoa	0.2	1.2
Cardamoms	0.1	0.2
Cinnamon Products	0.3	0.6
Citronella Oil	0.2	0.6
Arecanuts	-	0.7
Total	43.2	154.7

Source: Ceylon Blue Books and Statistical Abstracts of Ceylon.

TABLE 3

Quantities of Estate Products Exported
(In thousands)

	1938	1948
Tea (lb.)	235,739	296,000
Rubber (lb.)	114,624	207,287
Coconut Products		
Poonac (cwt.)	733	168
Fresh nuts (no.)	15,955	9,387
Dessicated (cwt.)	594	236
Fiber (cwt.)	732	654
Copra (cwt.)	1,504	1,089
Oil (cwt.)	1,508	1,515
Coir (cwt.)	92	51
Cocoa (cwt.)	72	46
Cardamoms (cwt.)	4	2
Cinnamon (cwt.)	47	37
Cinnamon Oil (oz.)	2,786	1,484
Citronella Oil (lb.)	1,604	1,568
Arecanuts (cwt.)	84	100

Source: Ceylon Blue Books and Statistical Abstracts of Ceylon.

TABLE 4

Value of Imports
(In dollars)

	1938	1948
Food, drink, and tobacco	18,033,270	87,267,890
Raw materials	5,682,352	17,917,310
Manufactured articles	15,826,890	60,289,070
Animals not for food	42,353	134,790
Total	39,584,865	165,609,060

Source: Ceylon Blue Books and Statistical Abstracts of Ceylon.

THE RURAL ECONOMY

Geographically there is no distinction between the estate or the plantation sector and the village economy, for rural Ceylon includes the estates.[6] Estates are typically nonurban both in character and location. They have continued to exist, sometimes for more than a century, without influencing the original settlers of these lands, the village peasants.

Although the progress of the plantation economy has been recorded for more than a century, hardly any information is available on peasant agriculture from 1850 onwards. Even government publications made only casual references to this sector of the economy on which more than one half of the country's population depended.* The census of 1946 disclosed

---

*The only useful records on the village economy were economic surveys in the period 1936 to 1948 of selected villages in the districts of Puttalam, Chilaw, Kurunegala, Kalutara, Galle, Matara, and

that 71.9 per cent of the population lived in the rural sector, 15.3 per cent in the urban sector, and 12.8 per cent in the estate sector. Even in the most urbanized district of Colombo, 58.5 per cent of the population belonged to the rural sector and 40.7 per cent to the urban sector. Assuming the 1946 pattern of distribution, out of the total estimated mid-year population of 7,550,000 as many as 5,428,450 belonged to the rural sector.

Although peasant agriculture did not improve significantly, there were factors which helped its survival not so much in the plantation districts but in other areas. From the mid-19th century, incentives were provided in the dry zones to sustain activity by the provision of irrigation facilities and alienation of land to the peasant. In the estate sector, however, many of the tea and rubber plantations encroached into the surrounding village areas, taking away a good part of the land that could have been used for village expansion. As a result, the peasant population was squeezed into the hospitable low-lying basins and river valleys, which were not very suitable for commercial crops such as tea and rubber. In this light, it is perhaps true that the development of the estate economy put peasants, particularly those in the hill country, into great hardship.

Recently some writers have taken the position that the expansion of estates was not a hinderance.[7] As against this, a study of income levels and other quantitative indicators of well-being of the peasant class tends to show that the growth of the plantation economy gave very few immediate benefits to the peasant class. The development of plantations offered limited opportunities of employment for peasants as they had to compete with very cheap and hardworking immigrant labor from India. Only seventy-five

---

Hambantota. Also see Preliminary Report on the Economic Survey of Rural Ceylon. Sessional Paper. No. 11 of 1951 (Colombo: Department of Census and Statistics).

years after the first plantations had been opened did Ceylonese peasants have the opportunity to seek employment on estates; and in the 1930's about 85,000 Ceylonese, or 12 per cent of the labor force, were estimated to be working on estates.

The typical village economy land holding was recorded in the Census Report of 1946 under town and village gardens. A town or village garden was defined as a holding of one acre or less carrying some form of cultivation and usually forming the compound of a dwelling house. There were 496,513 such units, chiefly in the Colombo and Jaffna districts.

Village gardens in the wet zone carried a mixed cultivation of jak, breadfruit, coconut, arecanut, kitul palms, mangoes, plantains, limes, etc. In the Jaffna Peninsula, cultivation consisted of tobacco, vegetables, dry grains, mangoes, and palmyra palms. In 1938, half the cultivators of paddy had less than one acre, and half the cultivators of coconut land had less than three acres. This minute subdivision of land, due to the system of inheritance, is a major problem in the wet zone, the more arable region of the country. The greater part of the population is concentrated in the wet zone, which occupies about one-third of the island. (Ceylon has been climatically divided into the wet zone and the dry zone, and topographically into the low country, meaning the plains, and the hill country, the highlands.)

Typical village garden were located between the large estates in the hill country and consisted mostly of paddy on the low-lying tracts and a few crops such as coconut and arecanut on the highland. The type of holding was determined by the general outlook of the peasant who was primarily concerned with self-sufficiency rather than commercial gain. Noncommercialization was due partly to backward technology used in cultivation and due partly to the limited resources, mainly land, that were available to the peasant.

The peasant was entrapped in a vicious circle because his landholding was small and he could not raise capital. This in turn kept his income at an apallingly low level. Furthermore, money was not easily obtained unless, of course, high rates of interest were paid. Until recently, loans were available at minimum rates usually exceeding 100 per cent. To service loans of this kind, the level of productivity had to be very high. Unless advanced technology and superior inputs were used, it would be extremely difficult for a peasant to produce a marketable surplus on an extent of land which did not even amount to half an acre.

Climatically, too, conditions were not conducive to hard work. In the wet zone, owing to the high incidence of rainfall and natural richness of soil, two seasonal crops of rice were easily obtained. As subsistence was the main consideration, the peasant was able to secure his requirements with a minimum effort. The system of tenure under which paddy lands were held was closely linked to productivity. Sixty per cent or 469,701 units of holdings were owned by cultivators, out of a total 771,908 units. The number of holdings under tattumaru ownership, where farmers take turns in cultivating the same plot, was 52,190 or 6.8 per cent, and lease holdings aggregated 28,069 or 3.6 per cent. And tenancies, where the cultivator was required to give a share of the crop to the landlord, was 199,934 or 25.9 per cent.

In 1946, the total area of asweddumized (a relatively new term meaning the preparation and sowing of land with paddy) paddy land was 899,969 acres, and the area under cultivation in the Maha season 1945-46 was only 607,510 acres.* Of the total under cultivation, large extents were found in Colombo

---

*Two paddy crops were obtained every year. The Maha, or the great crop, was cultivated from October to February; and the Yala, or lesser crop, from May to September. In the dry zone, where irrigation facilities are not available, only the Maha crop is possible.

(7.8 per cent), Jaffna (6.4 per cent), Batticaloa (6.8 per cent), Kurunegala (17.4 per cent), Matara (6.5 per cent), and Anuradhapura (8.8 per cent). The largest number of holdings of less than one acre was found in the Colombo district (68.0 per cent), Kandy (82.1 per cent), Matale (85.3 per cent), and Nuwara Eliya (75.4 per cent).

In most areas, other than those where absentee landlords predominate, paddy cultivation is strictly a family enterprise where all members share the tasks--tilling, ploughing, leveling, sowing, weeding, transplanting, harvesting, and threshing. During harvesting, however, outside labor is engaged because the paddy has to be taken off the field quickly before spoilage sets in. Payment for hired labor in the pre-war period was often in kind. Cultivation of land and irrigation works were heavily dependent on rainfall. Prolonged drought affected the main supply reservoirs creating water shortages at critical periods in the life cycle of the paddy plant. Ploughing was done by draft cattle, mostly buffaloes. Sowing, weeding, and transplanting were manual operations. Little effort was made by the government to improve the quality of seeds, to encourage the use of artificial fertilizer, pesticides, and to control weeds. Even where irrigation facilities were provided, yields have been very low, showing that high yields in paddy depend not only on water but on several other factors. Only about one-fourth of the paddy land had been provided with water in the period before 1947.

Although paddy is the predominant crop, the wet zone village economy differs somewhat from the dry zone. Chena cultivation was adopted by peasants in the dry zone jungles. This form of agriculture has been known as slash and burn cultivation, where the land rather than the crop is periodically rotated. There were 91,996 such plots in 1946 distributed in the Kandyan districts, notably Kurunegala, Ratnapura, Kandy, Badulla, Anuradhapura, Nuwara Eliya, and Matale. The aggregate acreage covered by chena land was about 221,395, of which only some 46,322 acres were found cultivated when the census was taken.

This land had crown title and did not belong to the peasant. But no ground rent was paid to the government. The cultivator usually had a permanent abode elsewhere.

From an economic standpoint, the objective of the peasant was to secure a good crop with minimum outlay. This was possible by using the rich soil that resulted from the cutting and burning of vegetation. These lands were generally fed by seasonal rainfall from October to April. Chena crops included kurakkan, maize, millets, pulses, gingelly, chillies, and vegetables. The actual choice depended on the location of the chena. Only limited extents of chena cultivation were found in the wet zone hill-country jungles and scrubland. No systematic studies have been made of chena cultivation but, it is observed that it is the mainstay of the poor peasant class in the dry zone.

Poverty and depressing conditions that exist in the villages are attributable to the lack of development of small industries. A few cottage industries provided sustenance to a part of the agricultural population, but they were in a relatively poor state of development up to 1938. Traditional cottage industries in the lowlands included spinning and weaving, pottery, metal work, lace making, curio making, manufacture of mats, baskets, brushes, and brooms, and coir spinning; they were confined to particular social groups where skills were handed down through generations. In the hill country, cottage industries consisted of brassware, lacquer work, woodwork, mat weaving, and curios, which were highly seasonal because of the lack of a steady market. Most often, cultivators were not always willing to take to craftsmanship because of the social stigma attached to certain trades. Certain trades were confined to different castes. A person belonging to a higher caste would not undertake a craft or vocation of those who were supposedly in a lower caste. Because of this there was considerable specialization, and it was not always easy for the peasant to take to more than one trade in order to better his living conditions.

Middlemen play a predominant role in the village economy. If it is not the itinerant merchant, the village boutique keeper acts as both middleman and creditor. The villager hands his produce to the boutique keeper who pays him in kind; cash does not enter into the transaction. The price for the villager's produce is low while that of the goods sold is high. Thus the intermediary or middleman makes a double profit. This system is prevalent because of unsatisfactory marketing arrangements for rural agricultural produce. The itinerant trader goes to houses, fields, and chenas to collect the produce regularly. Another point of contact is the weekly village fair, where the trader is able to make bulk purchases at relatively low prices.

The homestead of the peasant changed very little between 1930 and 1950. A typical house was constructed with wattle and daub, and roof-thatched with either paddy straw or dried leaves of the coconut palm. Such a house is the most important indicator of prosperity in the paddy growing regions. In the 1960's, cottages built of brick, mortar, and tiled roofs have gradually taken the place of wattle and daub houses.* Where chena cultivation exists, homesteads have not shown any significant change. Houses are of a make-shift type, often supported on a few poles carrying a thatched roof. In colonization schemes, however, the government has ensured that houses are built in accordance with a type plan.

As only about one-half of the village population depends on paddy, the rest who cultivate noncommercial crops, such as vegetables, suffer much hardship because of sharp fluctuations in prices over relatively short periods of time. A few who cultivate commercial crops such as tobacco, pepper, cardamoms, potatoes, onions, and chillies are fairly prosperous like their paddy growing counterparts.

---

*Today of a population of about 12 million, about 9 million are still resident in the villages; and from the standpoint of basic housing amenities, they are in considerable want.

There is little information available on the nature and the extent of economic links between the more advanced and the traditional sectors of the economy. It can be construed that before 1939 these links were not only weak but also were nonexistent in some areas. The village economies were completely cut off from the more urbanized and developed sectors. Only in the 1950's and 1960's has the modern "demonstration effect" had an impact on the village economy. But this too has not significantly changed the outlook of the village peasant. Although cash incomes might have sporadically increased in the 1930's, the wants of the village peasant, unlike those of the urban dweller did not increase at the same time. More than 60 per cent of Ceylon's peasants lived and depended on the rural sector. But nearly all the foreign trade and commercial links were with the modern sector, where more than three-fourths of the nation's exports in the 1930's originated; this is perhaps true even today. Moreover, the village sector had little or nothing to do with the processing of these exports. Even the labor came from the urban or semi-urban areas.

THE DUAL ECONOMY

From the foregoing it will be observed that a dual economy existed in Ceylon for a very long time.[8] In the traditional sector, except in the case of a few minor commercial crops, organization and technology were backward.

Dualism could be looked at in terms either of subsistence economy as against capitalism, or of monetization against non-monetization. The large plantations exhibit the most advanced forms of capitalist organization, where management and technology are advanced. In the subsistence sector, there has been no organization at all because the allotments under cultivation have been individually owned and the prosperity of each has been determined by the available resources of the individual, his outlook, and his general ability to increase productivity. Technology has been uniformly backward in most of the peasant regions. Until the late 1950's, the average paddy cultivator continued to use draft animals and organic fertilizers and was practically unconcerned about ecological factors. Moreover, it was difficult to introduce any change because of the conservative and inflexible attitudes of the farmer who was governed mainly by tradition.

Monetization was only a matter of degree in Ceylon because almost everybody used money. One hundred per cent barter was very rare. Money was wanted only to secure minimum requirements from village shops and boutiques, and there was no incentive to save money as an asset or as a source of wealth. In other words, money served only as a medium of exchange, and other functions such as a store of value were less important. In the 1950's and 1960's, with the development of steady markets for paddy and other food crops, this attitude has undergone a change; and the peasant of today likes to save money because he knows that it can obtain other goods and services, either immediately or in the future.

Another commonly categorized feature of the dual economy is the zero marginal productivity of labor. This perhaps is the basic economic criterion on which a distinction can be made between the traditional and modern sectors. The marginal product has been largely linked with the amount of land and the technologies that have been available. The typical pattern of inheritance and ownership in the villages is that all additions to a family continued to share the same allotment of land. Sometimes fragmentation takes place, but as time goes on most plots tend to be cultivated jointly by the same household. This tends to increase the economic burden, and even up to this day there is growing underemployment in the village economy.

Underemployment is not a new problem; it is the cumulative effect of a process which began more than fifty years ago. The magnitude of the problem increases as long as employment opportunities do not keep pace with the rise in population. It was also

TABLE 5

Estimate of Surplus Population in the Peasant Sector

Year	Cultivated area of the peasant sector	No. of persons supportable	Estimated rural population dependent on agriculture	Number of surplus	
				Population	Families
	('000 acres)	('000)	('000)	('000)	('000)
1871	1,207	1,086	1,814	728	162
1881	2,185	1,967	2,046	79	18
1891	1,691	1,522	2,182	660	147
1901	1,788	1,609	2,443	834	185
1911	1,755	1,580	2,782	1,202	267
1921	1,736	1,562	3,014	1,452	323
1946	1,710	1,539	4,305	2,766	615

Source: Data in Census Reports from 1871 to 1946.

partly due to the introduction of immigrant labor on plantations. Once peasants sought permanent settlement, their opportunities of securing employment were reduced. Until the middle 1950's the pressure of population on land has been increasingly heavy. Today, however, underemployment continues to be a problem despite employment opportunities available in the urban areas and higher productivity in existing small holdings.

Another noteworthy factor is the virtual lack of interdependence between the rural and modern sectors that existed with little change until the late 1940's. Coordination increased between the two sectors after 1948 when successive governments launched development programs. It has been pointed out that the lack of cohesion between the two sectors was due to the inherent characteristics of the two systems and the lack of common economic features that may have promoted contact. Apart from the development of irrigation facilities in the drier regions, policies were not designed either to increase productivity in the village economy or to encourage commercial crops such as tobacco and potatoes that might have helped to establish closer contact with the rest of the economy.

Dualism was not only economic and technological but also social. Social dualism continued and appeared to be even more marked until the free education system, introduced by the government in the 1940's, bore fruit by raising the standards of literacy and bringing the rural people into closer contact with their more socially and culturally advanced brethren. With the spread of compulsory education in the 1950's, not only did social dualism gradually break down, but it also helped to overcome technological dualism which existed in the peasant economy.

NOTES

1. Report of the IBRD Mission, _The Economic Development of Ceylon_ (Colombo: Ceylon Government Press, September, 1952), p. 1.

2. _Sessional Paper_. No. 7, 1947, p. 125. Also see B. B. Das Gupta, _A Short Economic Survey of Ceylon_ (Associated Newspapers of Ceylon, 1949), p. 28.

3. K. Williams. "Estimation of National Income of an Underdeveloped Export-Import Economy," _Bulletin of the International Statistical Institute_, XXXIII, Part III (1952) 147-160; K. Williams, _The National Income of Ceylon_ (Colombo: Ministry of Finance, July, 1952).

4. See Central Bank of Ceylon Annual Report for 1961, pp. 49-54, and Report for 1962, pp. 42-44 for further details.

The Central Bank estimates tended to give an

indication of the value of goods and services produced at market prices. Several new items were included in the Central Bank estimates such as public utilities, rents on houses, gross domestic investment, interest on bank services, and factor incomes from abroad that were not included in the Das Gupta estimates.

5. Report of the Coconut Commission. Sessional Paper. No. 12 of 1949 (Colombo: Ceylon Government Press), pp. 11-12.

6. See Sir Ivor Jennings, The Economy of Ceylon, 2nd ed. (London: Oxford University Press 1948), Chapter V.

7. See D. R. Snodgrass, Ceylon: An Export Economy in Transition (Homewood, Ill.: Richard D. Irwin, Inc., 1966).

8. For a detailed discussion, see D. R. Snodgrass, op. cit., pp. 4-15.

CHAPTER 2

ECONOMIC POLICY DURING AND AFTER THE KOREAN WAR BOOM UP TO 1955

BUDGETARY DEVELOPMENT PROPOSALS--THE SIX-YEAR PLAN

In the first post-independence budget, the Finance Minister announced that the government would embark on a Six-Year Plan of Development covering the period 1947-48 to 1952-53.[1] The purpose of the plan was to make Ceylon less dependent on imports for its supplies of essential food and manufactures. Considerable emphasis was laid on agriculture because the administration was aware that by increasing the output of food, imports could be minimized despite an increase in per capita consumption of food. In the late 1940's, imports of food, grain, and flour had increased only very slightly, showing that requirements were met, to some extent, by increased domestic production.

Production of essential foodstuffs was to be effected in two ways: by intensive and scientific cultivation of land already under cultivation, particularly in the wet zone, and by developing the vast areas of cultivable land in the dry zone. Accordingly, agricultural stations were opened up in many areas of the wet zone, and trained instructors were sent to teach the farmers scientific methods of cultivation. At the same time, agricultural producers' cooperatives were established throughout the island, and with the help of credit from cooperative banks, it was expected that farmers would be able to finance cultivation. Intensive cultivation in the wet zone was also to be encouraged by the repair of old tanks and channels, rehabilitation of abandoned paddy fields, and the provision of scientific irrigation, where necessary. In this way government hoped to bring under cultivation an area of 131,000 acres.

In the dry zone, large irrigation works which had been completed before the war were to provide the bulk of the irrigation facilities, and virgin jungle was to be cleared and land made suitable for cultivation and human habitation. Priority was given to restoring and increasing the capacity of ancient tanks or reservoirs built by kings. The reconstruction of the Parakrama Samudra was expected to cover an area of approximately 6,000 acres with water. This was to bring 54,000 acres under cultivation. The Minneriya and Giritale tanks and the Elahera canal which supplied water to them were repaired and their capacity increased to facilitate the cultivation of 30,000 acres. Similar restoration work on several other old irrigation tanks was undertaken. As planned, considerable progress was made, and by September, 1952, 41,000 acres of paddy land and 20,000 acres of high land had been brought under cultivation. The extension of the acreage under cultivation was made possible by the sale of large areas of government wasteland to farmers.

The largest project envisaged was the Gal Oya Development scheme. This project consists of a dam for providing water for irrigation and electric power. It was estimated to irrigate 100,000 acres of land and to reclaim a further 150,000 acres for rainfed cultivation. The targets indicated that by September, 1953, about 15,000 acres of land and 10,000 acres of high land would be reclaimed, and that the whole project, including colonization, would be completed by 1961. The original estimated cost of the project was $70.6 million, of which $33.6 million was to be spent on agricultural development.*

---

*The actual outlays on the Gal Oya Development

The government made a special effort to increase paddy production and, accordingly, began to subsidize the sale of fertilizer and agricultural implements and made available loans at low interest rates. By the end of this projected six-year-plan period, 47,272 acres had actually been developed as against the target of 48,257 acres, and another 14,600 acres were provided with irrigation facilities. Between 1947 and 1951, nearly 5,580 colonists had been settled, 19,800 were found employment in carrying out the various schemes, and 387 village irrigation works were restored or improved. The latter provided irrigation facilities for 10,559 acres of new land and 27,847 acres of existing land. The total expenditure incurred was $1.02 million.

Peasants were provided with more land by the acquisition of developed land in populated areas. By the end of September, 1952, 14,800 acres of private land had been acquired for distribution; and it was proposed to acquire a further 5,000 acres in the financial year 1952-53.

Experiments in dry farming methods were successfully carried out and adopted in two colonization schemes. At the same time, encouragement was given to the cultivation of subsidiary crops. In 1953, the country's entire requirements of gingelly and mustard were produced locally. The acreage under chillies had doubled by 1953. Improved cultural practices helped to increase the island-wide average yield of paddy by about 50 per cent.

Although efforts were made to increase food production, the government was, at the same time, aware that cash crops formed the basis of the economy and could not, therefore, be neglected. The Korean War boom delayed the replanting of rubber. In 1953, with the expansion of Ceylon's trade in rubber with China, the government began collecting a tax on

---

scheme have now exceeded $100 million. The return on this investment has been negligible.

rubber, and it was possible to grant subsidies ranging from $117.6 to $168.1 per acre for replanting with high-yielding varieties. Between 1947 and 1952, the acreage under tea increased from 554,072 to 572,008, or by 3 1/2 per cent, while the increase in production was 6 per cent.

Specific proposals were also made in the plan for the establishment of a number of manufacturing industries. The object was to initiate a policy of import substitution and to provide additional employment for the increasing population. Six government factories to produce cement, steel, caustic soda, textiles, paper, and hydrogenated coconut oil were to be established; and factories that had already been established during the war years, such as, glass, coir, plywood, leather, and ceramics, were to be rehabilitated. The outlays on these projects were estimated at $23.5 million. In actual practice, however, the government was able to pursue successfully its program of establishing manufacturing industries only to a very limited extent. By the end of the plan period, only one new factory, the cement factory at Kankesanturai, had started functioning. The cost of the plant was $3.6 million and its rated capacity was 80,000 tons. Along with the cement factory, a power station was built to supply electricity to the factory and to Jaffna town which was only a few miles away. The actual output of the cement factory was, for several years, far below its rated capacity. The ceramics and paper factories were under construction and the total outlays were in the region of $4.2 million. The paper factory was expected to produce about 4,000 tons of writing paper and 2 million kraft paper bags for packing cement.

Work had commenced on the vegetable oil factory at Seeduwa. This factory was to produce 825 tons of glycerine, 4,900 tons of fatty acids, 8,000 tons of refined oil, 1,050 tons of lauryl alcohol, and 58,125 tons of cattle food. The projected date of completion of the factory was 1953. The caustic soda factory with a rated capacity of 1,450 tons of chlorine, 750 tons of DDT, and 900 tons of hydrochlori acid was under construction and expected to be completed in 1953. Preliminary investigations were being carried out for the establishment of a cotton textile factory, and the government approved and voted money for the construction of steel-rolling, acetic acid, sugar, ilmenite, refining, and fertilizer factories.

Of the factories in existence only the plywood and shoe factories were reorganized at a total cost of $0.3 million. Industrial progress had been severely handicapped owing to administration by government departments that were subject to financial controls by the Treasury and whose procedures were unsuited for commercial undertakings.

Considerable interest was shown in developing the fishing industry with the object of reducing imports appreciably. Canadian aid was offered for this purpose. In 1952, imports of dried, salted fish and allied products amounted to $8.1 million. Between 1939 and 1952, the consumption of fish products had increased by more than 100 per cent.

In power, transport, and communications, the most significant achievement was the successful completion of Stage I of the Laxapana hydro-electric scheme, with an installed capacity of 25,000 kw. Between 1947 and 1953, the power generated by stations run by the Government Electrical Undertakings rose from 5 million watts to 12 million watts. The completion of the Laxapana plant enabled the department to meet the increasing load over the years up to about 1956. Since industrial progress was closely linked with the availability of an adequate supply of cheap power, the government decided to proceed with Stage II of the Laxapana scheme with a capacity of a further 25,000 kw. More than $8.4 million was spent on the modernization of railways, which included the commissioning of several new diesel locomotive units and the introduction of diesel electric power coaches for short hauls. The total expenditure on the port development scheme in Colombo, which included the construction of berths for passenger traffic and cargo, was about $13.4 million.

The Six-Year Plan was not a plan in an economic sense because it consisted of a few unrelated projects. The increase in output was not significant and the actual results achieved in its implementation were very disappointing. Government expenditure on economic development between 1947 and 1953 was estimated at $208.4 million, including outlays on several small projects which were not specifically mentioned in the plan. This made it more difficult to reach the original targets laid down in the plan. Besides, the growing financial crisis after the Korean War boom, made it necessary to curtail or abandon a number of projects originally included in the plan. The impact on industry and agriculture and on the import substitution of manufactured goods was not significant. There was some increase in the production of rice, but this was hardly sufficient to keep pace with the increasing population. The plan was also affected by the rapid rise and fall in the world prices of the three main export crops. In addition, the balance of trade was considerably affected by government policies which relaxed import restrictions during the Korean War boom and stimulated consumer demand. The general change in the economic situation after the boom forced the government to reorient its thinking on economic development.

A World Bank survey mission visited Ceylon in 1952, and its recommendations greatly influenced the government's policies on development. The World Bank mission's views on industrial development were these: "First considering the narrow limits of Ceylon's available capital resources the time is not yet ripe for really large investment in individual industrial projects, unless they have usually secure prospects of paying their way. Second, this is the time to lay the foundations of later development by close and systematic scientific study of raw material possibilities by promoting a wide variety of small projects as possible and by facilitating the acquisition of technical skills, managerial experience and a habit of industrial enterprise."[2] Because of this, perhaps, the government abandoned its intention to embark on a second six-year plan. In the meantime, work on many of the development projects was brought to a standstill, abandoned, or deferred because of the World Bank survey mission's recommendations. Those not seriously affected were the Gal Oya scheme, some minor colonization schemes, development of the Colombo port, and the rehabilitation of rubber.

BUDGETARY POLICY AND ECONOMIC DEVELOPMENT, 1949 TO 1955

In the third budget speech of 1949, the government affirmed that one of its primary aims and responsibilities was to maintain a high and stable level of employment and that out of national income a sufficient amount would be spent "to enable the wages of the whole working community to be paid". It also emphasized that henceforth the essence of budgetary policy would be the "employment of manpower and not of money alone".

As before, the budget stressed the importance of developing agriculture and industry. Government policy on growth and development was indicated in the Budget Speech for 1950-51 on the following lines: (1) the promotion of industrial development. This would provide employment in large-scale and cottage industrial establishments for the surplus population engaged in agriculture and for those agricultural workers who are unemployed during certain seasons; (2) the expansion of agricultural production; and (3) the adoption of policies designed to check inflation and to promote capital formation on a large scale.

There was no shortage of money and hence no reason to delay plans for development. But one of the major setbacks to industrial development policy at this time was the insufficiency of capital equipment and the lack of technical skills that were necessary to run modern industrial establishments. Development of agriculture had been given higher priority than industry, but the shortages and the high cost of fertilizer, machinery, and implements caused inordinate delays. Because of the proverty of the people, it was difficult to harness an adequate amount of capital for investment and to utilize capital in the most productive manner. In considering appropriate development policies, the high rate of increase in population resulting from a very sharp fall in the death rate was taken into account.

The most important factor contributing to economic stability in the post-Korean War boom was the government budget. In 1951, the cash operating deficit was reduced from over $33.6 million in the preceding two-year period to $1.9 million. The Central Bank did not have to restrict credit because commercial banks provided only the legitimate requirements of credit to the private sector. The Bank, however, discouraged the extension of credit for nonessential and speculative purposes, which included purchase of shares of estates. The actual volume of credit for productive purposes was confined to commercial credits for exports and imports. There was very little private sector borrowing for investment in industry and agriculture, other than for the plantation crops.

The resources available for expenditure on development were largely determined by the subsidy on rice. The Central Bank repeatedly urged that any further increase in consumer subsidies would be detrimental to the development effort and argued that if there was a rise in prices outside Ceylon, the subsidy weapon would become unwieldly and impractical and that it would perhaps throw upon the government the entire burden of paying for rising costs of essential commodities.[3] Towards the end of 1951, the subsidy problem had become acute because of higher prices for rice and flour imports and the fall in government revenue due to the decline in export incomes. The subsidy bill at this time, as indicated in Table 6, was running at something like 22 per cent of total government expenditure chargeable to revenue.

Whereas the subsidy problem considerably curtailed government expenditure on development, private investment in nontraditional undertakings hardly became worthwhile because of the import liberalization policies that were introduced during the boom. Import

TABLE 6

Food Subsidy

	Gross Subsidy on rice only (in millions of dollars)	Net subsidy on all food items (in millions of dollars)
1947-48	13.6	17.5
1948-49	8.9	16.1
1949-50	5.9	14.3
1950-51	22.7	21.3
1951-52	39.3	40.2
1952-53	24.9	20.8
1953-54	17.0	3.0
1954-55	19.5	5.9
1955-56	27.2	12.8

Source: Central Bank of Ceylon, Annual Reports.

control policy was used to circumvent the inflation resulting from the Korean War boom. The Government successively relaxed import controls in January, May, and July of 1951.*

RELAXATION OF IMPORT RESTRICTIONS AND TAXATION POLICY

The relaxation of imports was, from a private

*Imports of a few important commodities from all sources except Japan were brought under Open General License. Restrictions on dollar imports were, thereafter, considerably relaxed. There was also some relaxation in May when the areas from which certain individually licensed commodities could be imported were considerably extended. In July, the liberalization policy was carried even further when a large number of items were placed on Open General License.

sector development standpoint, unfavorable to businessmen who had plans for setting up new industries and postponed private sector industrial development by at least another ten years. But on the other hand, it was favorable to the plantation sector as it enabled to come in a wide range of essential materials and inputs for the plantation industry. The private sector thought it best that Ceylon should continue to import a wide range of manufactured goods from abroad rather than make an effort themselves to produce at home even the simpler products.* A further reason for the lack of initiative in the private sector had been the high returns obtainable from agricultural properties purchased from expatriate owners. This helped to retain in Ceylon profits that would otherwise have been remitted overseas, but at the same time it did not help to increase the national wealth.

What was required then was not so much a transfer of agricultural properties from non-Ceylonese to Ceylonese hands but the creation of new avenues of wealth. Therefore, the budget of 1951 attempted to render other forms of investment more attractive by reducing the abnormally high returns derived from export agriculture by levying duties. In 1950, the export duty on a pound of tea was 6.4 cents. This was raised to 8.9 cents in 1951. Until 1950, no export duty had been levied on rubber, other than a small tax. The new proposals introduced a duty of 2.5 cents per pound on dry rubber, and even with this duty producers were expected to receive a net profit of more than 16.6 cents on every pound of rubber. With regard to coconut products, the duty on copra was doubled with the object of maintaining a balance with the duty on oil, so that copra would not be exported to the detriment of oil exports. In

---

*Traditionally, the bulk of the Ceylonese entrepreneur class had been in the import trade and they found it rather difficult to get away from the established lines of import business that were extremely profitable and involved very little individual effort.

addition, a duty of 33.6 cents per pound was levied on pepper. Simultaneously, tax inducements were offered to encourage capital investment. Relief on income tax was given up to 33 1/3 per cent of the capital cost of houses for subordinate staff employed in business, 15 per cent on the capital cost of plant, machinery, and new fixtures, and 10 per cent on the capital cost of other buildings. New houses, which brought in a rent of less than $8.4 a month, were given a substantial rebate to set off against income tax for a period of five years.

Provision was made in the budget for 1951-52 to to increase the supply of finance to private individuals to develop agriculture and industry. The Government also promised to introduce new legislation dealing with general banking, mortgage, investment finance, and credit insurance to facilitate loan operations of commercial banks and other lending agencies. Furthermore, the country's financial and taxation policies were being redesigned to utilize the country's wealth and foreign aid received.

With a view to attracting capital to government sponsored corporations and new industrial undertakings, the budget indicated that investors would be granted relief from both income and profits tax for the first three years. Government-sponsored corporations were exempted from tax. New private sector industrial undertakings started after April 1, 1951, were liable to tax only on profits exceeding 5 per cent of the share capital for the first three years. Dividends up to 5 per cent on such capital were also exempted from taxes. It was stipulated that industrial undertakings had to be entirely new and not formed by the acquisition of an existing business or by the conversion or splitting up of any such business. They were required to manufacture or produce articles in Ceylon at any time within a period of three years from April 1, 1951. Each industry had to employ more than twenty-five persons and should use electrical energy or any other form of energy that is mechanically transmitted and is not generated by human agents.

For Ceylon, 1952 was a difficult year because

the country had to readjust itself to the new economic situation after the collapse of the Korean War boom. The loss of external assets had been extremely heavy. This was due partly to a fall in export incomes reinforced by rising import prices and due partly to a high level of imports sustained by an excessive expansion of the money supply, mainly to finance the budget deficit. As the money supply and income were sustained at a high level, consumers were able to sustain a high level of expenditure on imported goods. Imports in 1952 far exceeded export earnings plus other foreign income and resulted in a drain on external assets. Moreover, much of the Government deficit was directed towards consumption rather than economic development.[4]

THE AUSTERITY PROGRAM

To meet the worsening economic situation, the government launched an eight-point austerity program in mid-1952. This program was designed to conserve foreign reserves, to deal with the public finance problem of a deficit budget, and the external finance problem of a decrease in external assets. The main items in this austerity program were the following:

1. The rice ration was reduced by 1/4 measure for all categories of consumers.

2. The selling price of sugar was increased by 2.5 cents per pound.

3. A surcharge of 10 cents was imposed on all existing import duties.

4. A surcharge of 10 per cent was imposed on assessed income.

5. The betting tax was doubled from 10 to 20 per cent.

6. Strict control of expenditure on nonurgent items in the budget was introduced with the object of reducing total

expenditure by approximately $16.8 million.

7. The guaranteed prices of locally produced foodstuffs were raised in the case of paddy from $1.50 to $2.00 per bushel, maize from $1.20 to $1.30, kurakkan from $1.10 to $1.20, and sorghum from $1.20 to $1.30 per bushel.[5]

8. Import control, which had been relaxed in 1950 as an anti-inflationary measure, was intensified specially in respect of the dollar and the European Payments Union (EPU) countries.

Import control had to be intensified because of the exceptionally high purchases of dollar food-stuffs. These controls resulted only in a very small reduction in total imports, since supplies excluded from restricted sources were available from other sources, and the people were able to enjoy the same level of consumption they were accustomed to before the controls.

The general effect of the eight point austerity Program was lukewarm. Presumably it was not the intention of the government to use the program as an instrument for spearheading development in the private sector. It had no impact on private new investment. The tax reforms were intended primarily to raise more revenue for the government to meet committed expenditure. It was not going to release more funds for development because the object was to contain the large budget deficit that appeared with the increase in the subsidy bill.

The increased guaranteed price on cereals had some effect on private sector growth. Its object was mainly to encourage the domestic production of rice and other cereals and to cut down imports. It has been estimated that the cost of production of paddy varied from about $1.20 to $1.50 and the increase in the price stepped up paddy cultivation appreciably as it ensured a reasonable return to the farmers. The same was true of the other products that, of course, were far less important as subsistence crops.

With regard to the pricing of rice, the Central Bank Annual Report for 1952 commented as follows: "The policy of keeping the price of domestic rice far above the world price, that is already high, raises the question of how far it is advisable to go into stimulating domestic rice production at the expense of the consumer. The Ceylon consumer held the curious position of being able to buy his ration of imported rice at less than one-third the world price and having to pay far in excess of the world price for rice bought off the ration."[6] The unrationed rice was almost wholly home grown.

In 1953, import prices fell sharply, and with higher export prices the terms of trade improved to an average of 84 in 1953 as against 75 in the previous year. The trade deficit of $33.6 million in 1952 was reduced to $6.7 million. Despite these favorable trends, the demand for imports was still maintained at a high level. The resulting loss of external assets would have been unavoidable except under the most unusually favorable circumstances that prevailed in the period of the Korean War boom in 1950 and 1951

The roots of the crisis in government financial policy could be traced to the patterns which emerged earlier. In the previous three or four years, capita outlays, including expenditure on loan works and provision of working funds for state enterprises, had exceeded the financial resources available to government from current revenue and from loans out of domestic savings. The resulting shortfalls had to be met by running down government's rupee cash balances. From the financial year 1946-47 up to the financial year 1952-53 the government had depleted its rupee cash balances by an amount nearly equal to that accumulated from the financial year 1939-40 to 1945-46. Capital expenditure on loan works rose steadily each year from $5.4 million in 1946-47 to $37.1 million in 1952-53.

In the context of these trends, the government adopted in July, 1953, a series of measures designed primarily to improve its budgetary position. The price of rationed rice, which stood at 4.2 cents per measure since December, 1950, was raised to 8.4 cents per measure. In order to alleviate hardship to the consumer, the amount of the ration for manual workers was raised by 3/4 measure to the 1942 level of two measures (four pounds) a week. Meanwhile, the cut of 1/4 measure imposed in September, 1952, was restored to the other categories of consumers.* As a result of these measures, the expenditure on food subsidies was cut down to $21.3 million in the financial year 1952-53 as against a budgetary provision of $27.1 million. Next, there was also an increase in postal, telegraph, railway, and electricity rates. Higher duties were levied on a variety of imports including luxuries. For the first time, an excise duty was levied on locally grown tobacco processed into manufactured tobacco. However, with the reduction in the size of the deficit, government financial policy became more manageable; it also meant that in the future the government would not have to cut down development in order to finance consumption.

Next the emphasis in the budget was on productive investment. Postponable expenditure was cut down but total provision for capital works was sustained at a higher level. Towards the end of 1953, both the government and the Central Bank paid considerable attention to the feasible manner of financing--an expanded program of capital investment without imposing heavier taxation or without incurring excessive budget deficits. The Central Bank stated that with the steady decline of external assets, which had been built up during the Korean War years, additional funds for development purposes could come only from sources outside Ceylon. With regard to external

---

*There were three categories of persons who received rice on ration. The ration of the manual worker was the highest, next was designated "ordinary," and the smallest ration was given to infants.

borrowings, there were second thoughts, and the Central Bank Report for the year 1953 observed that the question of borrowing abroad has its own problems.

In the 1953-54 budget, it was proposed to give further relief to those engaged in plantation agriculture as an incentive to improve their assets. Earlier, the entire cost of replanting was given as a rebate only where the same product was produced. Provision was made in the new proposals to permit this rebate even when the old product was replaced by a new one. Experience had proved that the exemption of profits from taxation had failed to attract capital for new industrial enterprises and for developing new land for cultivation. Therefore, it was decided to provide greater incentives for relief in respect of capital expenditure on productive undertakings. Capital expenditure incurred in any particular year of assessment could be deducted from assessable income in arriving at taxable income for the succeeding year of assessment.* Furthermore, an approved investment was to be restricted to the purchase of ordinary shares of the first capital issue of any corporation, the capital of which was partly subscribed by government and is declared by the Minister of Finance as an eligible corporation.

---

*Capital expenditure not allowed in the ascertainment of statutory income applied to (1) any industrial undertaking in which the Commissioner of Income Tax is satisfied that certain conditions similar to those in Section VII(b) of the Income Tax Ordinance are fulfilled; (2) for the planting of tea, coconut, or paddy on any land not previously planted with these crops.

This relief was subject to the overall ceiling of $16,800 and could not exceed the total amount of tax that would be payable by any person for that year. Further, industrial undertakings were not permitted to cease operations within that period, and production should also commence within the period stipulated.

ECONOMIC RECOVERY--THE TEA BOOM

In 1954, Ceylon made a remarkable economic and financial recovery. The terms of trade improved and external assets rose. The terms of trade were on the average 22 per cent higher than in 1953. For the first time the government had an overall budget surplus in the financial year 1953-54. (The excess of revenue over expenditure was due to the higher export duty on tea. The export duty on tea, which was 12.5 cents per pound in October, 1953, was raised to 16.8 cents in November, 1954, and to 21.5 cents in January, 1955; with the fall in tea prices, thereafter it was reduced to 16.8 cents in April, 1955, and finally to 11 cents in September 1955.) Export values increased by $40.3 million to $304.0 million in 1954, while imports fell by $35.5 million to $234.8 million. This was due to unexpected trends in export markets, particularly the rise in tea prices. At the same time, there was a fall in outlays on imports that could be, in part, attributed to the reduction in government spending. It was also partly due to the fact that the private sector expenditure on imports did not simultaneously increase with a rise in incomes, unlike the experience following the Korean War boom in the early 1950's when outlays on imports did not decrease after the end of the boom. The export surplus also accrued in the form of dividends and profits to the large plantations, mainly tea companies.

The government bridged its budget deficit in 1953-54 by cutting down expenditure, chiefly on foodstuffs. The budgetary outturn for 1953-54 showed a net improvement far ahead of the surplus of $5.7 million that was originally anticipated. The final surplus turned out to be $15.6 million and the actual charge to revenue in respect of food subsidies in 1953-54 was $2.0 million as against $41.5 million in 1951-52 and $21.3 million in 1952-53. The size of the food subsidy bill was contained despite the increase in the rice ration which became effective in July, 1953. This was achieved partly by increasing the retail price of rationed rice. Another factor contributing to a saving on the food subsidy in 1953-54 was the decline in the import prices of rice, flour, and sugar. With the continuing decline in import prices the government found it possible to increase further the quantity of subsidized rice issued on the ration. In effect from November, 1954, the weekly ration was raised to two measures per person per week.

In the budget for the year 1954-55, emphasis was laid on economic development and monetary stability. The budget sought to achieve these objectives by increasing the total outlays on capital works and by maintaining and extending the tax incentives for investment, while monetary stability was sought by limiting total expenditure to what could be met from revenue and borrowing abroad. The original estimated revenue in the budget was $172.6 million, of which current expenditure was $123.3 million and capital expenditure $49.3 million. A deficit of $13.8 million had been programed. But the financial year 1954-55 ended with a net cash operating surplus of $21.4 million. An increase in revenue from the export duty on tea was one of the chief factors that contributed towards this surplus. The duty of 12.6 cents per pound at the beginning of the financial year 1954-55 was raised to 16.8 cents per pound in November, 1954, and to 21.8 cents per pound in January, 1955. As tea prices fell thereafter, there was readjustment in the duties.

In deciding the capital and development outlays for 1954-55, the government was guided by three principles. First, provision had to be made for commitments on relatively long-term projects started after 1954-55. The second principle was to speed up, where practicable, the rate of construction of projects started earlier. In this connection, special attention was given to the Gal Oya development scheme. The third guiding factor concerned the residue of funds available after providing for current commitments. Provision was also made in this budget for Stage II A of the hydroelectric scheme, Kalatuwawa water scheme, and for the continuation of surveys on the Walawe project.

With the object of enabling local industries to develop, import duties on certain categories of machinery and equipment were reduced. Local industries were permitted to import machinery on payment of customs duties at the rate of 2 1/2 per cent preferential and 12 1/2 per cent general, as against the existing rates of 17 1/2 per cent preferential and 27 1/2 per cent general. Machinery for making exercise books, component parts of such machinery, machines for making safety matches, and semi-automatic pastry moulds were also imported at low rates of duty. In order to stimulate local industry in the assembly of radio and wireless equipment, components were reduced to 10 per cent preferential and 12 1/2 per cent general, as against the prevailing rates of 25 per cent preferential and 27 1/2 per cent general. To encourage the growth of the textile cottage industry, the duty on dyes and dye-stuff was reduced to 2 1/2 per cent preferential and 12 1/2 per cent general. The following concessions were granted to agriculture. Manure, including animal bone which is used for paddy cultivation, was to be imported at the pre-1953 budget rate of 5 1/2 per cent as against 7 1/2 per cent in the previous year. Duty on imported eggs was doubled from 33 cents to 66 cents per 100 as a further measure of protection to the local poultry farming industry. Marine diesel engines to be fitted to fishing craft were allowed at the rate of 2 1/2 per cent preferential and 12 1/2 per cent general as against the existing rates of 17 1/2 per cent and 27 1/2 per cent, respectively.

NOTES

1. See Budget Speech 1948-49 by Mr. J. R. Jayawardena, Minister of Finance.

In a strict sense, the Six-Year Plan was not a formal plan. It consisted of a large number of proposals in the budget for 1948-49. Reference was made to the plan and progress reviewed in the two subsequent budget speeches for 1949-50 and 1950-51.

2. The International Bank for Reconstruction

and Development, Economic Development of Ceylon (Colombo: Ceylon Government Press, September, 1952), p. 25.

3. See Central Bank of Ceylon Annual Reports for 1950, 1951, and 1952.

4. In the financial year 1951-52 the total cash deficit was $43.2 million of which $42.7 million was spent on food subsidies. Expenditure on development out of loan funds and national development reserves was only $35.1 million. The Central Bank Annual Report for 1952 remarked: "The pattern of Government expenditure weighed higher consumption in the present more heavily than higher employment (through economic development) in the present and higher consumption (through greater production) in the future."

5. The guaranteed price is a floor price. At this price government purchasing centers would buy rice from farmers without restriction on quantity.

6. Central Bank of Ceylon, Annual Report, 1952, p. 9.

CHAPTER 3

ECONOMIC POLICY AFTER THE BOOM: 1955 TO 1960

Stress was laid on development in the budget for 1955-56. The government stated that budgetary policy should be geared to achieve rapid economic development while maintaining financial stability at the same time. Since it was anticipated that revenue receipts would be high and export earnings lower in 1955-56, the criterion of financial stability was to be met by a balanced budget. In actual practice, the government had a small overall cash operating deficit of $0.2 million as compared with a surplus of $21.4 million in 1954-55. A sharp rise in expenditure by $40.3 million was responsible for the deficit. Of this expenditure, $13.4 million was for food subsidies. When the budget was presented the government had made no provision for food subsidies out of revenue. But eventually the price trends of rice and sugar showed that the outlay on the subsidy would be higher than anticipated. The rise in the world market price of sugar reduced profits on the sale of sugar. On the other hand, the reduction in the price of rationed rice from 8.4 cents to 6.7 cents per measure completely changed the original budget forecast. Furthermore, increased purchases of locally produced paddy also contributed towards a rise in the cost of the subsidy.

FOREIGN INVESTMENT POLICY

Presented in the budget for 1955-56 was a six-year program of capital investment for the public sector covering the period 1954-55 to 1959-60. This plan is discussed in greater detail in the next chapter. Investment priorities in the development program were determined broadly on the lines recommended by the IBRD mission in 1952. With the renewed emphasis on long-term planning, in July, 1955, government issued a statement on foreign investment policy. The main points were as follows:

1. It was desirable for local capital to participate with foreign capital in the establishment of business enterprises. No rigid rules concerning such participation were laid down.

2. Importance was attached to the training of as many Ceylonese nationals as possible in businesses operated by foreign firms.

3. Remittances of dividends and interest as well as withdrawal of capital on liquidation were permitted freely.

4. For taxation purposes, foreign concerns were to be treated on equal terms with local enterprise. Whenever possible, the government would negotiate with other governments to relieve the burden of double taxation.

5. In the event of compulsory acquisition, foreign investors would be entitled to the fullest compensation.

The emphasis on foreign investment was due partly to the less favorable balance of payments situation after 1955, when the end of the tea boom was in sight and external assets began to fall. For the first time, an attempt was made to reorganize and rehabilitate several of the government industrial corporations that were functioning since the early 1950's. The government-sponsored Corporations Act No. 19 of 1955 enabled corporations to acquire and operate state-owned and state-operated industrial enterprises, and for the eventual replacement of these corporations by joint stock companies under the Companies' Act. In view of a subsequent change in policy, however, the Act had to be superseded by another piece of legislation governing the ownership and management of public enterprises. But importance appears to have been stressed on purely legislative aspects of making government-owned enterprises run efficiently. The problems in industrial corporations arose from Treasury control, deficiencies in management, and lack of proper technical staff.

INSTITUTIONAL CHANGES

It was evident that development of institutional arrangements for financing development was given much importance in the legislation of September, 1955, for provision was made for the establishment of the Development Finance Corporation of Ceylon. This was indeed the first specialized credit agency to be established in the post-war period and was long awaited because existing commercial banks were not geared to supply development finance to the private sector. The IBRD mission had recommended the setting up of such a finance corporation to provide the finance necessary to initiate new projects and to arrange and procure managerial and technical assistance for such ventures. The purpose of the corporation was to assist in the establishment, expansion, and modernization of private industrial and agricultural enterprise in Ceylon and to encourage and promote the participation of private capital, both local and foreign, in such enterprises.

The authorized share capital of the corporation was $1.3 million, consisting of 80,000 shares of $16.8 each. The issued and paid up capital was $1.2 million. By amendments to the act some ten years later, the authorized capital was raised to $4.0

million. Further, the act provided for the corporation to borrow from the government up to a sum of $2.7 million, free of interset. It was also empowered to obtain loans from the IBRD, and the government was authorized to guarantee such loans up to $4.0 million. The corporation was given considerable freedom in deciding the form of financing projects. It could grant loans with or without security, acquire shares in new or existing enterprises, underwrite new issues of shares, and guarantee loans from other private sources. In addition, it was vested with the power of furnishing managerial, technical, and administrative advice to private industrial, agricultural, and commercial enterprises in Ceylon. The corporation was at liberty to invest its idle funds and reserves in appropriate securities and to make funds available for reinvestment by selling any investment of the corporation as and when appropriate. Though the corporation was established with the support of the government, it had been designed to function as an autonomous private body without government control over its managerment. Accordingly, the general supervision, control, and administration of the affairs of the corporation were vested in a board of directors. The broad national interest of the country had been protected, and the majority of the shareholders and directors have been citizens of Ceylon at all times.

To further facilitate long-term lending, the State Mortgage Bank Act of 1932 was amended to permit exemption from stamp duty for the issue and transfer of debentures and to give the management authority to fix dates of redemption for debentures. In 1956, the government applied for membership of the International Finance Corporation. To overcome the technological gap that had hampered development in the earlier period, the Ceylon Institute of Scientific and Industrial Research (CISIR) was established. The main object of the institute was to study the technical and scientific aspects of projects referred to it by government and the private sector.

The government, moreover, assured the private sector that protection for new industries would be provided by high tariffs and import controls, and a standards institute was set up to lay down and enforce minimum standards for local products. The Taxation Commission, which submitted its report in 1955, recommended several incentives to promote development. Most of these were designed to encourage savings and capital formation in the private sector. The initial tax-free allowance given to business in respect of plant and machinery was increased by 10 per cent for machinery and 5 per cent for buildings; the new rates were made 25 per cent and 15 per cent respectively. In order to create a more favorable climate for private investment in new industry, tariff concessions were given. The duty on imports of fabricated sheet and metal items of iron, steel, brass, zinc, and aluminium were reduced to 2 1/2 per cent preferential and 12 1/2 per cent general, and reductions to 2 1/2 per cent preferential and 12 1/2 per cent general on heavy equipment like earth movers, agricultural machinery, and irrigation equipment were made. Also enjoying reductions in duty were raw materials, which included plastic sheets, wax, asbestos, fiber, and paper. From the foregoing it can be seen that the government hoped to deal with the problem of long-term economic development on several broad fronts.

END OF THE BOOM

The year 1956 was less favorable than 1955. This was true both from a balance of payments aspect and from the standpoint of productivity at home. The balance of payments showed a surplus of $12.6 million as against a surplus of $54.3 million in 1955. External assets increased by only $4.1 million in 1956 whereas the rise in 1955 was $49.6 million. In 1956, the value of exports fell and the terms of trade deteriorated. This less favorable economic situation was the result of a very severe drought and the fall in the world market price of tea together with a rise in the price of imports of consumer goods. Exports fell by 6 per cent in quantity and average price, causing a net decrease in earnings of $34.5 million. Simultaneously, the volume of exports of almost all major products contracted, but expenditure on imports due to an increase in prices rose by $28.6 million or by nearly 12 per cent. The contribution of tea to the aggregate value of exports declined from 61.6 per cent in 1955 to 60.2 per cent in 1956. Tea prices fell by 9.1 per cent and quantity of exports by 3.9 per cent. The net result was a reduction in the trade surplus from $80.7 million in 1955 to $17.6 million in 1956.

The object of budgetary policy in 1956-57 (presented by the new MEP [Mahajana Eksath Peramuna] government that took office in 1956) was to maintain the disposable income of the private sector and the development expenditure of the government at relatively stable and high levels. Despite this, the government's cash deficit in 1956-57 increased sharply to $33.0 million from $0.2 million in the previous year, while capital expenditure decreased respectively from $72.4 million to $65.7 million. During the year, underexpenditure was 22 per cent of the original estimates of capital expenditure of $83.9 million as against 30 per cent in the previous year. The charge to revenue because of food subsidies was $17.7 million as against $13.4 million. This increase was due to the reduction in May, 1956, of the retail price of rationed rice from 8.4 to 6.4 cents and of sugar from 10 to 9 cents per pound. Since these reductions were effected towards the latter half of the financial year 1955-56, their full impact was felt only in the following year. The world market price of sugar increased and reduced the profits on sugar. The cost of the subsidy would have been greater but for the fall in the import price of rice and the decrease in the purchases of locally produced rice; the price of the latter was considerably higher than imported rice. In 1956-57, purchases of paddy under the Guaranteed Price Scheme decreased from 205,000 tons to 155,000 tons.

The Finance Minister stated in his budget speech for 1956-57 "I shall disappoint honorable members who lately sat on these benches, because I have not a Six-Year Plan to offer in a five-year Parliament." In comparison, the budget for 1956-57 was nothing more than a prosaic statement of the economic situation of the country at that time; it contained hardly any proposals designed to encourage investment. This was possibly due to the fact that the new administration had insufficient time to devote to the preparation of an economic plan. Moreover, the elections of 1956 had taken an unexpected turn and caught the new government unaware. The government did not put forward any fundamentally new proposals for immediate consideration.[1] However, much emphasis was laid on expenditure on social services, health, education, housing, and land settlement. It was pointed out that the government should be concerned primarily with the welfare and well-being of the individual and that large outlays were made on education and health on account of the importance of "investment in men" for these are the "men we shall need for the development of the country's resources."[2] Coming to industrial development, the budget speech lamented that the previous government had left "a legacy of expenditures on the winding up of their ill-fated factories." The new administration declared that steps would be taken to rebuild these industries. It was also indicated that since domestic savings and investment were far below the levels desirable for progressive growth of per capita income, foreign capital would be most welcome.

A NEW ECONOMIC POLICY

On the institutional side, certain fundamental changes were contemplated as a result of observing shortcomings in the Six-Year Program. Referring to the plan, the Minister said, "These investments which were a strange mosaic of unrelated departmental schemes were impressively presented as a long-term plan, whereas the government's responsibility was for overall economic planning."[3] The government announced that a National Planning Council would be appointed and that the Planning Secretariat would be enlarged and made more effective. In September, 1956, the National Planning Council was established under the National Planning Council Act No. 40 of 1956. It was to consist of the Prime Minister, who was the chairman, the Minister of Finance, and fifteen others appointed by the Prime Minister. The function of the council was to define the planning of agriculture, industry, commerce, education, social services, and other matters pertaining to the national economy. Also defined in the act was the role of the Planning Secretariat. It was to function as a government department and its task was to provide advisory services and render any other assistance that may help the Council to perform its duties. The government further promised a plan which would "provide encouragement to private enterprise in its legitimate sphere and prevent the public investment program being clogged with fanciful schemes, gifts to favored constituencies, or grandiose brick and mortar operations."[4]

A policy declaration was made that the government would give high priority to industrial development and the control of basic industries while giving private enterprise every encouragement to participate in economic development. Industries were classified into three categories. The first consisted of industries to be exclusively owned and operated by the government, including cement, ilmenite, and salt. Reversing a decision made previously, the government decided not to transfer to the private sector, under the provisions of the government-sponsored Corporations Act No. 19 of 1955, the seven state enterprises manufacturing ceramics, vegetable oil, paper, cement, chemicals, leather, and plywood. The second category envisaged joint participation by the state and private enterprise in industries such as textiles and sugar. The third category, including the entire range of light consumer industries, was left open to private enterprise.

The Central Bank reported that Ceylon's financial position at the end of 1957 was not unsatisfactory. It pointed out that after a fall of $39.7 million, external assets stood at $157.1 million that was equal to a half year's imports. Despite the fall in export prices, the export volume, particularly of tea and rubber, had risen in 1957, but total receipts were $8.9 million lower than in 1956. Because of the less favorable trends, steps were taken to conserve foreign exchange. Restrictions were enforced on foreign travel, and transfers of capital were subject to more stringent control.

In framing the budget for 1957-58, the government was aware that an improvement in the foreign trade position would not be forthcoming. A deficit of $26.1 million was estimated, but in actual fact it was higher because of revised wage scales of government employees and unforeseen expenditure on account of the damage caused by floods in December, 1957. This deficit was financed by a reduction of $8.0 million in the government's cash balances and a net borrowing of $30.5 million. The expenditure on food subsidies in 1957-58 was $18.8 million as compared with $17.7 million in 1956-57. The increase in outlay on the subsidy was due partly to higher sales of rationed rice and due partly to the reduction in the price of rationed rice from 6.7 cents to 5.9 cents per measure in June, 1958. The food subsidy would have been even higher but for lower import prices of sugar and flour.

In the budget under review, the allocation of resources for development was discussed in some detail. To maintain a high level of expenditure on development, the government decided to put some restraint on current expenditures of a nondevelopment nature. New proposals were classified as follows: (1) directly productive activities such as agriculture, land development, and industry, (2) basic services and utilities, (3) social and welfare services, (4) administrative and security services. It would appear that allocations in the budget were made according to this order of priorities. The emphasis on health and education in the budget for the previous year 1956-57 was reframed to read, "health and education had to be contained within certain limits."[5]

The budget mentioned that although the Planning Council had not drawn up a plan it was of the view that, hitherto, too much had been spent on social services and too little on productive work and recommended certain priorities. The budget emphasized that there should be a slowing down of further expansion of social services and a change in emphasis from a "set of mere building programs to the real problems of agricultural and industrial development."[6]

The government attempted to solve the food production problem, which had become more acute with the less favorable balance of payments situation, by taking several steps. One of these was to bring new land under cultivation and increase the yields of existing lands under cultivation. To achieve this, research and extension services in paddy cultivation were suggested and a decision was taken to set up a Rice Research Institute. The subsidy on paddy fertilizer was increased.

The proposals in the budget for 1957-58 did not affect directly the level of investment. This was perhaps due to the relief given to "approved investments." Approved investments were defined in the Government Gazette and could qualify for tax relief, commencing April 1, 1958, if it was an original investment. The investment had to be over $336.1, and the total sum on which relief is claimed should not be greater than one-tenth in the case of a company and one-fifth in the case of an individual of the total statutory income after the deduction of all other reliefs. The maximum relief that could be claimed was $16,806. Further inducements were the reductions made on import duties on raw materials used by certain small industries and on wood working machinery and machinery for the local sugar industry. The duties on aluminium hollow ware and printed wrappers and labels were, however, increased as a measure of protection for local industries.

By 1958, there was some indication of the government's achievements in agriculture and industry, although they were restricted to a few spheres. The government was able to implement successfully the policy of increasing the domestic production of textiles. Beteen 1955 and 1957, about $0.84 million was spent on the development of the textile industry. Production of textiles by power looms went up from 44,200 yards in 1956 to 237,000 yards in 1957, while handloom production rose from 3 million yards to over 4.4 million yards. Imports of cotton textiles therefore fell by 12.8 per cent between 1956 and 1957. Industry in the private sector had expanded, and units had been established for the manufacture of torch batteries, asbestos cement sheets, electric bulbs, glassware, confectionary, razor blades, crown corks, gas mantles, tooth brushes, assembly of bicycles, surgical gauze bandages, and lint.

INCREASING BALANCE OF PAYMENTS DIFFICULTIES

Although the year 1958 had its share of misfortunes, the downward trend that began with the break of the 1955 boom was somewhat temporarily arrested in 1958. Physical output in many sectors rose appreciably, while the terms of trade moved in Ceylon's favor and the value of imports fell. Even this improvement did not strengthen the overall balance of payments position in 1958. Ceylon's export income rose by $4.9 million to $288.6 million in 1958. The balance of trade showed a deficit of $1.0 million as against a deficit of $20.7 million in 1957, while the terms of trade improved from 127 in 1957 to 135 in 1958. The output of tea rose by 15 million pounds to 413 million pounds in 1958 and exports were 12 per cent higher than in 1957. Rubber production increased by 5 million pounds although exports fell by 1.4 million pounds.

In reviewing the position, the Minister of Finance drew attention to the problems that the government had to face, particularly in 1957 and 1958. He stated, "Looking back on the past year it will be quite apparent that the government has not had the advantage of the most favorable conditions in which to carry out the tasks that devolved on it. The terms of trade have not been particularly favorable. The elements have been most hostile, but far more serious than this has been the part that sections of the people have themselves played in hindering the work of the government. This is equally true of the first year of our term of office. Notwithstanding the havoc caused by flood and drought and the wanton loss caused by frequent stoppage of work this government has done a great deal in its program for building up of a stronger economy."[7]

It can be seen then that the government's problems were two-fold. In addition to the economic problems, the country had been plagued with strikes, go slow campaigns, and industrial disputes, much of them arising from demands for higher wages.* Hence, no amount of coordination and programing would have helped the government to carry out its development policies to a successful conclusion. Furthermore, the long awaited development plan had not taken shape.

The proposals for development in 1958-59 were even more disappointing. Few new projects were envisaged and the government was content to go ahead with projects started much earlier. However, to afford some protection to a few nascent industries, duties on several items were adjusted. Import duties on raw materials required for the dry cell battery, the accumulator, electric bulb, and crown cork industries were reduced to 2 1/2 per cent. Duty reductions were also made on materials required in the manufacture of paper products, envelopes, plywood, brushes, and leather footwear. As a measure of protection to the foundry industry producing rice hullers and tea machinery, import duties on rice hullers and tea machinery were raised. Economic policy in this year seems to have been overshadowed by the implementation of the tax proposals of Nicholas Kaldor, consisting of a capital gains tax, wealth tax, expenditure tax, and a gifts tax, much of which proved ill-fated within a year or two of their introduction, when considerable modifications had to be made to the original scheme.[8] The relative slowing down of the pace of development is seen in the underexpenditure of $12.6 million,

---

*In the private sector alone in 1957 there were 304 strikes. The number of workers involved in these strikes was 367,300 and the number of man-days lost was 808,493. The only sector not affected by strikes in 1957 was the tea industry, where production reached the record figure of 397 million pounds.

or 22 per cent of the total loan fund expenditure, mainly for capital works.

The budget for 1959-60 was concerned primarily with the Ten-Year Plan, its contents, and its likely impact on accelerated growth. Chapter 4 examines the plan more closely. There were no taxation or tariff proposals worthy of individual mention in the budget.

In 1959, for the first time the country experienced a severe balance of payment crisis. There was a large trade deficit of $42.2 million, despite the improvement in the terms of trade and higher export earnings. The deficit was due to the sharp increase in the import bill to unprecedentally high levels. Further, Ceylon's external assets fell by $32.6 million, from $148.4 million to $115.8 million in 1959 as compared with $10.1 million in 1958. The Central Bank had repeatedly pointed out that the government's financial problems in 1959 and in previous years were due to an unrealistic approach to financing the budget deficit and, as financial adviser to the government, had at various times suggested a number of measures to reduce the budgetary deficit. They were, however, not wholly put into effect.

THE BALANCE OF PAYMENTS AND CORRECTIVE MEASURES

As the situation rapidly deteriorated in the second half of 1959, a concerted effort was made by both the government and the Central Bank to stabilize the situation. General economic policy had been influenced basically by two objectives: First, the need for effective action to bring about a rapid reduction in the level of imports, and outlays abroad; and second, to reduce inflationary pressures caused by monetary expansion. The Central Bank pointed out that in this context the government could have taken quick and effective steps in reducing imports by quantitative controls like quotas, licensing, and high import duties whereas action taken by Central Bank would relate primarily to the restriction of bank credit to the private sector.

In August, 1960, the Central Bank introduced monetary measures with a view to arresting the continuing fall of external assets. They were of a selective nature restricting bank credit, particularly credit for luxury and certain semi-luxury goods. They also included cash margins on letters of credit for the importation of specified types of goods, and a request was made to banks not to finance hire-purchase transactions in respect of certain goods except on the terms and conditions specified in the new regulations. Simultaneously, the Central Bank also increased bank rate from 2 1/2 to 4 per cent. By the end of 1960, there were indications that these measures had produced some results but were considered insufficient. Hence, the Central Bank urged that further steps be taken by the government to make the monetary measures even more effective.

The quantitative restrictions introduced by the government began in January, 1961. Forty-nine items that were previously under Open General License were brought under individual import license, and further items were added to the category during the course of the year. Also, the import of several items were prohibited. In July, 1961, import quotas were announced for thirty-one items subject to individual licenses, and no licenses were issued for many of the remaining items. As a result of these quantitative restrictions, imports of food and beverages fell by $4.4 million, motor cars by $7.6 million, watches by $4.3 million, and textiles by $3.7 million. Moreover, the sharp increases on import duties levied in January and July, 1961, contributed to a further reduction in imports. The impact of these measures are discussed in Chapter 8.

These balance of payments difficulties, from a long term perspective, were a blessing in disguise. They helped not only to revolutionize industrial policy but also brought to light the importance of a policy of import substitution and the need to look for foreign exchange from sources other than the traditional plantations.

Between 1955-56 and 1960-61 capital expenditure

had risen by $34.6 million while consumption outlays increased by $85.9 million to $261.3 million. The proportionately bigger outlays on current expenditure or consumption have been due to a very high charge on revenue of food subsidies and social services and have been discussed earlier. Had the subsidies been smaller it would have been possible to divert more resources to finance capital projects. What was lacking at this time were effective implementation procedures and financial resources, not an inadequacy of projects. The frequent subsidizing of rice also drained away resources which could have been utilized for development. The controversial element in the subsidy was that every person was entitled to it irrespective of his income level. The subsidy to the producer, however, has contributed greatly to higher productivity in paddy as this was the only substantial monetary incentive given to the farmer.

The progressive increase in the rice subsidy--it rose steadily from $13.4 million in 1955-56 to $41.7 million in 1960-61--has been a disquieting feature of government finance in the 1950's. Its implications for the 1960's were far worse as it became increasingly difficult for the government to sell rice at a more realistic price. It is unfortunate that subsidized rice has become a political weapon as a means of getting votes or discrediting one party. If one political party raises the selling price of rice or cuts the ration, the opposition will promise to reduce the price or restore the ration. On their own it is most unlikely that the people would take up the issue strongly. The consequences of this political game have been serious in that the government's financial position has deteriorated progressively and the consumption not only of rice but also of other goods has been maintained at an unrealistic level.

The progress achieved in this period could be summed up in terms of the Gross National Product. The figures in Table 7 do not indicate steady growth. In money terms the GNP fell sharply in 1956. After 1956 growth was largely arrested by increasing trade union activity and labor disputes. The rise in 1957

TABLE 7

GNP at Current Factor Cost Prices
(In millions of dollars)

	1955	1956	1957	1958	1959	1960
GNP	857.1	825.2	858.5	910.3	983.9	1021.8
Per cent increase or decrease	+ 6.8	- 3.7	+ 4.0	+ 6.0	+ 8.1	+ 3.9

Source: Central Bank of Ceylon Annual Reports 1955 to 1960.

and 1958 was not very marked. The performance was credit worthy only in 1959 when the increase in GNP was 8.1 per cent; this was due to an improvement in the balance of payments, which did not last very long.

NOTES

1. The Budget Speech 1956-57, Ministry of Finance, Colombo.

In the Budget Speech, the Finance Minister stated, "The time at my disposal in preparing the present budget has indeed been short, but it is not our intention to explain away the problems of our economy and our nation or to offer the country a hurried and patch-work solution to them with the pretence of implementing adequately the policy of our government. The budget I present today is only the prelude to the radical changes we intend to bring about both in policy and in the manner of administration."

2. *Ibid.*

3. *Ibid.*

4. *Ibid*.

5. *Ibid*.

6. *Ibid*.

7. Budget Speech for 1958-59. Ministry of Finance, Colombo.

8. Nicholas Kaldor, *Suggestions for Comprehensive Reform of Direct Taxation*. *Sessional Paper*. No. 4 of 1960 (Colombo: Ceylon Government Press).

CHAPTER

4

THE SUCCESSIVE ECONOMIC DEVELOPMENT PLANS

The proper choice of the means and techniques to achieve a satisfactory rate of growth has been of great importance. Experience has shown that it is possible to achieve a satisfactory rate of growth even without formal economic planning. There are innumerable means and methods which may be used to implement economic policy, and they could be changed frequently with advantage. The choice of an appropriate combination would depend on the political climate in the country, the aptitudes and aspirations of the people, and the available resources. This section deals primarily with three successive development plans all of which had to face problems that were anticipated only to a very limited extent.

It might be useful first to look at the country's development strategy in the 1950's and early 1960's. In Ceylon, as in most other developing countries, development planning has been confined to a period of about fifteen to twenty years. It will be recalled that in the budget speech of the Minister of Finance in 1948, a short development plan was presented with the object of promoting growth in certain specific areas in the economy.* But at that time there was

---

*In fact, economic planning of a sort began

little encouragement or urgency to put these policies into effect because the economy was relatively prosperous. The Korean War boom in 1950-51 resulted in a very substantial increase in national income, in the redistribution of income, and a sharp increase in external assets. The external payments situation was very satisfactory, and the country was able to liberalize considerably imports form the European countries as well as from the dollar area.

Moreover, in the context of the development programs of the early 1950's, the foreign exchange resources accumulated during the Korean War and available at that time were more than adequate to pay for imports of both consumer and capital goods. Of course, this adequacy of foreign exchange reserves was in relation to a development program of limited scope. If there had been a more ambitious program with greater emphasis on industrialization, higher agricultural productivity, and considerably higher target rates of growth, it would have been clear that the foreign exchange savings, even up to that time, would have been insufficient to meet commitments, unless of course, policies were directed at diverting a greater proportion of resources to the export sector.

In 1951, a World Bank team visited Ceylon and

---

even before independence; "Post-war Development Proposals" was issued in 1946. The objective in this plan was to "raise the standards of living by designed action, to maintain full employment, and to provide the opportunities to lead a fuller life". The plan did not represent a coordinated program for economic development. The proposal was to spend $292.2 million on capital projects; this was distributed as follows: Communications and Works, $94.1 million; Agriculture and Lands, $70.6 million; and Education, $62.5 million. The development of agriculture by promotion of dry zone colonization by peasant agriculture and the building of infrastructure were given greatest emphasis. Investment in industry was almost wholly ignored.

produced a report which carried a fairly comprehensive survey of Ceylon's development prospects, and it also drew up a development plan for the years 1953-59*. Over this six year period, the government was expected to invest $268.9 million. The emphasis was on agriculture, irrigation, transportation and power, health and education. The plan had very little impact on actual investment allocations thereafter because of the fall in commodity prices after the collapse of the Korean War boom and the political debate that took place over national priorities.

The strategy of development in the early 1950's, as it had been in the pre-war days, was mainly through the government budget.** In the budget, allocations were made through the various ministries to government departments for development work. These funds had to be voted annually by Parliament. The budget however, had serious limitations in these early years. First, as neither the people nor administrators felt any great urgency for development, a good part of the funds allocated for various projects remained unspent at the end of the financial year. Second, there was very little influence brought to bear on the departments by a central planning agnecy to ensure that the development programs for the year were carried out fully.*** The very slow pace of

---

*International Bank for Reconstruction and Development, The Economic Development of Ceylon. (Colombo: Ceylon Government Press, 1952).

**In British times, the sole instrument of development was the budget; there were no ministries and special government departments dealing with planning and implementation.

***There was no automatic relationship between the parliamentary sanction of money for capital expenditure and its full utlization for the appropriate activity. In all these years, underexpenditure particularly of monies voted for capital investment, was the keynote of government finances.

development in both the public and the private sectors in this period can be attributed to the inadequacy or the lack of appropriate techniques of programing and institutional arrangements for implementation.

After 1955, planning and economic development was taken seriously because of the failure of earlier efforts and the uncertainty of commodity markets. In this context, institutions and machinery for preparing a major plan were established.

SIX-YEAR PROGRAM OF INVESTMENT 1954-55 TO 1959-60

The first comprehensive national plan was presented by the United National Party Government in 1955. But the new political party, the Mahajana Eksath Peramuna (MEP) that took office in 1956 did not officially accept the plan, and instructions were given to reorient it to include a program for the private sector. Nevertheless, the plan is evaluated in this chapter because it was an important exercise in national planning and reflected the various priorities in development administration.

While the National Planning Council, presided over by the Prime Minister, was in overall charge of economic planning and policy, the Planning Secretariat was responsible for the actual preparation and coordination of development proposals and the determination of Priorities.* The Plan, known as the Six-Year Program of Investment 1954-55 to 1959-60, which

---

*Within one year of the issue of the Six-Year Program of investment, there was a change of government when the Mahajana Eksath Peramuna or the United Peoples Front came into power. This new government, which came into power in 1956, established the National Planning Council in September, 1956. A committee of the Planning Council was appointed to advise on interim measures including the policies to be adopted in the 1957-58 budget.

incidentally was prepared by the Planning Secretariat, covered the financing of economic development in the public sector only, and to this extent it was not a full national plan.

The Six-Year Program broadly sought to satisfy several objectives:

1. To safeguard the existing productivity of the major areas of the economy, since a deterioration in these sectors could affect or negate advances in other directions. This included a program for the rehabilitation or improvement of the major export crops.

2. To increase the total output in the economy through the expansion of existing economic activities and the creation of new ones. It included programs and projects for expanding the acreage and improving the yield of rice production, for improving the output of subsidiary foodstuffs and the fishing industry, extending the cultivation of tobacco, expanding animal husbandry, improving earnings from tourism, expansion of manufacturing industry, and other activities of a similar nature.

3. This included utility services and basic overheads of the economy as a whole. To a large extent, these were to be the exclusive responsibility of the state, and the emphasis was on essential services such as roads, harbors, telecommunications, railways and power. Substantial investments were to be made in these fields.

4. Since social services played a significant role in development by improving the quality and living standards of the population, provision was made for investment in water supplies, housing, hospitals,

schools, training institutions, and subsidiary social services.

The program attempted to utilize to the maximum the limited resources that were likely to be available in the six-year period. Limitations in resources implied that it would not be possible to satisfy the full complex of the country's needs. Priorities and outlays recommended by the IBRD mission were also taken into account, but the scope of the program was broader than that of the plan proposed by the mission. The total outlay was increased from $325 million to $425 million over the six year period. This had become necessary because the actual rate of development was higher than that envisaged by the mission.

The program of investment covered all but the very minor capital outlays of the central government over the six-year period. Investment expenditures of government, however, do not add up to the total investment in the economy because the latter would include the capital expenditure of the private sector as well as the local authorities. Because of its partial coverage, the Six-Year Program did not constitute an overall plan for the economy. At that time, because of lack of time and organization, it was not possible to prepare a comprehensive program including the private sector and the local authorities, time and organization.

The outlays mentioned covered the projected capital expenditures of the government over the six-year period 1954-55 to 1959-60. Projects to be financed were (a) continuing projects commenced before 1954-55 and (b) new projects to be started between 1954-55 and 1959-60. Both categories included a few projects which would be continued beyond the six-year period. Expenditure on continuing projects was to have a prior claim on total resources available for investment as projects could scarcely be abandoned in a state of partial completion. Of the total outlay of $702.0 million, during the period before 1954-55, $127.7 million had already been spent on projects in the first category and $149.2 million of the residual total was to be carried over for expenditure after the six-year period on projects that would still be in the process of being carried out. The magnitude of the investment program can be seen in the expenditure of $425.0 million required between the years 1954-55 and 1959-60. The allocation of this sum between four major areas of expenditure, as in Table 8, gives an indication of the priorities in the program.

Of the total outlay of $425.0 million, local expenditure amounted to $295.5 million, while $129.6 million was necessary for foreign goods. Of the total, $213.1 million, or 50.1 per cent, represented expenditure on commitments already made. The corresponding expenditure on new products was $211.9 million or 49.9 per cent of the total. If the estimated expenditure is further split up, the total includes the following items of expenditure:

Investment in land	-	$ 18.8 million
Buildings	-	$137.5 million
Equipment	-	$116.3 million
Other items	-	$150.6 million

Nearly 77 per cent of the outlays in the program are devoted to projects of an economic nature, which include agriculture, irrigation, and fisheries that will expand, in one way or another, the productive base of the economy. About 16 per cent of the total accrues to social services, like health, education, and housing, that improve the living standards of the people and would contribute indirectly to economic growth and 4.4 per cent to industry. The combined share of economic projects and social services in the program amounts to 93 per cent of the total. Civil administration and defense each receive about 3.5 per cent of the total investment.

The general pattern of priorities in the program indicates the broad requirements of an economy in a process of expansion. The outlays on administration and defense are of modest proportions. The expenditure on social services are substantial but not excessive in relation to other productive needs. The outlays on economic projects to include infrastructure

TABLE 8

Distribution of Estimated Expenditure

	Estimated Expenditure in Six-year Period		As a per cent of the Total	
	$ (000)	$ (000)		
Total		425,006.0		
Defense		15,903.0	3.74	
Administration		15,038.2	3.54	As a per cent of Administration
(i) Civil Administration	6,929.1		1.63	46.08
(ii) Police and Prisons	6,574.8		1.51	42.60
(iii) Law and Justice	1,702.4		.40	11.32
Social Services		67,687.1	15.93	As a per cent of Social Services
(i) Health	19,893.9		4.68	29.39
(ii) Education	24,554.8		5.78	36.28
(iii) General Housing	17,669.1		4.16	26.10
(iv) Unclassified	5,569.2		1.31	8.23
Economic Projects		326,377.8	76.79	As a per cent of Economic Project
(i) Public Utilities	140,776.6		33.12	43.13
(ii) Agriculture, Irrigation and Fisheries	150,059.2		36.48	47.57
(iii) Industry	18,789.7		4.42	5.76
(iv) Rural Development and Village works	9,672.3		2.28	2.96
(v) Tourism	2,080.0		.49	.64

Source: Six Year Program of Investment, 1954-55 to 1959-60.

investments involved the highest expenditure. Direct government outlays for industry were relatively small.

Agriculture contributed 54 per cent to the national output in 1953, and since more than 50 per cent of the population were engaged in agriculture, the agricultural sector ranked prominently among the economic projects, with a total expenditure of $150 million. Of this total, 41 per cent was allocated for irrigation, 24 per cent for land development, 18 per cent for agricultural crops, 10 per cent for assistance to peasants and village expansion, 6 per cent for improvements to nonexport agriculture, cooperatives, and marketing, and 1 per cent for forests. Agricultural development covered some 450,000 acres of land of which 125,000 acres were to be provided with irrigation, 25,000 acres were to be alienated for commercial crops, 120,000 acres for village expansion, and 180,000 acres for other agricultural development.

The amounts budgeted for the rehabilitation of three major plantation industries were rubber $17.6 million, coconut $2.5 million, and assistance to smallholders of tea $0.7 million. A sum of $7.2 million was provided for the alienation of underdeveloped crown lands to colonists for the cultivation of commercial and export crops like tea, rubber, and coconut. Five new major irrigation projects were to be undertaken, the Minipe extension scheme, Walawe scheme, Heda Oya scheme, Kirindi Oya scheme, and the Mahaweli Oya scheme. The total capital expenditure on these projects was $125.0 million.

For the expansion of fisheries $2.9 million was earmarked. The objective was to achieve self-sufficiency and to reduce imports. The program covered the machanization of craft, provision of ancillary equipment, experiments with trawler fishing, development of inland fisheries, and the construction of fisheries harbors, refrigeration plants, roads, and houses for fishermen.

On the development of industry, government policy was to encourage investment in the private sector and existing government industrial enterprises were to be reorganized. Small-scale industries were to be provided with government financial and technical assistance and research. The expansion of cottage industries, particularly the handloom industry, was also mentioned. A striking feature of the program was the relatively minor role accorded to industrial development although the expectation was that private investment would play a more important part. But the program did not specify in what way private enterprise would participate.

Given the duration of the program, the task was to determine its broad magnitude. Here it was necessary to face up to a serious limitation that has confronted the process of planning in Ceylon. This limitation was the absence of a reasonable degree of certainty regarding the future level of resources. Ceylon is an open economy where exports occupy a dominant place in the determination of national income. The prices of exports and imports are determined by external conditions and are subject to wide and unpredictable fluctuations that affect the levels of income, savings, and of government revenues. Accurate estimates of the future level of resources are, therefore, particularly difficult, if not impossible, to determine.

It would have been possible to make a series of hypothetical forecasts or projections for each of the major components of the future volume of resources. This would have provided a basis for determining the magnitude of the investment program; but such an approach would have been potentially artificial as it does not consider the real problems of unpredictable fluctuations in the volume of resources. In the preparation of the program itself a more flexible approach was adopted. The basic program was prepared on a working magnitude suggested by recent levels of government capital expenditures, and an average annual expenditure, in the period of the program, of $68.9 million to $72.3 million was broadly indicated. This implied a total program in the neighborhood of $425 million over a six-year period.

The possibility of fluctuations in the volume of future resources had then to be provided for. Therefore, supplementary courses of action to be pursued, if future resources permitted an expansion of the program, were included. The scope for reducing the capital outlays depicted in the basic program would, in practice, be limited. There are broadly three ways in which a program could be scaled down: (a) by postponing the date of commencement of new projects, (b) by retarding completion of new projects already under way, or (c) by abandoning projects in a state of partial completion. The last mentioned would prove wasteful while the second could not be permitted because of technical factors that would result in prohibitive costs. The flexibility of a program from the point of view of reducing the scale is, therefore, confined in practice to the postponement of new projects scheduled to be started in a given year.

FIRST INTERIM REPORT OF THE NATIONAL PLANNING COUNCIL

The first interim report of the National Planning Council, published in 1957, attempted to evaluate the the Six-Year Program of Investment and the problems connected with planning and plan implementation. Also included in the report were a number of reports of technical working groups and background papers. The Council had concentrated on three main tasks: (a) reviewing the progress of government revenue and expenditure and taking stock of the economic situation; (b) obtaining from departments details of proposed new projects and important projects carried over from previous years, along with ideas about longer term development; and (c) discussing with departments the special surveys and studies considered necessary for long-term planning.

The report essentially provides an approach to the problems of development and invites the widest measure of discussion and comment on the issues it deals with. It states that the task of overall planning for development must necessarily be approached on a long term basis and, as a first step, the planning organization must determine the major problems facing the economy. It must then define in the context of these problems the goals and objectives that must underlie planning and should work out a course of action that would be most effective and appropriate.

The report stated the basic goals and objectives that should, in the context of the country, underlie planning:

1. To expand output, income, and the standard of living

2. To remove unemployment

3. To alter the structural pattern of the economy and reduce instability

4. To secure a better distribution of income and to reduce where possible regional inequalities in development.

Attention has been focussed on the four major areas of development, namely, the export sector, the dry zone, the improvement of productivity in nonestate agriculture, and industrialization.

Some useful observations were made in the report on sectoral development priorities. Referring to exports and the export sector, it said that, because Ceylon was a small country, it cannot envisage a high level of development within the confines of what is described as a 'closed economy.' In the longrun, a prosperous and developed Ceylon will need to trade with the outside world to obtain a variety of imports, such as machinery, raw materials, and consumer goods. Since exports constitute the means of paying for these goods, it was necessary that Ceylon's capacity to export always should be maintained at a high level. Thus, all investments that aim at not merely sustaining but also expanding the potential of the export sector should receive high priority in any long-term plan.

About two-thirds of Ceylon still remains uncultivated and the bulk of this in the dry zone. The report emphasized that because of pressure of population, the dependence on imported foodstuffs, and the urgency to create avenue of employment, the maximum utilization of all productive and cultivable land, consistent with the needs of afforestation, should find a place in any long-term plan. This would, of course, mean the effective opening up of much of the dry zone. Since a primitive and backward agriculture can find no place in the long run, a vigorous and full scale drive involving modern techniques such as the use of selected fertilizer, better control over water, suitable organizational relations, and marketing facilities must constitute a vital part of any development effort to improve the productivity of nonestate agriculture.

Discussing industrialization, the report observed that the existence of an industrial base is often a potent factor in rapid development and, hence, it was precisely in this field that planning should seek to make an effective contribution.

This interim report of the National Council was primarily a statement on the philosophy of planning. Not much was said about the progress achieved in implementing the Six-Year Program because it did not get underway fully because of unforeseen economic difficulties that emerged in that period. The MEP government that took office in 1956 accepted the proposals relating to development priorities in the first interim report, and instructions were given to proceed with the preparation of a long-term plan in keeping with the view expressed by the National Planning Council that the task of overall planning for development must be approached on a long-term basis.

THE TEN-YEAR PLAN

The Ten-Year Plan prepared by the National

Planning Council was published in 1959.* It was the first attempt at drafting a comprehensive plan of development for the Ceylon economy covering the public and the private sectors. Earlier plans, particularly the Six-Year Program of Investment, were concerned only with investment in the public sector. The Ten-Year Plan not only presented program of development for the several important sectors of the economy, but it also brought them together to form a balanced and coordinated whole. The plan thus represented a further maturing of the planning progress in Ceylon.

The period chosen, namely 1959 to 1968, was in excess of the conventional five or six years usually covered by development plans. There were two important reasons for this: first, the economic problems of the country, particularly the very high rate of population growth, required a scale of development far in excess of what had been attained before. A relatively short planning period would not have provided a level of development commensurate with the requirements of an increasing population and a fast, expanding work force. The problem of employment was one of the key questions of relevance to planning in Ceylon, and the emphasis had to be placed on fields of productive activity where the future work force, which was estimated to more than double over the twenty-five year period ending 1981, could be found employment. Second, a large scale development effort

---

*The Six-Year Program of Investment, 1954-55 to 1959-60 was drawn up by the United National Party, which was in power from 1948-56. The UNP Government was in power only during the first year of the period of the plan. The Ten-Year Plan was prepared by the Mahajana Eksath Peramuna (MEP) that came into power in 1956. A new plan was prepared because the MEP government took the position that economic development was being mismanaged and there was scope for complete reorientation. It was convinced that industry should be given much higher priority in any national plan than had been hitherto given.

involved the initiation of several new projects and programs.

The basic objectives of the plan were (1) to provide employment for the increase in the work force and to bring about a reduction in existing unemployment and underemployment; (2) to aim at equilibrium in the balance of payments and to limit the current account deficit to a level that was capable of being financed by borrowing and grants from abroad; (3) in the long run to raise the standard of living, since this is the ultimate purpose of economic development; (4) to diversify the economic so as to make it less vulnerable to external changes; (5) to achieve an equitable distribution of national income.

The main operative part of the plan was the investment program that reflected the priorities that were considered relavant to a development strategy for Ceylon. Briefly, it provided for rapid industrialization; for the expansion of export earnings through raising the output of plantation crops; for import savings and the provision of domestic requirements of a variety of products in agriculture, animal husbandry, and fisheries, for meeting national needs in social services particularly education, health and housing; and for achieving levels of activity and expansion over different fields for the fullest absorption of the country's growing manpower resources. A number of assumptions were made, particularly that the terms of trade would remain the same as in 1957 and that a capital output ratio of 2.6 would apply to the economy as a whole. The Plan aimed at increasing national income by 5.9 per cent per year with an estimated annual increase in population of 3 per cent that would result in a 2.9 per cent increase in per capita income. This was to be achieved by raising the level of investment from 12.9 per cent of gross domestic product in 1957 to 21.1 per cent in 1968.

Over the plan period, the gross domestic product was expected to rise from $836.1 million to $1,587.4 million. The changes contemplated were not only quantitative but qualitative. An indication of the transformation of the economy was provided by the fact that the value of agricultural output was expected to rise from $448.7 million in 1957 to $726.7 million in 1968. Industry, construction, and electricity would expand at a much faster rate than previously, and the combined output of these sectors was to rise from $103.2 million in 1957 to $388.7 million in 1968, and their share in output would rise from 12 per cent to 23 per cent respectively. Correspondingly, the share of agriculture in total value of output was expected to fall from 54 to 45 per cent. The plan was expected to provide new employment for nearly 1.4 million people.

The total investment in the plan, covering the public and the private sectors over the entire ten-year period 1959-68, was $2,285.7 million. It was estimated that the country's savings could provide $2,056.5 million, and $214.3 million would, therefore, be needed from foreign sources. Of local resources of $2,056.5 million, $783.4 million would accrue from a current account surplus between 1959 and 1968. In addition, $132.8 million was to be received in loans and transfers from the private sector. These investments were distributed over the major fields of activity as in Table 9. The figures in Table 9 show the relative priorities in terms of outlays for the different sectors of the economy. The relatively high provision for industry and power (26.1 per cent of the total) reflected the greater emphasis on industrialization. One of the major objectives of the plan was to take a decisive step forward over the next ten years to industrialize the country. The provision for agriculture and fisheries (24.5 per cent of the total), though somewhat less than for industry and power, is also substantial. Transport and communications projects generally tend to be capital intensive; this is reflected in an investment of $327.1 million. In the category of social investments, housing is apportioned the largest share out of the total (20 per cent). This high investment was due primarily to the acute shortage of houses in the country. Public administration, which includes the construction of office buildings, secretariats, and items of office equipment for

TABLE 9

Ten-Year Plan: Total Gross Investment, 1959-68
(at 1957 market prices)

Sector	Amount ($ Million)		Per cent of Total	
Agriculture		522.7		22.9
Main export crops:				
Tea	85.2		3.7	
Rubber	69.1		3.0	
Coconut	52.9		2.3	
Other Agriculture and Animal Husbandry				
Irrigation and Land Development	183.5		8.0	
Specific Agricultural Crops and Animal Husbandry	131.9		5.8	
Fisheries (Excluding Fisheries Harbors)		36.6		1.0
Industry		456.1		20.6
Large and Medium	388.9		17.0	
Small Scale and Cottage	67.2		2.9	
Electricity		138.8		6.1
Transport and Communications		327.1		14.3
Roads	86.7		3.8	
Railways	50.6		2.2	
Posts[a]	62.5		2.7	
Aviation	8.1		.4	
Ports and Telecommunications	25.7		1.1	
Vehicles and Miscellaneous	93.4		4.1	
Construction		54.6		2.4
Social Services		600.2		26.3
Housing	458.0		20.0	
Health	75.0		3.3	
Education	67.2		2.9	
Public Administration		30.3		1.3
Other Services		119.5		5.2
Grand Total		2,285.7[b]		100.0

[a]Include provision for fisheries harbors.

[b]The small discrepancy between the total and the constituent items is due to rounding off of figures.

Source: Ten-Year Plan.

government departments, has a relatively small outlay. Expenditure on defense has been excluded from the investment program because it is conventionally treated as current consumption in systems of national accounts. The item "other services" includes investments in connection with the whole complex of service industries in the country. These fall almost exclusively in the private sector.

The plan does not envisage an even level of spending from year to year. The total investment was to be made through progressively rising expenditure. In the earlier period, increases in investment would be relatively moderate and in the later years the rise would be sharper. The rising level of investment would reflect at least three factors: (a) that physical capacities for consumption would expand progressively from year to year; (b) that resources for investment would be augmented as incomes and output increase; and (c) that investment needs will grow with expanding markets and consumer demand. Table 10 gives a phasing of investments by sectors over each of the ten years of the plan.

A comparison of the investment pattern to be realized by the end of the plan period, i.e. 1968, with that prevailing in 1957 reveals most clearly the nature and extent of the transformation in investment activity which the plan sought to achieve. Table 11 indicates the increases proposed for each of the major fields of the economy. Investment as a whole was expected to rise by 193 per cent from 1957 to 1968. The plan envisaged that the annual investments in all sectors of the economy would rise considerably by 1968, but especially in industry and housing. Investment in industry would exceed the 1957 level by over $50.4 million and investment in housing by $67.2 million. The increase in other fields, though not of such magnitude, are also considerable. This indicates not merely the stepping up of investment activity visualized by the plan but also the emergence of a pattern of development which aimed at radically changing the basic character of the Ceylon economy.

TABLE 10

Annual Investment Outlays, 1959-68
(At Market Prices of 1957
and
In millions of dollars)

Field of Investment	Base Year 1957	1959	1960	1961	1962	1963	1964	1965	1966	1967	1968	Total Outlay 1959-68
Export Crops												
Tea	4.7	5.6	6.1	7.2	7.6	8.2	9.1	9.4	10.3	10.6	11.3	85.2
Rubber	7.7	5.7	6.4	6.9	6.9	7.1	7.2	7.1	7.1	7.6	7.2	69.1
Coconut	4.0	4.5	4.9	5.2	5.4	5.5	5.5	5.5	5.5	5.5	5.5	52.9
Other Agriculture, Irrigation, and Land Development	15.1	8.6	9.7	13.1	15.0	16.8	19.2	20.8	23.9	26.1	30.4	183.5
Specific Agricultural Crops and Animal Husbandry		7.6	8.6	9.7	10.6	11.9	13.4	15.0	16.5	18.3	20.3	131.9
Fisheries (Excluding Fisheries Harbors)	0.8	2.5	4.0	5.5	4.2	4.9	2.9	3.2	3.4	3.4	2.7	36.6
Industry												
Large and Medium[a]	9.2	15.1	22.9	31.6	29.9	34.8	36.1	43.7	50.4	57.1	67.2	388.9
Small-scale and cottage		0.8	1.7	3.4	5.0	7.6	8.4	10.1	10.1	10.1	10.1	67.2
Electricity[b]	8.6	1.2	8.6	10.1	19.3	15.6	19.2	13.9	16.5	17.6	16.8	138.8
Transport and communications	19.7	18.8	25.5	30.9	34.1	32.6	31.4	33.3	35.6	39.8	45.2	327.1
Construction	1.3	1.7	2.0	2.5	3.0	3.4	5.0	6.7	8.4	10.1	11.8	54.6
Education	3.4	3.7	4.0	4.5	5.2	5.9	6.7	7.6	8.6	9.7	11.3	67.2
Health[c]	3.9	4.7	5.5	6.1	6.6	7.1	7.6	8.2	8.9	9.7	10.6	75.0
Adminstration	2.4	2.4	2.9	2.9	2.9	3.0	3.0	3.2	3.2	3.4	3.5	30.3
Housing	23.4	25.2	28.4	31.9	36.0	40.7	45.9	51.8	58.3	65.7	74.1	458.0
Other Services	7.1	8.2	8.9	9.6	10.4	11.3	12.1	13.1	14.1	15.3	16.5	119.5
Total	117.6[d]	116.3	150.1	181.2	202.0	216.3	232.8	252.6	280.7	310.1	344.5	2285.7[e]

[a]The figures are net of depreciation charges that have been included under Industry--Large and Medium.

[b]Included provision for Fisheries Harbors.

[c]Including Water Supply and Drainage.

[d]Includes increase in stocks of about $6.7 million ($2.0 million in tea and rubber). Any discrepancy between the constituent items and their totals is due to rounding off of figures.

[e]Totals may not add exactly because of rounding off of figures.

Source: Ten-Year Plan.

TABLE 11

Comparative Investment, 1957 and 1968
(At market prices of 1957)

	1957		1968		Increase over 1957	
	Amount $ millions	Per cent of total	Amount $ millions	Per cent of total	$ millions	Percentage
Export Crops	16.3	13.9	24.0	7.0	7.7	47
Other Agriculture	15.1	12.9	50.8	14.7	35.6	236
Fisheries	0.8	0.7	2.7	0.8	1.8	220
Industry: Large and Medium) Small Scale and) Cottage)	9.2	7.9	77.3	22.4	68.1	736
Construction	1.3	1.1	11.8	3.4	10.4	775
Electricity	8.6	7.3	16.8	4.9	8.2	96
Transport and Communications	19.7	16.7	45.2	13.1	25.5	129
Housing	23.1	19.9	74.1	21.5	50.8	217
Health	3.9	3.3	10.6	3.1	6.7	174
Education	3.4	2.9	11.3	3.3	7.9	235
Public Administration	2.4	2.0	3.5	1.0	1.2	50
Other Services	7.1	6.0	16.5	4.8	9.4	133
Total	117.6[a]		344.5		226.9	

[a]Including increases in stocks of about $6.7 million. Difference between total and constituent items is due to the stocks change (not specified) in 1957.

Source: The Ten-Year Plan.

PUBLIC AND PRIVATE SECTORS

The magnitudes discussed so far are national aggregates covering the economy as a whole and are the combined totals of investment to be made by both the public and private sectors. The programs of the sector were different in character; they were essentially in the nature of estimates of the performance that can be expected given the conditions and opportunities that would prevail over the ten-year period. Since the performance of the private sector can be closely influenced by government policies and measures, the latter means were to be used to encourage private investment. The investment totals in the plan between the government and the private sectors respectively are shown in Table 12. The figures are based on a division between investments to be made or financed by government and those to be made by the private sector. Non-monetized investments, representing the value of self-help contributions, are shown separately.

Though the Ten-Year Plan made a detailed study of only three leading industries in the public sector--cement, fertilizer, and sugar--the targets were never realized. In fact, the actual performance fell far short of the planned targets.

In the case of the cement industry, the target set for 1968 was 240,000 tons while the real output was only 80,000 tons. The actual performance did not even measure 33 per cent of the planned amount. This was so because the additional kilns at the existing factory at Kankesanturai and the new factory at Puttalam were not ready by then for commercial production.

Regarding the Fertilizer Corporation, the planned target for 1964 was 400,000 tons of ammonium sulphate. This target was not achieved even by 1970 because the tender for construction of the factory had not yet been awarded. In 1968, the actual performance was only 99,245 tons of fertilizer mixed out of imported ingredients, which is about 25 per cent of the planned amount. Moreover, it was expected that

TABLE 12

Government and Private Investment
by Sectors, 1959-68
(In millions of dollars)

Sector	Non-monetized	Government	Private	Total
Tea	-	26.2	59.0	85.2
Rubber	-	32.6	36.5	69.1
Coconut	-	6.9	46.1	52.9
Specific agricultural crops and animal husbandry	-	53.9	78.0	131.9
Irrigation	18.5	165.0	-	183.5
Fisheries	-	35.0	1.7	36.6
Large-scale industry	-	271.1	117.8	388.9
Small-scale industry	6.7	60.5	-	67.2
Electricity	-	138.8	-	138.8
Transport	16.8	277.6	32.6	327.1
Construction	-	15.1	39.5	54.6
Housing	73.1	152.6	232.3	458.0
Public Administration	16.8	155.6	-	172.4
Other Services	11.8	16.8	90.9	119.5
Total	143.7	1,407.7	734.3	2,285.7[a]

[a]The small discrepancy in totals is due to rounding off of figures.

Source: The Ten-Year Plan

the Fertilizer Corporation would be able to export the surplus after meeting the domestic requirements.

The planned targets in the sugar industry too were never achieved. The projected output for 1968 was 182,200 tons while the actual performance was 3,944 tons. The reason for the shortfall is that under the plan two factories were to be set up at Walawe with a capacity of 63,000 tons and an estimated cost of $9.7 million. These two factories have not been set up so far. Even making an allowance for 63,000 tons from new mills, the existing factories at Gal Oya and Kantalai have not been able to produce even 25 per cent of the estimated quantity. Reference to the sugar industry will be made in a subsequent chapter. The problem about sugar production in Ceylon is not a question of setting up sugar mills but that of growing adequate cane to feed the existing mills.

SHORT-TERM IMPLEMENTATION PROGRAM, 1962-63

As the Ten-Year Plan could not be effectively implemented, a Short-term Implementation Program was presented in 1962. Other reasons that led to the revised program were balance of payments difficulties and growing unemployment. The fall in export prices and the rise in imports produced pressures on the balance of payments. In this situation, the choice of projects was largely dependent on the availability of foreign aid; and in regard to the latter, the greatest opportunities were in transport, power, and industry. The pattern of investment in the Short-term Implementation Program was different from that in the Ten-Year Plan. It was less comprehensive and much private investment was excluded from the program.*

---

*Felix R. Dias Bandaranaike in his budget speech referring to the program said, "Economic development operates through forces and agencies whose potential, capacities and fitness are liable to change. Plans which most realistically reflect this character and condition of development are short-term programs."

The gross investment target was reduced to 16 per cent of the gross domestic product. With an estimated capital output ratio of 3.5 and a population growth rate of 2.8 per cent per annum, the projected investment was expected to provide an annual increase of 4.8 per cent in the gross domestic product and about 2 per cent in real per capita income. In the Ten-Year Plan the targets aimed at an increase in public sector industry by 22.1 per cent and in the private sector by 10 per cent, giving a total increase in industrial output of 32.1 per cent. In the Short-Term Implementation Program, the targets were revised to 15.4 per cent for public sector industry and 5.5 per cent for private sector industry, giving a total of 20.9 per cent. The total industrial output was below that envisaged in the Ten-Year Plan, partly because a number of investment projects in the public sector were not actually carried out and partly because of difficulties in the effective implementation of several projects that were started.

The Department of National Planning believed that there was considerable uncertainty in the forecasts made and that it was increasingly difficult to make specific proposals extending over a longer period. It would also be necessary to examine in detail the needs, resources, investment potentials, and implementation capacities when constant revisions had to be made in response to changes in demand and in the pace of growth in different sectors. The span of the development program was reduced to a period of two years and hence the name the Short-Term Implementation Program. It was proposed to achieve a very much higher rate of growth by selecting projects which would come into effect during the Plan period. The broad objectives of the Program were

1. To increase prosperity through productivity and by eliminating the three main bottlenecks--scarcity of capital, foreign exchange, and skills

2. To eliminate unemployment and underemployment

3. To diversify the economy so as to make it less vulnerable to unfavorable external changes and at the same time aim at obtaining equilibrium in the balance of payments on current account or at least keeping the deficit within manageable limits

4. To ensure the equitable distribution of national income

5. To keep the price level relatively stable.

The Short-Term Implementation Program attempted to lay down in a more complete and concrete form the investment pattern for the public and private sector over the two years 1962-63. While the private sector program was considered as somewhat uncertain because it had to be implemented indirectly by means of incentives,* the public sector program was clearly formulated and the capital budgets for the years 1962-63 and 1963-64 were consciously geared to the targets laid down in the plan. The program was drawn up in terms of the budget years and not calendar years. The investments in the Short-Term Implementation Program exclude provision made under public administration, other services, and the private sector component in agriculture, fisheries, and social services. Despite these, the totals show that there was a considerable reduction in the outlays as against those in the Ten-Year Plan. Table 13 shows the distribution of resources among the different

---

*Government decided to provide promotional assistance to the private sector, mainly through tax concessions. Under the auspices of the Department of National Planning, a committee consisting of representatives of the chambers of commerce, the Development Finance Corporation, and the Development Division of the Ministry of Industries was set up to act as a coordinating agency between the private sector and the planning organization.

sectors that were given priority in the program in relation to outlays in the Ten-Year Plan.

The estimated rate of growth in the Ten-Year Plan was 2.9 per cent while in the Short-Term Implememtation Program it was 2 per cent. Between 1951-57 the gross domestic product had increased at a rate of 3.9 per cent while population had grown at the rate of 2.8 per cent. The growth in per capita real income had thus only been about 1 per cent. This rate of progress was considered to be too slow, and at this pace it would take almost 70 years to double per capita income. Taking into account the various factors such as the availability of resources, the capacity of the economy to absorb planned investment, and the time required for the economy to attain an accelerated rate of expansion, a growth rate of 3 per cent in real terms in a two-year period was considered feasible. This would mean that with population growing at 2.8 per cent per annum, gross domestic product should grow at 4.9 per cent. To achieve this rate of growth it was felt that a total public sector investment on the order of $106.7 million in the first year of the program would be desirable. The government budget for the year 1961-62 was drawn up on this basis, and the program of current and capital expenditure and taxation was modeled with a view to achieving the objectives of the Short-term Program. Of an anticipated increase in income of $104.2 million during the plan period, about 17 per cent would be allocated for purposes of investment. The public sector, which included government corporations, was expected to contribute 60 per cent of the investment. Private consumption was estimated to take 62 per cent of the rise in income while government consumption was expected to rise slowly by about 9 per cent.

The program assumed that deficit spending by the government would be limited and capital investment would be financed by domestic non-bank borrowing from the private sector and foreign aid. The government hoped to raise funds to finance development from existing and new sources. In each year the national development tax was to yield $4.2 million

TABLE 13

Investment in the Short-Term Implementation Program and Total Investment in the Ten-Year Plan (In millions of dollars)

Sector	1961-62	1962-63	1963-64
Agriculture and Fisheries			
Tea:			
Under the Short-term program	3.5	4.6	5.9
Under the Ten-Year Plan	7.6	8.2	9.1
Rubber:			
Short-term program	3.4	3.4	3.4
Ten-Year Plan	6.9	7.1	7.2
Coconut:			
Short-term program	1.3	1.1	1.4
Ten-Year Plan	5.4	5.5	5.5
Other Agriculture:			
Short-term program	21.2	18.3	20.2
Ten-Year Plan	25.5	28.7	32.6
Fisheries:			
Short-term program	2.2	2.0	2.5
Ten-Year Plan	4.2	4.9	2.9
Industry			
Large Scale/Medium:			
Short-term program	18.8	22.3	43.1
Ten-Year Plan	29.9	34.8	36.1
Small Scale:			
Short-term program	1.3	2.2	2.6
Ten-Year Plan	5.0	7.6	8.4

Sector	1961-61	1962-63	1963-64
Power:			
Short-term program	13.6	15.8	13.0
Ten-Year Plan	19.3	15.6	19.2
Transport and Communications:			
Short-term program	29.5	30.6	13.0
Ten-Year Plan	34.1	32.6	19.2
Tourism:			
Short-term program	0.1	0.1	0.01
Ten-Year Plan	-	-	-
Social Services			
Health:			
Short-term program	5.7	5.9	6.2
Ten-Year Plan	6.6	7.1	7.6
Education:			
Short-term program	6.6	5.3	6.1
Ten-Year Plan	5.2	5.9	6.7
Housing:			
Short-term program	9.2	8.9	11.0
Ten-Year Plan	36.0	40.7	45.9
Total			
Short-term program	116.4	120.3	144.9
Ten-Year Plan	202.0	216.3	232.8

Source: The Ten-Year Plan and Short-Term Implementation Program, 1962-63.

TABLE 14

Sources of Finance--Public Sector Investment
(In million of dollars)

	1961-62	1962-63	1963-64
1. Surplus or Deficit of Revenue over Recurrent Expenditure (excluding Capital Maintenance Allowances)	-3.2	+0.2	-8.4
2. National Development Tax	4.2	4.2	4.2
3. Domestic Borrowing from Non-bank Sources	25.2	29.4	30.3
4. Self-financing by Corporations and Receipts from Tea Tax, etc.	3.2	6.9	7.6
5. Capital Maintenance Met out of Recurrent Revenue of the Central Government	12.6	12.6	12.6
6. Foreign Aid	19.7	21.5	21.8
7. Total Resources Available	61.7	74.8	68.1
8. Total Resources required	106.7	114.3	116.0
9. Uncovered Gap	45.0	39.5	47.9

Source: Short-Term Implementation Program, 1962-63

from domestic borrowing on the average $25.2 million;* self-financing by corporations and receipts from the tea tax were to rise progressively from $3.2 million in 1962 to $7.6 million in 1963-64. About $21.0 million in foreign aid annually was also anticipated. Non-bank sources were expected to contribute a good proportion of the capital expenditure and were expected to come from small savings, provident funds, life insurance business, and undistributed profits of corporations. In practice, only a very few corporations had a surplus that could have been used for development. The Cement Corporation was the only one that was expected to provide nearly $2.0 million.

The plan laid considerable emphasis on increasing productivity in the plantation sector. The strategy was that attempts to develop existing industries would positively help to improve the balance of payments position in a very short time. The relative investment in tea was increased substantially, but less emphasis was given to the replanting program partly because higher yields could be obtained from the application of fertilizers. However, the outlay on the replanting program increased because of the raising of the subsidy from $420.20 to $630.30 per acre. With regard to the rehabilitation of rubber at an annual rate of 15,000 acres, it was expected that the acreage to be replanted by the end of 1964 would reach approximately 230,000, which is about half the total area under cultivation.

Attempts were made to step up appreciably the export of coconut products from $32.9 million in 1962 to $37.0 million in 1964. Expenditures on irrigation, land development, colonization, and village expansion were also increased during the plan period. About 43,000 acres of land were to be brought under irrigation during the three-year period, and

---

*The National Development Tax was levied on all government and semi-government employees and was in the form of a percentage deduction from monthly emoluments.

the total expenditure on irrigation and land development was about $35.8 million.

With a view to attaining self-sufficiency, investment in non-export agriculture, especially paddy, was given equal importance. Considerable attention was also paid to the development of subsidiary crops. For instance, sugar was singled out for development. Owing to shortcomings in organization, the output from existing plantation at Gal Oya and Kantalai had been too low. Whereas in 1961 a harvest of 18,000 acres was expected to yield 34,000 tons of sugar or 3.5 tons per acre, only 2,000 acres were harvested, yielding 2,297 tons of cane or 1.4 tons of sugar per acre. This low output had serious repercussions on the two factories at Katalai and Gal Oya and materially affected their economic operation. In fact in 1961, these factories were supplied with only 8 per cent of the cane required for their optimum operation, requiring in high costs of production. Under the program it was expected that by 1964 about 34 per cent of the cane requirements of the factories would be supplied.

It was estimated that approximately 6,000 tons of raw cotton would be necessary to meet the requirements of the local handloom industry and the textile mills in the country. The program envisaged that by the end of 1964 half these requirements would be met by bringing 12,000 acres under cultivation. In 1961, a sum of $0.8 million was spent on the import of 1.35 million pounds of unmanufactured tobacco for cigarettes, and $1.2 million on the import of beedi and beedi leaves. (Beedi is the cheapest brand of cigarette smoked by the low income groups. It does not contain tobacco. A certain variety of leaf is wrapped round to form the cigarette. It has now been found that the beedi leaf grows wild in the jungles of Ceylon.) The targets set for the cultivation of beedi in 1963-64 was 2,000 acres. Considerable attention was also paid to the exploitation of forest resources in the country. An outlay in excess of $0.5 million each year was proposed, and timber output from the government sector was estimated to rise from 6 million cubic feet in 1961-62 to 8 million cubic feet in 1963-64.

Investment on industry was lower, but a part of the emphasis was on heavy industry that included a steel mill and a petroleum refinery. The volume of investment in power transport and communications was slightly higher because they were regarded indispensable for economic development; and, furthermore, foreign finance could be relatively easily obtained for such projects. Investment targets were cut back least in the infrastructure.

The Central Bank annual reports for 1963 and 1964 stated that the investment targets in the plan were not achieved. Production targets were almost achieved in tea, rubber, coconut, and paddy. The increase in real per capita income was much lower than the target of 2 per cent. In 1963 real per capita income declined because of an adverse movement in the terms of trade resulting from a rise in the prices, particularly of food imports. From the point of view of performance of public sector industries, the actual level of output in most enterprises was below the predetermined annual targets. Table 15 shows that performance fell short in cement, textiles, paper, fertilizer, tires and tubes, and salt.

The attempts at development planning in this period were far less successful than was expected because the strategy of plan implementation was not properly conceived. More emphasis seems to have been devoted to the preparation of elaborate paper documents rather than to the project content of the plan and how best it could be implemented to produce quick results. Here too the main instrument of carrying out the Short Term Implementation Program continued to be the budget. The Planning Secretariat was mainly an advisory body that was entrusted with the task of formulating a plan. This approach was not without some defects. The function of the National Planning Council was limited to issuing broad directives to the Planning Secretariat on the choice of projects and the sectors in the economy that required considerably higher rates of growth; it had very little to do with reviewing progress and implementation. The program was drawn up on the basis of various reports which the Planning Secretariat obtained

TABLE 15

Short-Term Implementation Program:
Projected Figures for Public
Sector Enterprises for
1962-64
versus Actual Performance
(Value of output in millions
of dollars)

	Projected figures			Actual figures		
Public Sector Enterprise	1962	1963	1964	1962	1963	1964
1. Hardboard	0.265	0.479	0.182	-	-	0.003
2. Industrial Estates	0.860	-	-	0.383	0.533	0.261
3. Iron and Steel	1.681	5.055	5.378	-	2.271	4.528
4. Cement	2.830	4.029	4.740	1.828	2.597	3.067
5. National Textiles	1.908	0.672	2.521	0.024	0.861	0.032
6. Ceramics	0.450	0.588	0.588	0.430	0.442	0.033
7. Leather	0.365	0.034	0.019	0.511	0.027	0.045
8. Eastern Paper Mills	0.662	0.588	-	0.270	0.373	0.299
9. Mineral Sands	0.353	-	-	0.045	0.084	0.134
10. Fertilizer	0.076	-	5.210	-	-	0.015
11. Tires and Tubes	1.008	2.521	4.370	0.248	0.737	3.377
12. Paranthan Chemicals	-	-	-	-	-	0.081
13. Oils and Fats	-	-	-	0.027	0.028	0.006
14. Plywood	-	-	-	0.019	0.020	0.028
15. Salt Corporation	0.114	0.103	0.470	0.008	0.028	0.080

Sources: The Short-Term Implementation Program; Central Bank: Documents maintained by the Social Accounts Division

from a large number of government departments. Many of the departmental projects were conceived individually without some relationship to the overall objectives of current development policy. Proposals were formulated without verifying whether individual projects would be viable or whether there would be any interdependence or relationship between the different investments. A general criticism has been made that the plans were unsuccessful because they were a little too ambitious and because the financial resources necessary were not easily available.

CHAPTER

5

AGRICULTURAL DEVELOPMENT POLICY BEFORE 1962

MEASURES TO INCREASE PADDY PRODUCTION

Progress in agricultural development in the first few years since independence has been achieved largely by bringing in new land under irrigation. For instance, between 1948 and 1954, a total extent of 168,184 acres was brought under irrigation. Considerable attention was also paid to land development programs. These schemes were mostly in the North Western and North Central Provinces and were linked to major irrigation works. The results of agricultural policy up to 1955 was not encouraging, and after 1956 the government had to reorient its strategy by adopting more positive measures to improve agriculture in Ceylon.

In peasant agriculture, the emphasis was primarily on increasing the output of paddy. Paddy production increased from 31.3 million bushels in 1956-57 to 48.1 million bushels in 1961-62, representing an increase of about 70 per cent in a period of six years. Table 16 shows the trends in productivity. As against this, there was also an increase in the average yields per acre and in the area under production. Between 1956 and 1962, the acreage under paddy increased by 329,968 acres or by about 27.3 per cent. This was due chiefly to more land being brought under cultivation in the colonization schemes

TABLE 16

Paddy Productivity

	Total Production (millions of bushels)	Average Yield Per Acre (millions of bushels)	Total Acreage under Cultivation
1956	31.3	31.7	1,205,984
1957	36.6	34.8	1,387,184
1958	36.4	36.3	1,330,219
1959	43.0	36.8	1,468,406
1960	43.1	36.4	1,471,983
1961	48.0	37.6	1,535,952

Source: Administration Reports of the Department of Agriculture, 1956-61.

of the dry zone. Between 1956 and 1962, 58,949 acres of paddy land had been alienated to 21,143 colonists at a total cost of $2.7 million. In the same period, 97 major irrigation works were undertaken that improved irrigation facilities to 83,300 acres of land. The total cost of these schemes was Rs 166 million.

The higher yields in paddy were achieved by increased use of fertilizers. In the period 1956-62, fertilizer consumption increased by about 250 per cent; this is reflected below:

Fertilizer Consumption (in tons)

1956-57	14,139
1957-58	16,942

(Continued)

Fertilizer Consumption (Continued)
(in tons)

1958-59	26,341
1959-60	20,173
1960-61	29,041
1961-62	38,075

Source: Administration Reports of the Department of Agriculture, 1956-62

This increase was the result of the Government Fertilizer Subsidy scheme that had been in existence since 1951. In 1958, the scheme was modified and made applicable to all paddy cultivators in the country. A subsidy of 50 per cent was given to cultivators who purchased fertilizer through the Department of Agrarian Services, and 33 per cent was given to those who made purchases through cooperative societies. Simultaneously, a network of district stores to carry stocks of fertilizers was set up. By the end of 1962, forty-two stores had been constructed. Another important factor contributing to improvements in agriculture was the development of credit facilities, especially after the establishment of several new multi-purpose cooperative societies and the opening of the People's Bank in 1961. The role of credit in agricultural development is discuss in a subsequent chapter.

Crop insurance on paddy was introduced in the Maha 1958-59 season on an experimental basis. With the Maha 1962-63 season, insurance facilities had been gradually extended to cover some 65,000 acres. The scheme sought to increase paddy production by guaranteeing farmers against loss of crop caused either by natural hazards or by adoption of new cultivation practices. Crop insurance has helped to increase the creditworthiness of the farmer and has ensured that in the limited areas where this scheme operated, cultivation would not be disorganized as a result of crop failure in the preceding season. Efforts were made to introduce the more widespread use of pure line seed paddy. With this in view, private seed farms were encouraged, and a premium of $0.30 per bushel was paid in addition to the guaranteed price of $2.0 per bushel, if the seed paddy was up to standard with regard to purity, viability, and moisture content. The Government was also able to bring in more land under cultivation as a result of the salvinia eradication campaign. (Salvinia is a floating weed that quickly tends to clog waterways and reservoirs.) Up to the end of 1962, the total area freed from salvinia was 32,868 acres.

Improved techniques had further contributed to higher levels of production. Tractors were widely used in paddy cultivation; in 1963 there were 7,736 agricultural tractors registered in the country as against 559 tractors in 1955. Precise information on improved practices like weeding and manuring is not available. But the Statistical Abstract for 1963 reported that in the Maha 1961-62 season, of the 958,388 acres of paddy land sown, about 63,381 acres were transplanted, 5,379 harrowed, and 50,484 acres were sown with pure line seed.

THE GUARANTEED PRICE SCHEME

Apart from the incentives offered to increase production, effective price incentives also were offered. Paddy was the first item to be brought under a guaranteed price. The history of the guaranteed price scheme dates back to the late 1940's. A committee comprising government officials decided in 1948 that certain food items could be produced in adequate quantities locally and that to encourage production of such commodities guaranteed prices should be fixed. The committee, which later reported on the actual working of the scheme, recommended the following steps:

1. Guaranteed prices should be assured to producers of certain commodities.

2. The Agricultural Products (Regulation) Ordinance should be reintroduced.

3. The Marketing Department should buy the produce at guaranteed prices.

After approval by the Cabinet, the Agricultural Products (Regulation) Ordinance was reintroduced in December, 1949, to cover the following commodities: dried chillies, black pepper, coffee, green gram, mustard, turmeric, red onions, and tamarind.

The collection of produce under the government Guaranteed Price Scheme (GPS) on the lines indicated by the Agricultural Products Regulation Board in 1948 was initially undertaken in 1949.* The object of the scheme was to encourage increased production by assuring the producer a guaranteed price and to ease the flow of peasant food crops to domestic markets by lessening the economic stranglehold of the middlemen. The purchase of products was financed from two advance accounts. The Agricultural Products Ordinance advance account applied to dried chillies, green gram, red onions, black pepper, mustard, turmeric, and coffee; and the home garden food advance account applied to gingelly, kurakkan, and maize. For products under the Agricultural Products Ordinance importers were required to obtain prior approval from the Marketing Commissioner and to sell the home grown product along with imports.

---

*The GPS operates in the following way. The government authorizes a cooperative society to act as its agent. The society buys produce from the peasant at the government set price and subsequently resells it to government after keeping a small commission for itself that is in the nature of transport and handling charges. If the produce is paddy, it is sent to a government-owned or a government-licensed private mill for milling. Other produce is sold by the government through the Marketing Department or private retailers to the consumers.

Paddy is the largest peasant crop that has been brought under the GPS. Up to February, 1950, the guaranteed price was $1.20 per bushel of paddy; in March, 1951, it was raised to $1.30 and through two further successive revisions to $2.00 in 1952. The guaranteed price produce was collected in the respective areas of cultivation through 152 cooperative agricultural production and sales societies, 24 marketing department branches, and 28 private agents in areas where there were no cooperative societies. The Marketing Department continued to function in this capacity until the end of March, 1950. Thereafter, the collection of produce was transferred to the Food Ministry. The scheme, which was worked under the supervision of the Food Commissioner (Supplies) and later the Director of Food Production, was retransferred to the Marketing Department with effect from December 1, 1953.

Since 1954, guaranteed price purchases have been made through nearly 600 cooperative agricultural production and sales societies. These societies obtained marketing loans from the Director of Food Production in order to purchase the produce. However, the Guaranteed Price Scheme has not always functioned satisfactorily. From its inception, complaints have been received that several cooperative societies did not purchase guaranteed price products while others did not accept all the produce offered. It was also stated that certain societies made their purchases from traders or middlemen and not from bona fide producers. This has been so mainly because many corrupt officials had entrenched themselves in these cooperative societies. To eliminate these malpractices, societies were required to maintain registers showing the name of the producer and the quantity purchased. These registers were periodically inspected by officers of the Marketing Department and the Cooperative Department. Further, government agents were authorized to send out flying squads to the field and to societies in order to check the purchase of paddy, the use of marketing loans, and to penalize any society that committed irregularities. In areas where societies failed to make purchases, government agents were authorized to set up separate organizations for purchasing paddy.

In operating the Guaranteed Price Scheme, it was found that the bulk of the surplus paddy came into government hands. As any delay would compel cultivators to sell their paddy to middlemen at well below the guaranteed price, the government decided to take certain supplementary measures. These include setting up in producing areas more cooperative agricultural production and sales societies that would be easily accessible to farmers, to encourage societie to put up paddy stores, and to introduce close supervision to prevent traders operating in the name of societies or exploiting producers.

In 1958, the Department of Agrarian Services was responsible for the overall administration of the Guaranteed Price Scheme. The purpose of this transfer was to ensure greater coordination of food production activities and guaranteed price purchases. By the end of 1958, some 3,000 multi-purpose cooperative societies were functioning, and storage facilities for paddy had been considerably increased. In 1960-61, the scheme was given legislative sanction by the passing of the Agricultural Products (Guarantee Prices and Milling) Act No. 33 of 1961.

THE DEPARTMENT OF AGRARIAN SERVICES

Among the institutional changes that were affecte in the 1950's, the establishment of a separate department for agricultural development, the Department of Agrarian Services was a landmark. This department was constituted in October, 1957, out of the former Department of Food Production. The Agrarian Services Department was set up in a permanent capacity in constrast to the temporary nature of its predecessor. The functions of this department are quite distinct from those of the Department of Agriculture. The tasks of the latter are to organize the technical research and extension necessary for agricultural development. The Department of Agrarian Services renders complementary services, mainly with a view to promoting food production and the improvement and stabilization of farmers' incomes. The direct measure taken by the Department are (1) to improve minor irrigation facilities for the irrigation or drainage of new existing arable land, (2) the supply of free seed paddy to needy farmers, (3) the control of salvinia infestation, (4) the operation of the Guaranteed Price Scheme and rice milling. The indirect measures include (1) the reform of the paddy land tenure designed to provide incentives to the tenant farmer and to give him security of tenure, (2) credit and marketing facilities to farmers, (3) subsidization of inputs such as fertilizer and seed paddy, (4) crop insurance, (5) administration of the Food Production (Estates) Act that makes it obligatory for estates to cultivate food crops.

THE PADDY LANDS ACT

In addition to a direct incentive in the form of a guaranteed price for produce, tenurial reforms had to be affected for land under paddy cultivation because agricultural progress does not solely depend on better methods of cultivation. The system of tenure of paddy land has been prevalent in Ceylon from time immemorial. About 40 per cent of the land, or approximately 400,000 acres, have been cultivated by some 300,000 tenant farmers. The tenant was generally expected to give the bulk of the produce to the landlord, who owned the land. Tenant farmers, in terms of local terminology, are known as Ande cultivators. Where the Ande system was in existence, the landlord either provided a part of the cost of cultivation or he would supply inputs in kind, such as fertilizer and seed paddy. In some instances, the landlord would secure about 50 per cent of the crop, without bearing even a part of the cost. This traditional system of agricultural tenure was found to be unsatisfactory for promoting higher levels of productivity in paddy cultivation. It tended to kill incentives because the farmer did not always have the freedom to enjoy the benefits of his efforts.

In December, 1957, during the debate in Parliament on the Paddy Lands Act, members of the House of Representatives frequently referred to the under-privileged position of the paddy cultivator in a society where feudal elements were still dominant. The minister who sponsored the bill felt that the Paddy Lands Act would bring about a fairly fundamental, economic and social change in the rural economy. The Paddy Lands Act was thus enacted on February 1, 1958. Its main objects were to give security of tenure to Ande cultivators and to increase productivity. As a good proportion of paddy lands were not owned by the cultivators, indebtedness was rampant. The farmers then became the victims of a vicious cycle where poor economic conditions have resulted in a very low output.

The Act was expected to bring relief to a large number of peasant farmers by giving them a permanent and secure right to the land, as far as possible, by providing incentives to increase production. It made the eviction of tenants unlawful and introduced the principle of inheritance of tenancies. By these means, security of tenure was ensured and the fragmentation of lands cultivated by tenants would cease. The Act also eliminated payment of higher rents to the landlords. Thereafter, rents were determined by the Commissioner of Agrarian Services, subject to a maximum of 15 bushels per acre or 1/4 of the total yield, whichever was less. The Act further provided for a maximum rate of interest for loans of seed paddy, for hire of tractors, buffaloes, or other agricultural implements by the landlord.

The Paddy Lands Act has set in motion an organization at the village level called cultivation committees composed of cultivators themselves who were to manage their own affairs governing agricultural activities. These committees deal with the issue of water, repairs to minor irrigation works, management of cultivation in specified areas, meet problems such as pest and animal damage, and ensure agricultural supplies such as fertilizer and agro-chemicals. They also act as institutional devices to protect the tenant cultivator and the small owner cultivator by collecting and paying landlords' legal rents and guaranteeing loans to farmers from institutional sources. Cultivation committee members are elected from among owner cultivators and tenant cultivators of paddy lands. A committee is composed of twelve members who hold office for three years. Each committee covers about 400 acres of paddy land and is vested with strong legal powers under the Paddy Land Act in the management of paddy fields. About 3,750 committees have been set up since 1958, and several more are being presently formed.

Cultivation committees have undertaken programs to bring in direct benefits to paddy cultivators. One of their main tasks has been to develop irrigation facilities. Between 1958 and 1965, these committees have undertaken minor irrigation contracts to the value of $1.4 million and completed self-help schemes where committees contributed 50 per cent of the value of their work in labor while the government contributed the rest. These committees also undertake maintenance functions under the Irrigation Ordinance. Many committees have spent part of their funds in further subsidizing fertilizer purchased by them under the Fertilizer Subsidy Scheme from government.

These committees have also been entrusted with the preparation of crop lists, which are estimates of the yields of each parcel of paddy land; this data has been very useful for government in making purchases under the Guaranteed Price Scheme. Cultivation committees have been primary reporters of data on paddy production for the Department of Census and Statistics. They also maintain paddy lands registers, which contain the names of owners, tenant cultivators, and owner cultivators. Although in practice the efficiency of these cultivation committees has varied considerably, they seem to have filled a void in the organization at the village level. Their importance lies in the fact that this was the first instance where leadership was offered to the farmer himself. Earlier, the traditional leadership in the village had been either with the older, well-established families or the professional class in the village, such as the school teacher or the village physician. This was a historical development emerging from the older feudal system that tended to push back the importance of the peasant as an economic unit in the village. When cultivation committees have been set up in certain areas where tradition cannot be easily uprooted, there have been instances where persons, other than cultivators, such as the physician, school teacher, or the village financier have been able to engineer themselves to secure important office in the cultivation committee. This pattern is likely to continue until such time as the peasant is educated enough to take an active interest in his own affairs and assume leadership.

The need to reform the cultivation committees and eradicate corruption is closely linked up with the very slow but important process of educating the farmer. But the problem is likely to solve itself with the increasing influx of educated people who probably will have to go back to the villages because of the lack of job opportunities in the towns. The overall impact of the agrarian reforms resulting from the Paddy Lands Act are

1. It vested in the tenant cultivator the right of undisturbed cultivation of the plot he cultivates, provided he maintained a satisfactory standard. Except for the payment of the stipulated rent, the tenant has no further obligation to the landlord.

2. It registered the cultivation interest of every parcel of paddy land. There is now a person, either owner or tenant cultivator, with permanent cultivation rights. A form of joint cultivation known as Tattumaru would, under this scheme, gradually disappear.

3. It has enabled cultivators to excercise very wide control over all aspects of paddy cultivation in their villages. Certain minimum management functions were specified as the statutory duties of the cultivation committees.

4. The control and management of paddy cultivation is being done systematically

in terms of a plan for the area in which the paddy lands are situated and in the context of overall development policy.

On March 1, 1958, one month after the act came into force, its provisions were put into operation in the districts of Colombo and Hambantota. On September 20, 1958, the act was extended to four more districts--Kandy, Kurunegala, Kegalle, and Ratnapura. The act is now in operation in most of the paddy growing districts. Each district is divided into cultivation committee areas, and the average cultivation committee area consisted of about 150-250 acres. Several assistant commissioners and divisional officers of the Department of Agrarian Services were appointed and trained to equip themselves to carry out various functions under the act. In addition, a very large number of agricultural instructors and village cultivation officers were given basic training in the implementation of the act. Nearly 150 other officers, mainly district revenue officers, were also given a training in the law relating to eviction.

Soon after the act became operative, eviction assumed alarming proportions. By the end of 1958, there were more than 10,000 eviction inquires in hand and up to 1965 the Department of Agrarian Services had received about 27,000 complaints of eviction. To look into matters of this kind, a board of review was appointed on August 15, 1960, under Section 50 of the Paddy Lands Act. In districts where the act did not fully apply, there was provision for the review of evictions to restore tenancy. In districts where the act has been in operation, there is provision for prosecution and penalty for wrongful eviction. But despite these, the number of complaints of eviction have increased steadily.

To correct certain legal shortcomings that were encountered when the act was being implemented, it was necessary to amend the original act on more than three occasions. A fairly comprehensive set of amendments was introduced in 1964. Looking at the working of the act during the last twelve-year period, it may be said that the results of the Paddy Lands

Act have fallen short of expectations. An existing land system cannot be easily changed without bringing about appropriate social changes. Since this has not occurred, it is inevitable that there has been organized resistance to the act from the land-owning class.

SUBSIDIARY CROPS AND PRODUCTS

With regard to other crops, efforts were made to increase the output of potatoes. Potato cultivation in Ceylon was encouraged by the government around 1956. As a first step, four seed potato stations were established in the Nuwara Eliya district. Total potato production rose from 677,712 pounds in 1958 to 1.25 million pounds in 1961.

In this period, Ceylon reached self-sufficiency in egg production. Prior to 1958, the bulk of the eggs consumed had to be imported form India. Apart from the very heavy spoilage, the import trade in eggs was used as a means of remitting funds out of Ceylon and evading exchange control regulations. Hence, a total ban on egg imports was imposed in 1961. The planned program of egg production was initiated by the Department of Agriculture with the cooperation of private traders throughout the country and the liberal financial aid given to small producers by the People's Bank. The foreign exchange savings from this project has exceeded $0.7 million per annum and also helped to foster a profitable and viable domestic industry.

After 1956, increasing attention was also paid to animal husbandry. The National Milk Board was established in 1954 but functioned effectively only after 1956. The Milk Board established the Colombo Central Dairy in 1957, with a capacity of 45,000 pints of milk. After 1957, several collection and processing centers were set up at important milk producing towns such as Kotagala, Galle, Ambawela, and Kundasala. In 1961, the Department of Agriculture initiated work on eight new dairy farming projects at a cost of $0.8 million with a recurrent expenditure of $0.6 million. The major schemes under this were the Tamankaduwa livestock project, with the ultimate program of producing 50,000 pints of milk per day, and the Bogawantalawa and Ambawela farms.

Production of subsidiary crops has been encouraged by the alienation of land to peasants under village expansion schemes. In addition to the guaranteed price of paddy, the government maintained throughout this period a price support scheme for red onions, maize, kurakkan, chillies, green gram, tamarind, pepper, mustard, and potatoes. The impact of the Guaranteed Price Scheme is seen in Table 17. In order to market their produce at fair prices, producers and cooperative societies were provided with nine additional collecting centers that were set up between 1956 and 1962, bringing the total number of such centers at the end of 1962 to 29. In the same period, the government also opened six new shops managed by the Marketing Department to make essential foodstuffs available to consumers at reasonable prices.

ASSISTANCE TO PLANTATION AGRICULTURE

Government policy was directed not only towards improving the viability of domestic agriculture but also of plantation industries. Ceylon's principal export crops have had to face constant competition from other producers, mostly in the Southeast Asian region. While many countries producing tea, rubber, and coconut have made much improvement in the techniques of cultivation and raised productivity considerably, Ceylon seems to have lagged far behind. In the ten years preceding 1962, tea, rubber, and coconut continued to play a very dominant role in the economy because new manufacturing industries were only just emerging. Especially after 1955, the government took active steps to improve the economic position of the plantation industry so that it may be able to meet competition from other countries.

The total value of exports in 1964 amounted to $309.6 million, of which $298.0 million was contributed by the three main plantation industries. Of this

TABLE 17

Production of Subsidiary Crops

	1955	1961
Kurakkan (bushels)	506,255	726,606
Maize	248,569	363,535
Menneri	26,583	54,162
Gingelly	129,694	257,652
Dhal	-	120
Groundnuts	-	52,534
Sorghum	18,034	52,947
Green Gram	59,782	66,841
Cowpea	36,205	44,437
Manioc (cwt.)	3,823,362	5,842,624
Sweet potatoes	916,855	1,148,039
Potatoes	9,290	77,232
Chillies	378,063	410,468
Mustard	14,624	410,468
Red Onions	818,882	14,424
Ginger	72,034	81,856
Turmeric	28,408	36,212
Pepper	102,923	224,997
Cardamom	44,978	23,236

Source: Supplement to Budget Speech, 1963.

figure, tea brought in $191.9 million, rubber $48.7 million, and coconut $57.3 million. The contributory share in national income of each of these industries throughout has been proportionate to their relative shares in the total value of Ceylon's exports. Even with the emphasis on industrialization after 1961, tea, rubber, and coconut have continued to contribute about three-fourths to the total national income. This shows that the prosperity of the country is closely linked to the plantation economy despite structural changes that have taken place in the last few years. It also shows that policies should be formulated to maintain the efficiency of the plantations. Even today, this sector brings in approximately 95 per cent of Ceylon's foreign exchange earnings, which are vitally necessary not only to maintain essential imports but also to finance industrialization. Since 1960, priority has been given to the rehabilitation particularly of tea and rubber because the competitive position of Ceylon tea has weakened with the very sharp fall in prices. Rubber has also had lean times because of the threats from synthetics and the frequent releases from U.S. commodity stockpiles. Coconut has had to contend with other natural oils and synthetic substitutes.

In the following section the rehabilitation programs for the three major plantation industries will be reviewed and some assessment will also be made of their impact on economic growth and the competitive position of these industries.

Tea

Before 1958, the scheme of assistance for the rehabilitation of tea was very inadequate. A sum of $8.40 was paid as an outright grant to the producer, and a further sum of $15.10 per acre was given as a short-term loan. This assistance was channeled through tea producers' cooperative societies to tea holdings of less than 20 acres in extent. The total assistance granted under the earlier scheme, including recoverable loans, was only $0.3 million spread over the five year period ending 1956.

Between 1955 and 1962, the acreage under tea rose by 4.4 per cent and output increased by 23 per cent with average yields per acre rising by 27.7 per cent. This increase in production has been to some extent the result of steps taken by the government to assist the tea industry. In 1958, the government drew up plans for the rehabilitation of the tea industry because many of the plantations were 70 to 80 years old. Little or no replanting of uneconomic and old tea lands had been done because of the very high cost involved and the lack of experience and knowledge of the advantages of vegetative propagation as against other methods of introducing new plants.

The Tea Replanting Subsidy scheme was introduced in 1959 in order to induce estates to embark on a regular and systematic replanting program with high yielding strains of vegetatively propagated tea. (Vegetative propagation is a technique, first developed in the post-war period, where new plants are propagated from cuttings and not from selected seed, which was the earlier method.) This scheme was intended primarily for large estates of over 100 acres. The Tea Rehabilitation scheme, which was simultaneously introduced, was meant for small estates of less than 100 acres. Though the vast majority of large estates had been efficiently run and continued to be well maintained, the same was not true of the smaller estates and small holdings. Large estates have not required financial assistance for current expenditure such as the general maintenance of the plantation in good condition. The only assistance they required was for replanting the uneconomic tea with high yielding strains and improving manufacturing facilities by the introduction of modern machinery and equipment. Under the Tea Rehabilitation scheme, subsidies are paid to smallholders for improving the agricultural condition of tea lands by the application of fertlizer and the adoption of soil conservation measures.

The estimated cost of replanting tea has varied considerably and ranges from about $672.30 to nearly $1008.40 per acre, depending on the nature of the land and the planting density. It was, however, intended to subsidize the entire cost of replanting under the scheme. When the scheme was originally introduced, the subsidy payable was $420.20 per acre in six installments for replanting with proved varieties of vegetatively propagated teas. In 1963, this sum was found inadequate; and as progress was not very encouraging, the subsidy was raised to a maximum of $630.30 per acre. But still there was hesitancy on the part of some estates to initiate replanting because of the uncertain future prospects for the industry. The target set for replanting was 50,000 to 60,000 acres over a 10 year period commencing from 1959. The introduction by the Tea Research Institute* and other estates of high yielding varieties of tea giving yields of over 4,000 pounds per acre, as compared with the yield of 815 pounds per acre in the early 1950's, has given a tremendous impetus to increase output.

The Tea Replanting Subsidy scheme did not apply to areas to be newly opened up. The program consisted of uprooting the old plants and replanting vegetatively propagated tea, or planting areas with vegetative propagated tea, which hitherto was not under tea, while eradicating an equivalent area of old tea belonging to the same applicant. Representations were made by some owners that they were in possession of large extents of uncultivated lands, which they were prepared to plant with tea, but as they did not have any uneconomic areas to eradicate against new areas to be planted, they were unable to receive any benefit for the tea subsidy scheme. This proposal did not meet with much approval from the government because of the possibility that planting of new land would result in encroachment into land that would be required for village expansion.

The Tea Replanting Subsidy scheme is administered by the Tea Controller assisted by a board known as the Tea Subsidy Advisory Board consisting of the

---

*The Tea Research Institute (TRI) of Ceylon was established in October, 1925. Its work was financed by a tax of 0.017 cents per 100 lbs. of tea.

Chairman of the Board of the Tea Research Institute, a director of the TRI, representatives of the Planters' Association and the Low Country Products Association, and a senior planter with considerable experience in the tea industry.* Certain matters of general policy to be observed in the administration of the scheme were worked out in consultation with the Tea Research Institute, the Planters' Association of Ceylon, and other representatives of the industry. Because of the very skilled technical assistance required for replanting with high yielding planting material, for bringing new tea into bearing, and the high cost involved, it was agreed initially to restrict the scheme to estates of over 100 acres. As a result of representations made by planting interests in 1960, it was decided to allow, in special circumstances, replanting in certain areas with tea seed where soil and climatic conditions were not altogether favorable for the vegetatively propagated material, subject to the condition that an equivalent area is replanted with vegetatively propagated tea. In 1964, the Tea Replanting Subsidy scheme was extended to smallholders as well because the Tea Rehabilitation scheme had been a success and the target set up to the end of 1968 had been exceeded by 1962.

Under the Tea Rehabilitation scheme, owners of estates of less than 100 acres in extent were originally given subsidies totalling $100.80 per acre. After 1963, it was increased to $135 per acre, in three installments of $50.40 per acre for the supply of vacancies, $16.80 for soil conservation, and $67.80 for meeting half the cost of use of land for a period

---

*The Tea Control Department was set up in 1933 to carry out Ceylon's obligations under the International Tea Agreement. Under the Tea Control Act No. 28 of 1949 and the Act of 1957, the Tea Controller is responsible for collecting statistics, for registration of tea lands and factories, for issuing permits for the planting of new areas, and for the replanting of worn out tea lands

of five years. In the first four years, applications received under this scheme exceeded the target acreage of 60,000 laid down in the Ten-Year Plan. Because of the volume of applications received, the scheme was administratively suspended in 1963, except in the case of colonists who had alienated land in government village expansion and colonization schemes. If the Tea Rehabilitation scheme were to achieve the targets laid down in the Ten-Year Plan, it would have meant that a greater percentage of the total subsidy fund would have to be alloted to small holdings and small estates, and only a smaller percentage of funds would have been available for the replanting scheme. Furthermore, the tax at that time of .07 cents on tea exports would have to be increased. This proposal has not been looked upon with favor because the tea industry cannot afford an increase in the tax, while a reduction in the replanting program will severely affect the long term interests of the industry.

The total production of tea in 1958, the year preceding the introduction of tea replanting and the tea rehabilitation schemes, was 413 million pounds. In 1962, output rose to 467 million pounds, and a steady increase in production has been recorded in subsequent years. The average yield per acre rose from 671 pounds in 1955 to 790 pounds in 1962. In 1965, an all-time production of 503 million pounds was recorded.

While the subsidies were designed to help productivity, the tea export duty rebate scheme, which was introduced in September, 1956, was instrumental in helping the development of exports. Under this scheme, the export duty of 5.9 cents per pound was reviewed on low price teas as an interim measure of assistance to the producers of medium and low grown teas, particularly to the smallholders.

In 1962, the government launched a further scheme known as the Rubber and Tea Replanting Subsidy scheme for the replanting of uneconomic rubber land with high yielding vegetatively propagated tea. These lands, because of elevation and other factors, were unsuitable for replanting with high-yielding rubber but were found suitable for tea. A subsidy of $252.10 per acre was offered, and the target acreage under this scheme to be replanted with tea was fixed at 8,000 acres.

Rubber

The replanting of rubber lands was advocated in the pre-war years, and this was one of the main recommendations in the report on the rubber industry.* The Rubber Replanting Subsidy scheme came into operation in 1953, shortly after the signing of the Rubber/Rice Trade Agreement between Ceylon and the People's Republic of China.** In terms of this

---

*E.W.Whitelaw and S.F.H.Perera, Report on the Rubber Industry of Ceylon. Sessional Paper No.18 of 1947 (Colombo: Ceylon Government Press).

This report indicated that about 175,000 acres were uneconomical because the trees were well past their most productive age. The committee urged that a replanting program should be started without delay.

**The rubber industry has had a fairly long history of assistance and regulation. The rubber research scheme came into operation in 1913 and was later subject to the provisions of the Rubber Research Ordinance of 1929. The Rubber Research Board, which was set up under this ordinance, was financed by a tax of one-eight of one cent (Ceylon) on every pound of rubber exported. Between 1934 and 1938, rubber exports were restricted under the Stevenson Restriction scheme, and Ceylon's export quotas were announced. The Rubber Control Department was established in 1934 to implement the international rubber regulation scheme. Thereafter, new planting was prohibited except on the authority of permits issued by the Rubber Controller in terms of the Rubber (new planting) Ordinance No.38 of 1939, as amended by the Rubber (new planting) Ordinance No.49 of 1949. The Rubber Commissioner's Department was set up in 1942 primarily

scheme, owners of uneconomical rubber lands who were prepared to replant their lands with proved varieties of high yielding rubber were paid subsidies on the following basis: (a) if the area to be replanted is an estate of 100 acres or more, the subsidy was $117.60 per acre; (b) if the area is between 10-100 acres, the subsidy was $151.30 per acre; (c) in the case of smallholdings, under 10 acres, the subsidy was $168.10 per acre.

The average period for high-yielding budded rubber to come into bearing is about six years. So that plantations are satisfactorily maintained after the replanting is completed, the subsidy is paid in four installments in the case of estates and five installments in the case of smallholdings. The first installment is paid immediately after the old rubber has been uprooted, and the second is paid after the new plants have been introduced, the third and the subsequent installments of the subsidy are paid at yearly intervals provided the new plantation is maintained in a satisfactory condition.

The replanting scheme as originally envisaged aimed at replanting 65,000 acres of old rubber with high-yielding varieties in a five-year period, 1953-57. In 1955, the pace of the replanting program was stepped up, and the target area to be replanted increased from 65,000 to 90,000 acres. In practice, this revised target also was exceeded, and the actual area replanted by the end of the projected period in 1957 was 90,206 acres.

At the end of the first five-year period, the government decided to extend the replanting subsidy for a further period of five years ending in 1962. The target was to replant 110,000 acres in the second five-year period, totalling 200,000 acres under high yielding rubber from the inception of the scheme up to the end of 1962. It was estimated that

---

to purchase and ship to the United Kingdom Ceylon's entire rubber output in the war years.

when these new plantations came into full bearing the total production of rubber would increase by about 60 per cent. The success of the scheme in this this ten-year period encouraged the government to proceed further with the replanting program. During 1962-67, a further acreage of 75-90,000 acres was expected to be brought under new rubber, which would increase production by about 80 per cent.

In the first five years of its operation (1953 to 1957), the Rubber Replanting scheme was financed by a tax on rubber. At the end of 1957, this levy was suspended because of the severe depression in the rubber market; and alternative arrangements were made to finance the scheme from 1958 onwards. The cost of operating the replanting scheme had been approximately $3.4 million a year. Under the Economic Aid Agreement signed in Peking between Ceylon and China in September, 1957, the Government of the People's Republic of China agreed to give Ceylon economic aid to the value of $2.5 million annually for a period of five years, ending in 1962. China also agreed to finance a part of the cost of the rubber replanting scheme, while Ceylon agreed to provide the balance of approximately $0.8 million. After the expiration of this agreement, a further economic agreement on the earlier lines was signed in October, 1962, for a five-year period ending in 1967. Under this agreement, China agreed to give Ceylon a free grant of technical and economic aid valued at $8.4 million spread over five years at $1.7 million per year. This aid was not specifically used to subsidize the Rubber Replanting scheme, which has since then been financed by annual grants from the consolidated fund. Between 1953 and 1962, 193,266 acres, or a little more than 20 per cent of the total acreage under rubber, had been replanted. The increase in productivity after 1958 (between 1958 and 1962 yields increased by 20.2 cent while the acreage under rubber increased by 2 per cent) was attributed to the replanting program rather than to newly opened up plantation.

Steps were taken after 1956 to assist actively the smallholder by supplying high-yielding planting material and fertilizer through government rubber depots. Free advice was given by the Rubber Research Institute on the control of disease and maintenance of properties. After 1960, further measures were taken to improve and extend the rubber replanting scheme. The emphasis, thereafter, was primarily on replanting uneconomic lands with high yielding clones. In 1963, with the extension of the replanting scheme for a further period of five years, the government decided to increase the rate of subsidy per acre.

Coconut

The agricultural census of 1952 showed that about 25 per cent of the coconut acreage was in estates, and of this, only 17.1 per cent on estates of more than 100 acres in extent. The coconut industry thus consists primarily of smallholdings, and this is also the case in village gardens and land around low country houses. Unlike in tea and rubber, because of the pattern of ownership, the coconut grower has paid scant attention to fertilizer use and securing higher yields. To arrest the decline in the island's coconut industry and to improve the condition of estates and smallholdings, the government decided to launch a coconut rehabilitation scheme in 1956. This two-pronged scheme was aimed at stepping up the pace of replanting on worn-out coconut lands by supplying high grade coconut seedlings at subsidized rates and by improving the yields of estates and smallholdings by the supply of fertilizer at subsidized prices.

Most of the island's palms are over 50 years of age and only a very few estate owners and smallholders have regularly replanted their worn-out coconut lands with young palms. (Coconut is the one crop for which there is a substantial market at home. The per capita consumption of nuts is about 120 per annum.) The rehabilitation scheme of replanting worn-out areas is aimed at remedying this defect and is operated by the Coconut Research Institute. To produce the necessary seedlings, the institute has set up a number of large coconut nurseries at

Ratmalagara, Walpita Farm, Ibbagamuwa, Hettipola, Wilpotha, Battulu Oya, Dematawela, Kalawewa, Kilinochchi, Alampil, Mylambavely, Koggala, Eraminigolla, and Wellawaya in the principal coconut growing districts in the island. The institute distributed approximately 1,175,000 high-grade seedlings during 1958 that were sufficient for new planting or replanting approximately 19,600 acres, while the seedlings distributed in 1959 were sufficeint for new planting or replanting of 20,000 acres. The seedlings, which cost the institute about 12 cents each to produce, are sold to estate owners and smallholders at the subsidized rate of 5 cents each. The resulting loss is met by an annual grant from Parliament.

The rehabilitation scheme of supplying subsidized fertilizer for the use of coconut estates and smallholdings is operated by the Coconut Rehabiliation Department.

One-third of the cost of fertilizer is met as a subsidy from the government in the case of estates (i.e., coconut lands over 20 acres in extent) and one-half of the cost of fertilizer is met by the government in the case of smallholdings, (i.e., coconut lands 20 acres or less in extent). The subsidy is an outright grant from the government and is not a repayable loan.

Application for fertilizer permits are made direct to Coconut Rehabilitation Department. In the case of smallholdings however, the choice of applying either directly to the department or through the nearest cooperative agricultural production and sales society or multi-purpose cooperative society has been given. Smallholders are encouraged to apply through cooperative societies, but if they are able to find their own transport and prefer to deal directly with the department, they can do so.

During the year 1958, 34,758 tons of subsidized fertilizer were distributed under the scheme to estates and smallholdings, totalling about 350,000 acres in estent. The corresponding figures for 1962 were 45,000 tons of fertilizer for 384,623 acres. The acreage covered in 1958 represents about one-third of the total extent of coconut lands in Ceylon. Figures of coconut production in 1956 and 1962 are given below:

Year	Annual Domestic Consumption of Nuts (No. of nuts)	Annual Exports (No. of nuts)	Total
1956	1,048,000,000	1,429,484,876	2,477,848,876
1962	1,294,000,000	1,536,358,753	2,830,358,753

Source: Supplement to Budget Speech, 1963.

The above table shows that the rehabilitation program has had a fairly marked impact on productivity over a relatively short period of time. Output has increased by about 20 per cent over a period of six years.

Minor Export Crops

Cinnamon, cocoa, cardamons, and pepper come in importance as principal export earners among the minor agricultural crops. Available data on these crops have been unsatisfactory throughout. Even in the case of cocoa, which is cultivated on more organized lines than other crops, production data has been very unrelaible.

Cinnamon is grown along the coastal areas of the low country wet zone, mostly in the Colombo, Galle, Matara, and Negombo districts. The bulk of the cinnamon plantations are in the form of smallholdings. In 1957, there were about 29,000 acres under cinnamon while exports amounted to about 45,000 cwts. Ceylon has always been the world's largest exporter of cinnamon.

Ceylon's cocoa plantations are concentrated in the Kandy, Matale, Kurunegala, and Moneragala districts. In 1957, production was 85,000 cwts. while exports were about 52,000 cwts. Until 1964, the government had not shown interest in rehabilitation of the cocoa industry although export prices had risen appreciably in 1954-59, and the future prospects of the crop were favorable. The replanting subsidy scheme was launched in 1964; the target was to replant 1,500 acres per year. The project turned out to be a failure partly because individual proprietors were reluctant to cut down old trees as long as they were bearing and the uncertainty regarding title to cocoa land.

Cardamons flourish best at high altitudes and is mostly cultivated in Nuwara Eliya, Matale, and Kandy. In 1957, there were about 6,500 acres under the crop, and production was 18,000 cwts; of this, 2,700 cwts. were exported. A good part of the cardamons comes from estate production; a very small percentage is grown by smallholders. In the early 1960's it was found that many of the existing cardamon plantations were past their best years of bearing and a replantation program was necessary.

Production of pepper was about 55,000 cwts. in 1957 while exports were only about 10 per cent of this output; the rest was consumed locally.

Except in the case of cocoa, there have been no rehabilitation programs for any of the other minor crops. As mentioned earlier, such assistance has been found necessary in the case of cardamon. Even more important is the formulation of a concerted program to extend the area under each crop, because since 1966, they have fetched very good prices in export markets and have been substantial foreign exchange earners. Such a program would be consistent with the policy of crop diversification, particularly of lands under tea, that has been advocated by successive governments.

THE FISHING INDUSTRY

Although Ceylon has an unbroken coast line surrounded by deep seas that are ideal for fishing, the fishing industry does not even today have a policy for systematic and scientific development. Despite this, fish production has doubled since 1958; output in 1964 was valued at $30.3 million. The increase in output is attributable mainly to the introduction of small mechanized inshore fishing craft. But since 1964, Ceylon imported 120,000 tons of fish at a cost of nearly $12.6 million. Total fish consumption is estimated at about 215,000 tons, or approximately 44 pounds per capita. Although the waters around Ceylon are reported to have more than 500 varieties of edible fish, much of the resources still remain unexploited because fishing has been confined virtually to a zone within five miles of the coast. From the early 1950's, several reports have been submitted by specialists on the prospects for the development of the industry; and it is stated that Ceylon can be self-sufficient in fish, but very little seems to have been achieved.* This perhaps is due to the absence of a proper long-term program and lack of continuity in policies. Only piecemeal measures were taken up to about 1966.

After 1956, the government sold mechanized fishing boats to fishermen on hire-purchase terms. Between 1958 and 1962, 1,002 fishing boats valued at $3.2 million were sold. Loan recoveries on the boat purchase scheme have been unsatisfactory and the default rate very high, which ultimately led to its abondonment. This was followed in 1961-62 by a

---

*One of the more recent studies was by an FAO/IBRD team in 1965. Their report is entitled Draft Report of the Fisheries Project Preparation Mission to Ceylon (Colombo: Ministry of Planning and Economic Affairs, 1966).

One reason for low productivity has been the relatively small number of fishing days; in 1961-63 it was only 182 days for mechanized craft. The relatively low efficiency of mechanized craft has been due to the lack of shore facilities for repair and maintenance and from the difficulties and inconveniences inherent in marketing and distribution.

new scheme of mechanizing local craft such as outrigger canoes. Under this scheme an initial deposit of one-third of the cost of the engine was required, and repayment was to be spread over eighteen months. Loans for fishing gear were also provided up to a maximum of $336.10, and the rate of interest was 6 per cent. The fisheries factory at Mutwal, constructed with Canadian aid, was completed in 1957. It has a freezing capacity of twenty-four tons per day and can produce up to forty tons of ice. In 1962, with Japanese assistance, a Fisheries Training School was established. This school provides instruction in the repair of mechanized boats, handling of fishing gear, and in new methods of fishing and preserving the catch. Between 1956 and 1962, fish production, other than trawler catches, rose from 765,312 cwts. to 1,516,000 cwts.; trawler catches aggregated 20,230 cwts. in 1962.

CHAPTER 6

IMPACT OF THE COOPERATIVES AND NEW FINANCIAL INSTITUTIONS ON AGRICULTURAL PROGRESS

The cooperative movement in Ceylon has existed for over sixty years. During this period, it has, with varying degrees of success, entered into traditional economic activities where, as in several other countries, cooperative principles have had some influence. This includes consumer cooperatives, where people get together with the object of providing themselves with goods at fair prices and sharing the profits resulting from sales. The movement also includes production, marketing, and the provision of credit facilities for industry and agriculture. The use of cooperatives as an instrument for the effective diversion of credit to the rural economy is of vital importance in the recent development of the cooperative movement.

A review of the economic development of Ceylon in the five decades preceding the 1950's would show that development has taken place largely without the intervention of cooperative principles in production and marketing. This is easy to understand because the pre-independence economy was geared to the production of the three main export crops. The predominance of the plantation sector in the economy tended to eliminate the cooperative as an instrument for achieving a higher level of productivity and growth. Most plantations consisted of big estates or holdings run according to the best capitalist traditions. Ownership was either in the hands of companies or proprietors, and the financing of production and movement of produce was undertaken by commercial banks.* The little influence that cooperatives had in this period was confined entirely to the rural economy.

THE BACKGROUND

The first cooperatives were financed by the Local Loans and Development Fund, which continued to be the sole source of finance until 1929, when the cooperative central banks took over. Up to 1947, credit extended by the cooperative movement for agriculture was through a network of credit societies with a small and select membership. The average loan was small and its use restricted. In 1947, the government proposed a scheme for liberalizing credit for the development of nonplantation agriculture and to free peasant farmers from the clutches of indigenous money lenders on a much wider scale. With this end in view, a network of cooperative agricultural production and sales societies was set up to provide cheap credit to cultivators of paddy and other crops. The government undertook to finance these societies for short-term and medium-term requirements as well as for working capital for the purchase of produce. Interest on loans was 2 per cent to societies, and they in turn offered loans to members at 4 to 6 per cent at a time when the bank rate was 4 1/2 per cent. Cooperative banks were allowed 1/2 per cent for servicing these loans. Credit was also available for the construction of godowns (warehouses) and buildings and for the purchase of tractors.

In 1957, multi-purpose cooperative societies were set up to gradually replace the cooperative agricultural production and sales societies whose activities were generally restricted. The government

---

*Before 1939, all the banks in the country were branches of foreign banks; they were either British exchange banks or banks with head offices in India.

anticipated that multi-purpose societies would play a dominant role in development. The agricultural credit scheme, which had hitherto been operated by the Director of Food Production, was extended to the multi-purpose cooperative societies. However, a change in the institutional set-up appeared with the establishment in 1957 of a specialized department, the Department of Agrarian Services. This department was to operate the government's agricultural credit scheme and the Guaranteed Price Scheme for a variety of crops.

PRESENT ORGANIZATIONS

The role of the cooperative institutions in agricultural financing cannot be examined without reference to the organization and structure of the cooperative movement. The cooperative movement in Ceylon consists of three categories of institutions--the primary society at the village level, the various middle tier organizations at the district level, and the apex organizations at the national level. A distinction cannot easily be drawn, for these organizations are closely linked to each other. With greater efforts at integration, there now appears to be considerable overlapping, and even at the village level district organizations have emerged. At all levels, there is official contact either with the Cooperative Department, other government departments, or the banking system.

The primary societies have been the backbone of the cooperative movement from its very inception; the strength of the movement can be assessed from their numbers and viability. At present, Ceylon has over 14,000 primary societies with an active membership of 1,518,823, giving a ratio of one society to every 850 of the population. Of these, about 5,000 are listed as production and sales and multi-purpose cooperatives, 4,000 as credit and savings societies, 2,000 societies connected with schools, 1,100 industrial, 675 agricultural, 650 consumer stores, and 270 associated with the fishing industry. About 30 per cent are said to be inactive; and even of the 5,000 classified as production and sales and multi-purpose societies, about 1,200 are not engaged in many lines of activity but confine themselves to consumer distribution. In actual practice, only about 2,700 are engaged in two or more functions; they are the truly multi-purpose societies. Of the 3,600 credit societies with unlimited liability, about half are said to be inactive and little has been done in practice to revitalize them.* The financial turnover of the movement in the year ending September, 1967, was $351.3 million.

Despite the gloomy picture of the bulk of the societies being in the generally inactive category, there are at least 1,000 primary societies that have progressed and perform a vital function in the provision of agricultural credit. These societies compare well with those found elsewhere. It is necessary to emphasize here that it is not the numbers that matter but the ability of a few organized societies to act as useful instruments of economic development.

The existence of a strong secondary and apex organization is an indication of the maturity of the system. These institutions do not seem to have made much headway. At the middle tier, the most important organizations are the 124 multi-purpose cooperative society unions. They function generally as wholesale organizations concerned with the supply of consumer goods. At this middle level there are also some 70 credit unions, which functioned earlier as supervisory bodies when credit societies constituted the greater part of the movement. In addition, there are 24 district unions with very little financial viability and limited financial support.

Between the primary and apex levels there are seven cooperative banks. Before the establishment

---

*See Report of the Royal Commission on the Cooperative Movement in Ceylon. Sessional Paper. No. 2 of 1970 (Colombo: Government Printing Office, 1970).

of the People's Bank, there were 17 cooperative banks, some of which have been absorbed at the national level by the People's Bank. At the apex level there are two groups of institutions. The first group includes six which are entirely cooperative. In the second group there are two that are hybrid, being partly cooperative and partly public corporations. The six in the first group include cooperative unions of agricultural producers, coconut producers, industries, fisheries, consumers, and the Cooperative Federation of Ceylon. The six organizations in the first group have not been able to gather confidence and strength behind them. In view of this, the movement does not have a strong parent body that could provide leadership and guidance in business management, technical assistance, planning, and training of personnel that it badly needs. The Cooperative Federation itself is not an active body concerned with formulating policy and, in general, directing the movement. The two institutions of importance in the second category are the Cooperative Wholesale Establishment and the People's Bank. These two institutions are linked closely with the cooperative movement, but they have been constituted as state corporations with a certain measure of government control.

The Cooperative Wholesale Establishment is the central wholesale organization for the cooperative trade, but in practice it functions chiefly as a state corporation with its business interests spread into noncooperative areas. It is also designed to compete with the private business interests in the country, particularly those in the retail and wholesale trades. In the case of the People's Bank, half its shares are held by cooperative societies. The shareholding cooperative societies elect three of the eight directors of the bank; and three of the nine directors in the Cooperative Wholesale Establishment are nominated by the Cooperative Federation. In 1967, the People's Bank lent $12.9 million to cooperative societies,including cooperative banks. The seven cooperative banks lent $1.4 million to societies and unions in addition to a sum of $46.6 million withdrawn by them on overdraft account.

The cooperative movement, as it exists in Ceylon today, is basically concerned not with the diversion of funds raised by the movement itself to finance agriculture. Instead, it is an instrument of the state responsible for channeling more than 30 per cent of credit to small farmers and small industrialists. It is also responsible for supplying more than 65 per cent of the food requirements of the people. About 25 per cent of the paddy produced today is marketed through the cooperative societies. Before the reduction of the rice ration in 1966, about 50 per cent of the rice was channeled through the Guaranteed Price Scheme which is operated by the cooperatives.

The cooperative movement originated in the rural areas, and its purpose was to serve the rural population. In certain respects, such as the marketing of agricultural products, it has not made much progress. Even in the marketing of paddy, there is more scope for the cooperatives to participate because this is almost entirely in the hands of millers. These weaknesses seem to stem from the financial inadequacies that have plagued small societies in the villages and also from the lack of proper organization and managerial skills. Very few multi-purpose societies have volunteered to supply a wide range of agricultural inputs that are vitally necessary for increasing productivity in agriculture.

Cooperatives have made their greatest impact in the channeling of credit to the producers. The funds so disbursed come either from the government or government agencies. As mentioned earlier, cooperatives have very limited funds, which are hardly adequate to meet the fringe requirements for agricultural development. Today, most of these multi-purpose credit societies depend on advances from the Central Bank. These advances are guaranteed by the government and are channeled through the People's Bank. A development of singular importance is the establishment of rural banking departments in many of the multi-purpose societies.

COOPERATIVES AND DEVELOPMENT PLANS

In successive economic development plans, there was little or no attention paid to the possible role of the cooperative sector. Presumably, the cooperative sector has been treated not as a source that could initiate and direct development but merely as an instrument that could be utilized at times as an adjunct to other methods of promoting development.

Despite the lack of direct interest in the cooperative sector, the functions of the cooperatives in national development have been fully recognized by government; but the extent to which this machinery has been utilized is somewhat limited. The economic progress achieved through cooperatives in India and Japan will show that cooperatives could be used to a much greater extent in national development. The Agricultural Cooperative Society Law of Japan states, "This law has for its purpose to promote the development of the national economy by increasing agricultural production and improving the economy and social status of farmers through the development of cooperative societies." The Indian fourth Five-Year Plan specifically mentions that for the achievement of growth and stability, both agricultural cooperatives and consumer cooperatives occupy a central position. It also refers to the role of institutions in increasing credit inputs and other resources required in agriculture, and for this purpose an efficient and viable cooperative system could make a substantial contribution.

AGRICULTURAL CREDIT BEFORE 1966 AND THE HIGH RATE OF DEFAULT

One of the drawbacks in the agricultural credit scheme operating in the 1950's was the inadequacy of funds made available to farmers. Only members of cooperatives who were considered creditworthy by the committee of management could borrow; and assuming that each member owned only one share worth $8.4, the maximum credit limit of a member was five times the subscribed share, which, in effect, meant that a member could borrow only up to $42.0. A member who owned three acres was also entitled to the same amount of credit. As the maximum cultivation loan was $29.4 per acre, the total amount of credit available in any one season was hardly sufficient to cultivate 1 1/2 acres.

Statistics of loans granted by the government under the credit scheme in the twenty-year period from 1947 to 1967 are not very encouraging. In 1947-48 the amount granted was $732,100, and the figure rose progressively to $3,087,395 by 1955. After reaching a peak of $3,686,386 in 1956-57, there was a sharp decline to $1,792,773 in 1962-63. In 1963-64, the amount granted was $5,813,109. Despite the erratic trend in the annual disbursements, there has been a steady increase in total loans outstanding. In 1947-48, loans outstanding were $304,537. In 1957-58, it was $3,469,243, in 1964-65 it had risen $9,109,243, and in 1966-67 the amount had risen sharply to $13,327,731.

What is remarkable in this loan program was essentially the high rate of default. Levels of default in the period 1947 to 1953 are not available. But statistics published after 1953 indicate that defaults have risen progressively from $998,319 in 1955-56, representing 32.4 per cent of total loans outstanding, to $4,351,932 in 1963-64, representing 59.8 per cent, to $9,489,747 or 71.2 per cent in 1967. From 1947 to September, 1967, total loans granted amounted to $52.8 million. Very little effort, particularly before 1965, was made to carry out an exhaustive study of the reasons for the very high rate of default. It would appear that this could be attributed to the relative inefficiency of the Agrarian Services Department that loaned the money to the peasant farmers, the lack of follow up procedures, and the inadequacy of security.

With the increase in the supply of credit, the output of paddy rose steadily over the 1950's and early 1960's, but the gains were not spectacular, as the figures below show, except in 1968 and 1969.

Paddy Yields
(Bushels per acre)

	1960	1961	1962	1963	1964	1965	1966	1967	1968	1969
Maha	36.10	35.93	38.02	37.84	38.60	34.11	35.91	40.85	47.49	51.23
Yala	36.82	36.46	37.69	38.04	38.92	34.70	35.04	42.01	44.59	48.24
Total	72.92	72.39	75.71	75.88	77.52	68.81	70.95	82.86	92.08	99.47
Average	36.46	36.19	37.85	37.94	38.76	34.40	35.47	41.43	46.04	49.73
Increase in yield	-	-0.74	4.59	0.24	0.82	-4.36	1.07	5.96	4.61	2.69

Perhaps this is because efforts were not made to cultivate all available paddy lands, and an increase in credit was not fully associated with other improved inputs because farmers has a tendency to use credit given for production for consumption purposes. The high rate of default could be attributed to this factor too.

Several committees were appointed to look into this question. Many of them submitted reports on the existing distribution of credit, but no attempts were made to study the problem of default so that remedial measures could be effected. One such committee reported in 1962 that only 65 per cent of the paddy cultivators in Ceylon were members of cooperative societies and that about half the number were share capital defaulters and, therefore, not entitled to borrow. It further reported that one-third of the cooperative societies were not considered creditworthy and were ineligible to receive loans from the government. As most members purchased only one share, their maximum borrowing capacity was considerably restricted. This committee recommended that the maximum credit limit to a member should not be the face value of shares held by an individual but his need for credit for productive purposes.

After 1961 the practice of giving what were known as "cultivation loans" by the Department of Agrarian Services was abandoned and cultivators were granted loans for specific purposes. For instance, a cultivator of one acre of paddy land could obtain credit for the following purposes:

Seed paddy	\$4.0
Fertilizer	\$6.10
Transplanting & row seeding	\$4.20
Weeding	\$4.20
Plowing	\$6.70
Harvesting	\$4.20

The committee further recommended that the credit limit should be \$19.30 per acre with a maximum of \$168.10 per member. Where the same land was cultivated twice a year, the maximum credit limit should be fixed at one-and-a-half times the above limits, but not more than \$29.4 per acre or \$168.10 per member should be granted in any one season. In 1963, the government took active steps to induce more farmers to join the cooperative movement so that there would be less attendant risks involved. On the basis of recommendations made by official committees, the government decided, inter alia:

1. That the Guaranteed Price Scheme should purchase produce only from members of cooperatives. This was to serve as an inducement for farmers to join cooperative societies.

2. That the Cooperative Societies Ordinance should be amended to provide for compulsory recovery of share installments from payments due to members under the Guaranteed Price Scheme.

In terms of the scheme launched in 1963, fresh loans were to be granted to defaulting cooperative societies for distribution to nondefaulting members. The government, moreover, decided to introduce a compulsory scheme for loan recovery by cooperative societies from their members. As a result of this policy, there was a sharp increase in loans given.

The loan granted to a member was fixed at $29.40 per acre and the maximum credit limit for a member who held one share was raised to $84. Share capital payments were to be made in ten installments of 80 cents per harvest. Loans amounting to $5.46 million were granted in 1963-64 as against $1.80 million in 1962-63. The reorganization in 1963 of the agricultural credit program, however, proved to be a failure because the government did not enact legislative amendments to the Cooperative Ordinance that were recommended under the scheme, and those that were effected came in too late. The other reason was that credit was given without adequate safeguards for recovery of loans. The government regarded the cooperative society merely as a channel of credit to farmers and not as the borrower itself. The societies themselves felt that they were not responsible for the recovery of loans; and since the money was channeled to the cooperatives from a government department, borrowers looked upon it more as a welfare measure than as a commercial proposition.

THE NEW AGRICULTURAL CREDIT SCHEME

In 1966, an official committee was once again appointed to review the role of the cooperative movement in relation to the provision of credit to farmers and to what extent the system could be geared to achieve higher levels of productivity in agriculture. The recommendations of this committee resulted in the introduction of one of the most significant experiments in agricultural financing that the country had hitherto undertaken. The scheme has been referred to as the New Agricultural Credit scheme. The success of the cooperatives in increasing productivity should be examined purely in the light of the achievements of this scheme.

The essential feature of the scheme is that credit to the cooperative system was to be fed through the People's Bank and other commercial banks. The Central Bank in turn was to refinance the People's Bank and the commercial banks and issue a guarantee up to 75 per cent on loans from these institutions.

The Central Bank was to refinance at 1/2 per cent and charge an additional 1/2 per cent for the guarantee. The People's Bank was, in fact, the only bank that participated in this scheme. It loaned money to societies at 5 per cent, and members had to pay 9 per cent per annum. A penalty of 3 per cent was added in case of default, making the effective rate 12 per cent on the amounts in default. The latter was applicable both to members and societies. The lending rates were raised to more realistic levels in order to make the borrower realize the seriousness of his obligations. Experience showed that credit on easy terms was unlikely to result in good borrowing because there was a natural tendency for the borrower to give priority to loans carrying higher rates of interest. Under the earlier schemes, the lending rates were subsidized; this was in addition to the other subsidies that the farmer received. The increase in demand for credit in earlier years was due partly to the low lending rates. The present rates under the New Agricultural Credit scheme are in keeping with rates in other Asian countries:

Country	Government lending	Lending Rates of Cooperatives
Burma	3%	12%
Taiwan	14.4%	13.3-16%
India	4.25-7.8%	6.8-9.4%
Japan	3.65-5.5%	10.95%
Thailand	0%-8%	10%-12%

The government decided to write off all unpaid balances that were outstanding from cooperative societies as of October 31, 1966, out of loans granted before October 1, 1958; and the societies in turn were to waive these amounts from the members. The defaults on loans granted to societies between October, 1958, and October, 1966, because of partial crop failure was also to be waived for societies and for members. The maximum loan for paddy cultivation was raised from $29.4 per acre up to a maximum of 6 acres to $37 per acre up to a maximum of 10 acres per cultivator.

Where the societies' loan repayments during the first three years of operation of the new scheme were satisfactory, the waiver of the remaining debts to the Department of Agrarian Services would be considered. Members who do not repay loans on the due date would be required to surrender to the societies their rice ration books and those of their families, and coupons would be detached at the rate of one coupon per one rupee. This process would go on until overdue loans were recovered. Recoveries from rice coupons would not, however, be made in the event of crop failure. The initial success of the scheme encouraged the government to enhance facilities available under it. In 1968, the loan per acre of paddy was raised; and in special project areas under improved varieties of seed, where larger amounts of fertilizer were found necessary, additional sums were given.

The New Agricultural Credit scheme began with the Maha season commencing in September, 1967. In the Maha season 1967-68, loans for paddy cultivation were given at the rate of $37 per acre up to a maximum of 10 acres per farmer.* The money was released in three stages. In the first stage, the aggregate sum required for plowing, seed paddy, transplanting, row seeding, and weeding was released and the maximum installment was $23 per acre. The second stage of the loan was paid by the People's Bank directly to the Commissioner of Agrarian Services to supply fertilizer, seed paddy, and agro-chemicals to societies.

---

*Before the scheme came into operation, the by-laws of the cooperative societies limited and indebtedness of a member to not more than ten times the face value of shares held by him. Under the new arrangements, the relevant by-laws were amended permitting a member to borrow up to twenty times the face value of shares.

For further details of the scheme see H.N.S. Karunatilake, Banking and Financial Institutions in Ceylon (Colombo: Central Bank of Ceylon, 1968).

The last installment of $4.20 per acre was released for harvesting.

Under the present arrangements, although credit is provided by the People's Bank, the government bears 74 per cent of the default minus half per cent of the total funds lent, which accrues to the Bank as the guarantee fee.

For the Maha season 1967-68 a sum of $13.10 million was approved by the People's Bank, but only $10.30 million was actually utilized by cooperative societies. In Maha 1968-69 the actual sum loaned was even less, *i.e.*, $7.7 million. Credit released in Maha 1968-69 and Yala 1969 was only 74 per cent and 8.5 per cent, respectively, of credit utilized in the corresponding previous seasons. This shortfall in the utilization of credit was due principally to an overestimate of credit requirements and also because earlier defaulters were ineligible to borrow. Others had been disuaded from borrowing because of the need for hypothecation of rice ration books. Many borrowers did not expect the government to insist on the surrender of rice ration coupons till the loan was fully repaid. The amount of loans approved and actually utilized in the Yala 1968 has been smaller than in the Maha 1967-68. In part, this is because the physical acreage normally cultivated under Yala is little over half that of the Maha. Out of the sum disbursed in the Maha 1967-68 cultivation season, voluntary repayments amounted to 69.4 per cent of all loans while recoveries through the surrender of rice ration coupons was $1.4 million, or 7.5 per cent, giving a total recovery rate of 76.9 per cent of total loans given. In the Maha 1968-69 season, voluntary recoveries declined to 51 per cent. At the end of June, 1969, $22.9 million had been disbursed under the New Agricultural Credit scheme. Of this, $13.7 million, or 59.5 per cent, had been recovered. Of the total sum outstanding the amount in default was $3.6 million, or 15.6 per cent.

In the Maha 1968-69 season, the sum loaned per acre was increased from $37 to $44. Credit limits had to be increased because of the higher costs of fertilizer and plowing rates. The loan of $4.20 for harvesting was abandoned, and instead a sum of $4.20 was given for the purchase of pesticides. Under the revised scheme disbursements were made in three installments.*

The inability to repay loans as a result of crop failure was treated differently from that of negligence or willful default. In such cases, repayment was extended over the next three seasons and was payable in three installments. As a result of crop failure, 4.9 per cent of the loans were extended for repayment during the following seasons. If allowance is made for crop failure, the actual amount of loans in default in 1967-68 would be 18.2 per cent of the total. As against this, in the previous year when the scheme was administered by the Department of Agrarian Services, only 45.9 per cent of the amounts disbursed was recovered. Apart from the hypothecation and surrender of rice ration books for Maha loans, defaulters for Maha 1967-68 season were not entitled to borrow until the full amount of the loan was recovered. If the failure to repay is certified as being due to a farmer's inability to

---

*Basis of disbursements:

	Purpose	$ per acre	
1st Stage	Seed paddy	5.40	
	Plowing	10.10	
	Pesticides	4.20	
	Total 1st stage		19.70
2nd Stage	Fertilizer	16.0	
	Total 2nd stage		16.0
3rd Stage	Hand weeding	4.20	
	Transplanting or row seeding	4.20	
	Total 3rd stage		8.40
	Total all stages		44.10

dispose of his crop, he will not be denied credit facilities for the next season.

Problems in the operation of agricultural credit schemes in Ceylon, given below, have been a handicap and continue to be of some hindrance under the better arrangements that now exist.

1. Some farmers look upon loans as outright grants and therefore do not consider it obligatory on their part to repay loans. Further, habitual defaulters of the earlier schemes have also been given credit, without any consideration of the causes for default. The unsatisfactory level of voluntary repayments has been a significant factor in reducing the number of farmers eligible for credit.

2. Some farmers have shown a preference for repayment of loans through rice ration coupons. This is due to the valuation of rice ration coupons at 17 cents per measure, which is higher than the guaranteed price for paddy. At 17 cents per measure, the value of a bushel of paddy is $2.60 as against the guaranteed price of $2.40. Repayments with rice ration coupons make farmers ineligible to borrow till such time as they have fresh coupons for hypothecation.*

3. Credit limits are determined on a national basis rather than on the basis of regional requirements. The need for credit in certain areas was less than the amounts given, and there was a tendency for some farmers to use borrowed funds for other purposes.

---

*From June, 1970, hypothecation of rice ration coupons has been discontinued.

4. The existing indebtedness to other creditors results in the latter collecting their dues from the threshing floor leaving the farmer without an adequate balance to repay. Part of the present strategy should be to eliminate the dominant position occupied by indigenous lenders in some regions.

5. The declining trend of credit disbursements, if unchecked, could be a serious setback to the peasant farmers' capacity to adopt improved cultivation practices requiring higher financial commitments.

6. One of the fundamental weaknesses of the scheme continues to be the inadequate supervision of loans given by cooperative societies.

THE PEOPLE'S BANK AND COOPERATIVE FINANCE

The People's Bank is now the chief financier of the cooperative movement. The bank has the largest number of branches in the country (over 90), forming a network throughout the different districts. The objectives of the bank are "To develop the cooperative movement of Ceylon, rural banking, and agricultural credit by furnishing financial and other assistance to cooperative societies, approved societies, cultivation committees and other persons". It is also empowered to transact all other types of business of an ordinary commercial bank. Further, there is provision for the government to lend to the Bank as and when necessary as authorized by a resolution of the House of Representatives. The bank may raise money by the issue of debentures guaranteed by government. The shares of the bank are held in equal proportions by the cooperative movement and by the Ceylon government.

The cooperatives have obtained finance from a number of sources, and, of these, as the Table 17 shows, the People's Bank and government have supplied the bulk of the credit.

TABLE 18

Debts of Cooperative Societies, 1967
(In millions of dollars)

People's Bank	6.2
Cooperative District Banks	3.5
Cooperative Societies Deposits	.03
Local Loans and Development Fund (Government)	15.2
Members' Individual Deposits	4.1
Others	3.1

Source: Administration Reports of the Commissioner of Cooperative Development.

In 1967, the cooperative district banks had borrowed $1.6 million from the People's Bank. In the same year, the People's Bank loaned $1.8 million to cooperative societies and cooperative unions for marketing, in addition to an additional sum of $11.1 million for other purposes. Societies and unions have undertaken pawnbroking as agents of the People's Bank, and under this category a sum of $0.9 million has been given.

In 1963, the People's Bank launched a scheme of extended rural credit, which is another source of institutional credit to the rural sector. Under this scheme, cooperative societies with a good credit performance were selected, in consultation with the Cooperative Department, and overdraft facilities were made available to them for relending for approved purposes to their members over and above those available to members from other sources. The overdraft limit given to a cooperative society ranges from $1,680 to $8,403. Loans could be used for a number of purposes and were not limited to purely productive activities. In addition to production, they included bringing new land under cultivation, animal husbandry, cottage industries, electrification, housing, redemption of debts, and consumption. The maximum loan for any of the first three purposes was $420.20 and for consumption purposes $84. A member may obtain a loan for consumption and other purposes provided the aggregate does not exceed $504. The loan had to be repaid in full within a period of five years. At the end of 1969, the scheme was being operated by 72 cooperatives as against 69 at the end of 1968. The overdraft limits authorized by the People's Bank were $0.3 million and the amount utilized increased by $80.7 million.

RURAL BANKS

At present the kingpins of the cooperative credit system are the multi-purposes societies that have opened rural banking departments, the third main source of institutional credit for the farmer. A description of cooperative institutions will be incomplete without reference to them. The People's Bank launched the rural banking scheme in March, 1964, with a view to extending banking services to the villages. The purpose was to provide agriculturists with credit for production, consumption, housing, emergencies, and the redemption of debts. The latter were also the prime objectives of the extended rural credit scheme. The People's Bank has been instrumental in setting up banking departments in certain select multi-purpose cooperative societies, taking into account the economic importance of the area served by the society and the level of viability that these particular multi-purpose cooperatives had attained. A selected multi-purpose society must have a membership of at least 250 and should have been in existence for at least three years. Rural banks are not branches of the People's Bank. They are actually loans and savings departments of multi-purpose cooperatives. The management of rural banks is in the hands of the societies, while the People's Bank provides them with the technical assistance to open banking departments. The People's Bank has assigned to each rural bank one of its officers who has been carefully selected and who has received special training. His duties at a bank are to train its credit manager, check on security measures, introduce proper procedures, function as an adviser, and to periodically submit reports to the People's Bank. Rural banks have been provided with office equipment on easy terms by the People's Bank. All these banks have overdraft facilities with the People's Bank where credit is available at 7 per cent, and the banks in turn could grant loans to members at a rate not exceeding 12 per cent.

Every rural bank is required to set up a credit committee and recruit a credit manager. The credit manager is expected to have an agricultural background and training in cooperation. The society is advised by the bank to pay him a suitable salary. The society has to supervise the loans given, and the credit manager is normally expected to undertake on the spot inspection. The maximum credit limit for rural bank loans to individual members is now $840.30. Loans are given in kind and technical advice is available when necessary. Loans are released in installments and there is end-use supervision. Loans above $84 have to be supported by collateral, and repayment is determined according to the purpose of the loan and the capacity of the borrower to repay. The maximum period of repayment is five years. While loans are given only to members, rural banks transact pawnbroking business with members and nonmembers alike. Every member applying for credit is required to open a savings account. By this means the rural banks have promoted the savings habit and at the same time helped the borrower to enhance his capacity to repay. The People's Bank has carried out regular inspections of rural banks, and it has been observed that the banks have been functioning very satisfactorily.

The first rural bank was opened in March, 1964, and before the end of the second quarter, two others had commenced business. All three were in selected areas in the Central Province. These banks are among those which have the largest number of accounts today. The first rural bank had 1,629 savings accounts amounting to over $33,613 at the end of

TABLE 19

Maximum Credit Limits by Purpose:
A Comparison of the Extended Credit Scheme
and Rural Banks

Purpose	Maximum Credit Limit in Dollars	
	Extended Credit Scheme	Rural Banks
Production (e.g., Agriculture, Livestock, Farming, Cottage Industries)	420.20	840.30
Redemption of Debts	420.20	840.30
Housing	420.20	840.30
Electrification	100.80	100.80
Consumption	84.00	84.00
Emergencies	33.60	33.60

Source: Rural Credit Department, People's Bank.

August, 1969. Its short-term advances were a little over $60,504, and the bank had made a profit on its business. The third bank, which was opened in the same year, had 1,478 savings accounts and had made a profit of $2,672 in the year ending August, 1969. In 1965, five rural banks were opened, and, unlike the first three, they were located at distant places in the country. Each of these banks has more than 400 savings accounts and one exceeds 1,000 accounts. In 1966, five more rural banks were established, and today all except one have over 400 savings accounts. In 1967, 14 new rural banks began operations. In 1968, there was a marked acceleration of the pace at which rural bank facilities were provided when 17 banks were established in different parts of the country. The number of rural banks continued to increase in 1969 when 24 new banks were opened. At the end of November, 1970, there were 90 banks in operation as against the four that were established in 1964. Thus, in a period of five years, the number of rural banks has increased more than twenty-fold, averaging about 12 per year. Present indications are that because of their popularity, it is likely that many more banks will open in the near future.

Rural banks have, from the very inception, received both savings and fixed deposits. The majority are savings accounts. In 1969, total savings amounted to $960,150 and comprised 28,626 accounts. Fixed deposits were few in comparison; there were 724 fixed deposits totalling $77,339. The most noteworthy feature is that these banks have been able to match their short-term advances against savings deposits. Rural banks as a whole have ceased to be dependent on the finance of the People's Bank. In 43 banks, deposits were in excess of advances, while advances exceeded deposits in 25 banks. At the end of 1969, the banks had given 7,893 short-term advances. The average loan increased from $109 in 1968 to $118 in 1969. If the sum total of savings and fixed deposits is taken into account, total short-term advances are less than the sum of savings and fixed deposits.

Rural banks have also engaged in pawnbroking business. In 1969, the banks had 11,367 pawnbroking accounts, and the total sum loaned was $216,332. With regard to these loans, the need to back them with savings and fixed deposits does not arise because the valuables against which loans have been issued are adequate security, provided of course, a correct appraisal of the value is made.

The majority of customers of the rural banks are farmers. With increasing prosperity in the rural areas, as a result of higher levels of productivity, savings deposits have multiplied. This is particularly true of the banks that were established in 1964 and 1965. People have taken a genuine interest in developing the savings habit because in rural banks the possession of a savings deposit is a pre-condition for credit. A great many of the rural banks are located in areas that grow paddy or subsidiary foodcrops. This in itself is an indication that the banks transact mostly with the rural farmers and that they have been established with the object of benefiting them. At the same time, the increase in savings deposits is an indication of the growing prosperity in the rural economy, which is the result of improved techniques and the use of better agricultural inputs. It, moreover, reflects the potential for creating a surplus in an agricultural economy.

Of the sixty-eight rural banks, thirty-nine have been showing substantial profits. Even those that have shown a loss, those losses do not exceed a few hundred rupees. It is yet premature to comment on the overall profitability of these banks because many have been established during the past two years. Those that were in existence in 1964, 1965, and 1966 have, on the average, shown profits, while those that showed slight losses were established in the first seven months of 1969. Statistics relating to savings deposits indicate that rural banks services could be extended to areas which have hitherto had no such facilities. Furthermore, the success of the rural banks is an indication that for banks with progressive policies, there is tremendous scope for expansion and development. Even those that have commenced with a sense of uncertainty could become viable and profitable within a period of four to five years.

Although the history of the cooperative movement in Ceylon is fairly long, the success of the movement has been recent. As the foregoing account shows, with proper policies and better organization, cooperatives can be made to work effectively. Until the early 1960's, cooperative societies were unable to make any useful contribution to the country's development because of the weakness of the apex institutions. With the establishment of the People's Bank this has been overcome. Today, the multi-purpose societies are the source of vital inputs such as credit and fertilizer, and greater productivity is attributable to the latter. Achievements in agriculture, more specifically since 1965, will be discussed in a subsequent chapter.

CHAPTER

7

DEVELOPMENT OF MANPOWER RESOURCES

The population census of 1953 revealed that the total number of gainfully occupied persons was 2.9 million, representing 37 per cent of the total population at that time. This means that for every hundred persons 63 were dependent on the labor of the remaining 37. According to a United Nations study, the percentage of economically active people of all ages is 42.5 per hundred for Asia and the world.[1] The percentage of economically active found in Ceylon in 1953 was, therefore, somewhat lower than the average for the world. The results of the March, 1963, census are not yet officially available, but on the basis of sample surveys that have been conducted recently, it is evident that the total number of gainfully occupied people in Ceylon today is even less than that 1953.

The sample survey of employment, unemployment, and underemployment carried out by the Department of Labor in 1959-60 showed that only 30.5 per cent of the population was gainfully employed. The sample survey of consumer finances conducted by the Central Bank of Ceylon in 1963 estimated that 31.7 per cent of the country's population was in the economically active category. The reasons for the low participation of the population in economic activity could, to some extent, be attributed to the present age structure of the population.

TABLE 20

Economically Active Population

Year	Total Population	Economically Active Population	Per cent of Total
1921	4,498,600	2,220,700	49.4
1946	6,657,300	2,611,500	39.2
1953	8,097,800	2,993,000	36.9

Source: Census Reports 1921, 1946, and 1953.

In Ceylon today nearly 42 per cent of the population is below 14 years of age, whereas in the developing countries the percentage varies from 22 per cent to 30 per cent. Since children below the age of 14 are not in the economically active category, this factor may be significant. Those in the age group 15 to 64 years, which generally supplies the manpower for economic activity, form about 55 per cent of the total population, whereas in the developing countries the percentage is normally above 65.

Economists and planners did not pay much attention to the importance of developing manpower resources until the 1960's. In the pre-war decades, education was looked upon as an end in itself and was not recognized as a means of increasing the national wealth of a country. In many developing countries, greater emphasis has been placed on the mobilization of manpower resources because experience has proved that deficiency in manpower could hinder the pace of development.

Economists today recognize that manpower is an economic resource as important as equipment, machinery, and money. In an economic sense, manpower consists of managerial, scientific, engineering, technical skills and craftsmanship that are essential for the initiation, operation, and management of economic institutions. Hence, the government has directed its attention to creating the essential skills by the development of manpower resources through education and training, and secondly in the generation of employment opportunities to take maximum advantage of manpower potentialities.

The Ten-Year Plan was the first to recognize and emphasize the need for technical training and the role of education in economic development. This plan indicated:

> The problem of education merits special attention in view of its close relationship to general development. Planning in this field must satisfy at least three requirements.
>
> 1. The magnitude of the expansion program for schools must bear some relationship to the size of the future increase in the school-going population.
>
> 2. Measures must be devised which meet this objective in the most economic way so that the claims made on the resources of the country are not excessive.
>
> 3. And, perhaps, the most important of all, from the angle of development, the type of education imparted and the relative proportions between different kinds of skills produced must be closely geared to the needs of economic growth as set out in an overall plan.[2]

The plan went on to emphasize that "the educational system must now be more aggressively geared to the needs of development with a greater bias to technical and scientific education. This would require a greater provision for technical and practical courses in schools (the present curriculum is unduly academic) and a larger flow of pupils into higher technical and scientific courses in specialized institutions and universities."[3]

FREE EDUCATION AND MANPOWER

Since October, 1945, three years before the country attained independence, Ceylon has had an universal free education scheme, *i.e.*, from the kindergarten to the university. Ever since, there has been a marked increase in the number of pupils enrolled in primary and secondary schools. In 1947, there were 1,025,836 pupils, and by 1964 the number had increased to 2,620,927, or by about 155 per cent in a period of 17 years. The enrollment in the age group 5 to 14 years in 1964 was 2,207,366, which corresponds to about 80 per cent of the population in that age group.

Year	No. of Students of All Ages in Schools
1938	741,017
1945	852,042
1953	1,548,198
1959	2,098,941
1960	2,192,379
1961	2,313,852
1962	2,347,757
1963	2,461,374
1964	2,620,927

It can be surmised that by 1970 the total enrollment in schools would exceed 3.2 million. The availability of free education has tended to increase school attendance and to decrease the labor force participation of the population of school going age. Consequently, with the increase in the student population, a sharp increase in government expenditure on education has resulted in the last 25 years. In 1964-65, total expenditure on education was $58.8 million per year and in 1969, $67.2 million, which was about 20 per cent of the government's estimated revenue, or about 5 per cent of the GNP.

Although the economic implications of free education were not examined in the early years, it was, however, the government's view that a scheme of free education would enable the great majority of children to benefit from the scheme. Thus, many children, especially from the rural areas who could not afford an education at fee levying schools, had access to free education and opportunities of securing positions of standing in the country's administration and business. A large number of students who are now in the universities, possibly more than 85 per cent, are those who have benefited from free education; the bulk of those who have secured jobs in the public service since 1965 are in this category.

Implications of the free education scheme for development of human resources and manpower have been very significant. Despite any defects in the scheme, the principle that every individual in the country should have access to education is one of the fundamental principles of a proper manpower planning policy. The free education scheme was introduced at a time when development proposals were not closely linked to the manpower requirements of the economy. The first few development plans, excluding the Ten-Year Plan, paid scant attention to the need to gear manpower to the country's development program and resources. A complacent attitude had been adopted by administrators that trained manpower resources would emerge automatically and fit easily into the pattern of the development program. Perhaps this aspect of economic planning was ignored because in developing countries emphasis was placed on the development of human resources only during the last twenty years. Had the development plans paid sufficient attention even in the late 1950's to the manpower requirements of economic development, it is likely that the entire basis on which the free education scheme operated would have been altered.

It does not mean that the total outlays on education should be reduced, but the content of the courses and the present emphasis in education could have been suitably reoriented. The present defects of the free education scheme could be attributed to the lack of coordination between economic planning and the system of education. A manpower plan formulated with foresight would have indicated the changes necessary in the curriculum at the secondary school and university levels and specified the requirements of human resources for different projects and categories of work.

As a result of the lack of coordination and appropriate policies, there has been a surplus of manpower in some fields while in others there has been a shortage. From the outset, emphasis in schools and in universities has been primarily on nontechnological training. Ceylon inherited a system of education introduced some 125 years ago by the British. It was geared exclusively to the production of clerical and junior officers who could assist expatriate officials in administration; and for this, people with a broad formal education without any specialization in technical fields were required. The emphasis in schools then was on the arts and the humanities. This system of education continued even after Ceylon gained independence without any efforts being made to reorient the system to meet the requirements of manpower and skills.

In the 1960's, some attention was paid to reorient the system of education. With efforts at accelerating the rate of growth, more attention was given by planners to the training of manpower. Consequently, attempts were made to set up administrative and technical training facilities in schools and universities. A general weakness in the system of education in Ceylon is that vocational training has lagged far behind general education. There continues to be a dearth of manpower at the technical level, mainly foremen, draughtsmen, supervisors, and mechanics, whereas there is a surplus of persons holding academic degrees in arts subjects but with very little practical background.

The Planning Committee on Education and Manpower was of the opinion that senior secondary education had to be reconstructed not only to meet the new and emerging cultural needs but also the most essential manpower requirements of the country. It said that the reconstruction program would have to be looked at from a quantitative and qualitative standpoint. Qualitatively, the curriculum should be made less academic and more vocational. Quantitatively, the program should entail the gradual change of the current 85 per cent enrollment in arts classes and 15 per cent in non-arts classes at the General Certificate of Education (Ordinary Level) to approximately 60 per cent arts and 40 per cent non-arts.[4] The implementation of these proposals will require the further establishment of science laboratories, agricultural science laboratories, woodwork, and metal work shops.

REPORTS OF COMMITTEES ON MANPOWER RESOURCES

The formulation of an appropriate manpower policy has not been easy because adequate attention has not been paid in the past to investigating the manpower components of the development programs. Nor have attempts been made to collect and analyse data on various aspects of manpower and its utilization. Only two systematic inquiries have been conducted in the pre-1965 period. The International Labor Organization sponsored a survey on manpower covering 1951-61; and in 1958, the Planning Secretariat conducted a survey of engineers in the context of technical skills for the Ten-Year Plan. In 1961, the Commission of Inquiry on Technical Education also carried out a survey on manpower requirements.

After the establishment of the Ministry of Planning, a committee was appointed in 1965 to examine specifically manpower needs; their report was issued in May, 1967. The committee emphasized that they were handicapped in their deliberations by the lack of adequate and reliable statistical data on manpower and the absence of a clear and comprehensive program of economic development over the next five-year period. Moreover, they pointed out that there was no central organization to coordinate the manpower aspects of the development effort, that sufficient attention had not been paid to a comprehensive manpower survey of the country or to secure up-to-date information. Supporting the recommendations made by the earlier Commission on Technical Education and the views expressed at the Colombo Plan seminar on manpower, the report urged that a directorate of manpower be set up in the Planning Ministry as a matter of high priority. Therefore, in 1966 a manpower unit was set up in the Ministry of Planning and Economic Affairs, and at the same time a planning unit was created in the Ministry of Education to undertake work on education planning and research. To overcome the statistical gap, the committee supported the view of Albert Waterston, in his Report on Recommendations on Economic Planning in Ceylon published in 1966, that the Department of Census and Statistics should be brought under the Prime Minister and should function as an integral part of the Minister of Planning.

The development of technical education has been examined by the Commission of Inquiry on Technical Education and, on the basis of recommendations made, a separate unit has been set up in the Department of Education for this purpose. This unit has taken steps to increase the supply of technically trained personnel, yet the supply is inadequate in comparison to the country's development requirements. This unit also has been handicapped in estimating the actual requirements of manpower because of the absence of systematic manpower surveys. The present expansion program of technical education has been based on statistics of future requirements of trained manpower as given in the Report of the Commission of Inquiry on Technical Education.

TECHNICAL SKILLS

The demand for engineers in Ceylon has been studied by several committees. In 1958, the Planning

Secretariat carried out a survey of employment of engineers with a view to ascertaining future requirements. The survey showed that there was an immediate demand for 1,960 engineers to meet new requirements as well as to fill vacancies created by extensions and retirements over the five year period ending 1962. As Table 21 illustrates, 200 additional engineers would be required to meet the demand from the public and private sectors. Fairly accurate forecasts of the demand for engineers were not made because of the absence of information relating to current employment prospects in the private sector. The committee observed that the demand would depend eventually on the investment targets proposed in the new development program and the growth rate envisaged for the industrial sector.

TABLE 21

Estimates of Additional Annual Requirements of Trained Technical Personnel

Category	Number
A. Engineering and Industry	
(a) Technologists (Engineering 200, Architects 25, Applied Scientists 25)	250
(b) Technicians of all types	1,000
(c) Craftsmen of all types	5,000
B. Agriculture	
(a) Scientists (Technologist Grade)	25
(b) Agricultural Technicians	700
(c) Trained Farmers (including 'craft' grades)	12,000
C. Commerce	
(a) Managers and Executives	200
(b) Sub-Managers and Supervisors	200
(c) Vocational Grades	22,000

Source: Report of the Commission of Inquiry on Technical Education, 1963.

At present the training of engineers is chiefly undertaken by the faculty of engineering at the University of Ceylon and to a smaller extent at the Institute of Practical Technology of the Department of Technical Education and Training. With the expansion of the faculty of engineering at Peradeniya, the turnout of engineering graduates has increased progressively from 55 in 1960, to 80 in 1967, and to 100 in 1970. In addition to graduates of the University of Ceylon, there also are others who take professional exams conducted by foreign universities, and it has been estimated that about 20 engineers would be available from these sources. The newly established College of Technology is the third source from which engineers will qualify, and by 1972 the turnout of engineers is expected to be in the required neighborhood of 200 per year.

The training of architects is undertaken by the Institute of Technology and by the Department of Architecture of the University of Ceylon, Colombo. These two institutions are expected to provide about thirty architects per year. At present, there are no courses for the training of applied scientists, and proposals have been made to develop such courses at the post-graduate levels in local universities.

Facilities for training managers in the field of commerce is now handled by the Ceylon Technical College and the junior universities while the University of Ceylon conducts a degree course in commerce. Since 1966, the Department of Management Studies at Vidyodaya University has provided courses in business and public administration both at the undergraduate and graduate levels, each leading to a degree. Already over 200 graduates in business administration have found employment in the private sector and in government enterprises. In addition, those who have received higher degrees, the Masters degrees in Business Administration and Public Administration that qualify them for higher executive posts, hold key position in government administration and in the private sector. These facilities are being expanded gradually to cater to the increasing need.

Technicians are normally in the middle order of engineering and industrial employment. This category includes inspectors, foremen, surveyors, and draughtsmen. The Technical Working Group on Skills reported in 1958 that there were approximately 6,000 persons in the technician level consisting of 3,800 engineering technicians, 900 draughtsmen, 850 surveyors and foremen, and 450 others.[5] The survey conducted by the Commission of Inquiry on Technical Education revealed that in 1961 there were nearly 7,000 technical employees both in the public and private sectors. Of this, 1,000 had recognized technical qualifications and over 3,000 were departmentally qualified. At the end of 1965, there were some 6,500 technicians employed in government departments and about 800 in the public sector. It has been estimated that the ratio of engineering technicians in the public sector should be 1:4. In practice, however, this ratio has varied considerably from establishment to establishment. In the State Engineering Corporation the ratio of engineers to technicians is 1:2; in the Public Works Department 1:6; in the Irrigation Department 1:4; and in the Ceylon Government Railway 1:14. The Colombo Plan Bureau has suggested that countries in Southeast Asia should aim at an average ratio of 1:5 between engineers and technicians.

The number of vacancies in the technicians grade at the end of 1965 was estimated to be about 400. At a replacement rate of 4 per cent per year, the total requirements of the public sector would work out to 750. The majority of technicians in Ceylon have been trained at the Ceylon Technical College and at the Institute of Practical Technology at Katubedde. The latter institute conducts two-year full term courses in civil, mechanical, and chemical engineering and a one year course in draughtsmanship, surveying, and levelling. The Hardy Institute of Technical Training at Amparai, run by the River Valleys Development Board, also provides a two-year course in practically the same areas. The Ceylon Government Railway conducts a five-year apprenticeship course, and the Irrigation Department has a scheme for training technical assistants in the Department. Similar schemes are operated by the Electrical

Department (now the Ceylon Electricity Board), the Colombo Port Commission, and the Survey Department. The total number of qualified trainees from these sources up to 1966-67 has been estimated to be about 2,500. The present development programs can absorb 2,800 new technicians. Steps have already been taken to fill this gap, notably by the establishment of junior universities and technical colleges in several towns. Plans have also been finalized to set up more provincial polytechnics and to expand existing facilities at the Institute of Practical Technology at Katubedde.

The Commission of Inquiry on Technical Education estimated that the demand for craftsmen for industry and engineering would be approximately 5,000 per annum. It was reported in 1967 that the turnout of craftsmen from all sources was about 1,000 per year. To overcome this shortage, it was proposed to establish polytechnics in the provinces, trade schools at the Ceylon Technical College, to reorganize the Basic Technical Training Institute, and to establish five junior technical schools every year beginning in 1966. From these institutions about 500 have qualified as craftsmen every year. Today there are more than twelve junior technical schools that offer instruction at the trades level, which leads up to the National Certificate for Craftsmen. It generally takes about four to five years to train a skilled craftsman. But since there is an immediate demand in development projects, it has been suggested that intensive courses of training be followed so that craftsmen could qualify within a period of about two years.

TRAINING IN AGRICULTURE

More recently, with the intensive drive towards agricultural development, steps have been taken to place agricultural know-how at the disposal of farmers. Many traditional farmers do not have an adequate theoretical and practical training in agriculture. This has been one of the main reasons for static techniques and for low productivity. The stepping up of agricultural productivity requires extension services and training facilities for people in the rural areas. There is also another reason for increased emphasis on agricultural education and training. An end result of the scheme of free education has been that the number of those who leave school to enter the labor market in search of white collar jobs has increased progressively from year to year. Since opportunities for white collar jobs are limited, many remain unemployed and, therefore, unproductive. An almost exclusively theoretical bias in the educational system is one fundamental cause for the imbalance between the large number of those who leave school and opportunities for employment. One method of overcoming this would be to impart education with a strong agricultural bias because it will provide greater diversity of self-employment opportunities to those who have had a formal general education but who have only minimum capital resources.

The average farmer in Ceylon does not receive a comprehensive and systematic training in agriculture. The present extension services merely provide him with advice and better inputs. He is ignorant of the most elementary principles about soils, the impact of rotation of crops, and the economics of marketing; this is also the case with younger generation because of the inadequacies of the system of agricultural education today.

Agricultural education in Ceylon dates back to 1884 when the first school of agriculture was established. Since then, efforts have been made to expand gradually agricultural education in the country. But rapid changes in emphasis, the dislike for agricultural pursuits by educated people, lack of appreciation of the role of agricultural education, and the absence of a coordinated program at all levels have contributed to the failure of agricultural education in Ceylon. The aim of agricultural education in Ceylon should be primarily to achieve maximum production, thus enabling a large section of the increasing labor force to find suitable employment opportunities. For this purpose it would be necessary to teach pre-vocational agriculture as a compulsory subject in the schools. The curriculum of vocational agriculture should be designed to cater to the needs of school leavers at various levels of education. Agriculture education should also form a part of higher education.

Higher education in agriculture with courses leading to a degree is at present available only at the University of Ceylon. Since the Faculty of Agriculture was set up in 1948, the total number of graduates turned out up to 1968 has been only about 125 because of the very limited demand for graduates in this field. In relation to the importance of agriculture, it has been estimated that there should be at least 10,000 agricultural graduates in Ceylon. One reason for the relatively poor demand has been defects in the courses available at the university; the courses have had an academic rather than a practical bias. To overcome this, the degree courses should be modified to give a practical bias and should also give coverage to such fields as marketing, food processing, canning, and sales promotion so that employment opportunities for agricultural graduates could be widened. At the diploma level, courses in agriculture have been provided at two farm schools, one for men and the other for women.

HIGHER EDUCATION

In 1965, the total enrollment of persons for higher education was 14,300, which is less than 1 per cent of the population in the age group 18 to 24. This ratio might compare favorably with the trends in the other developing countries, but the question is how many of them are following courses which are vitally essential? Nearly 76 per cent of the students in universities follow courses in arts and only 24 per cent are enrolled for science courses. This imbalance in the scheme of enrollment has been due to several factors. First, there are shortcomings at the secondary school educational level where there is a preponderance of arts subjects, with poor facilities for teaching science and lack of teachers. Second is the failure in the past to formulate programs of higher education in a positive and systematic manner geared to the manpower requirements of the country. Then there are also the outmoded teaching techniques that are still prevalent throughout the country. This is principally so because teachers have not been able to adjust themselves to new developments in the field of education and in techniques of teaching.

The vast majority of students who enter the universities today are in the arts areas, and the most popular subjects are Sinhala, history, geography and economics. Of these subjects, only economics has some relevance to development. This situation is likely to continue till such time as the secondary school curriculum gives much less emphasis to arts subjects. The alternative would be to restrict the numbers that are presently taken in by the four universities. The four universities are The University of Ceylon, Colombo; the University of Ceylon, Peradeniya; Vidyodaya University of Ceylon; and Vidyalankara University of Ceylon. Three of them are in the Colombo district and one outside. The lowering of standards of admission has further contributed substantially to the greater intake of students for arts studies. As a result, the quality of the average graduate has fallen considerably. This could also be attributable to the fact that the courses are conducted in Sinhala, and the paucity of Sinhala texts leads to very restricted reading. What little knowledge is gained is through the lecture notes, which are reproduced with varying degrees of accuracy at the examinations.

Despite the implementation of recommendations, there is little or no fundamental improvement in the skills and quality of those who graduate at the four universities. What is required urgently then is the implementation of recommendations at the secondary school level, which have been ignored. Science education at the junior and secondary school levels has received a severe setback due to the shortage of qualified teachers, the lack of equipment, and suitable text-books in the official language. A further limitation is funds for providing laboratories and other equipment for science education. Science education in general has been less attractive for the average student because of the poor background provided at the elementary school level and also because of the overemphasis on arts courses in the preceding two decades; the average student finds science education less attractive. Several junior universities and institutes of higher technical education have been established for those unable to secure places at universities. The junior universities and technical institutes are oriented towards subjects in the field of commerce, accounting, management and science education. It still remains to be seen whether these institutions will, in practice, produce the training and skills that are urgently required by government and the private sector.

Several commissions and committees of inquiry have reported on the inadequacy of the present system of higher education and have urged early reorganization. One recommendation has been implemented, and that is the establishment of a National Council of Higher Education to assist the minister in the following aspects of education: (1) The apportionment and control of expenditure on higher education; (2) the maintenance of academic standards; (3) the administration of universities and other institutes of higher learning; (4) the coordination of university and higher education with the needs of the nation for social, cultural, and economic development; and (5) any other matters which the minister may refer to the council.

The influence of the National Council of Higher Education on reorientation of work at the universities has been negligible.* It has been concerned more with the finance and administration of universities than in developing and introducing courses that are vitally necessary to make a positive contribution to

---

*The new government that took office in May, 1970, has decided to replace the National Council of Higher Education with a University Grants Committee.

the development effort. Although the admission of candidates is within its purview, no limits have been imposed on those entering the arts faculties. If it is to make any useful contribution, the National Council of Higher Education should have some influence over the system of education as a whole because the curriculum cannot be changed merely by making adjustments in the content of courses at the university levels. Changes should be effected at the primary levels and progressively brought up over a period of time. The National Council of Education has been criticized by the public, the university staff, and the students because of its failure to make radical changes in the system of higher education.

EMPLOYMENT AND UNEMPLOYMENT

There has been a rapid increase in population in Ceylon during the last two decades, resulting mainly from a sharp fall in the death rate. This has resulted in a corresponding increase in the size of the workforce. It is estimated that the workforce has been increasing at the rate of about 106,000 per annum between 1953 and 1960. In a study prepared in 1959 by the Planning Secretariat, it was estimated that the workforce of 3.4 million in 1956 will double to 7 million by 1981.[6] The extent of the future increase in the workforce is an indication of the magnitude of the problem that the country will face in the field of employment and manpower planning.

There are two important aspects to the manpower problem in Ceylon. As one sees it today, there is a surplus of labor both in the traditional as well as in the developing sectors of the economy, and this has appeared in the form of employment and underemployment. On the other hand, there is an acute shortage of technical skills and qualified managerial staff. These, however, are not independent and separate issues. They are intimately related to each other because the coexistence of unemployment and the shortage of skills indicate certain shortcomings in harnessing the present manpower resources. In other words, these problems have arisen because of defects and imbalance in the education structure.

The sample survey conducted by the Department of Labor in 1959-60 showed that nearly 340,000, or 12.8 per cent, of the country's labor force, or 4.5 per cent of the total population, was unemployed.[7] This survey also showed that 11.8 per cent of the labor force in the rural areas and 18.3 per cent in the urban areas were unemployed. Similar results were shown by the Central Bank Consumer Finance Survey 1963 where 457,000 persons, representing 13.8 per cent of the island's labor force or 4.4 per cent of the total population, were unemployed. The survey also showed quite distinctly that unemployment was higher in the urban than in the rural areas. The population census of 1963 has tentatively reported that unemployment was 265,000 in 1963.* Mr. Evans in his Report on Rural Employment Problem issued in 1965 stated that the unemployed population was about 475,000, or 13 1/2 per cent of the workforce.

Date on unemployment is available from the numbers of registrants at the employment exchanges, but they do not reflect the true position for a number of reasons. For instance, unemployment in the rural areas is not indicated because it is mostly the urban and semi-urban dwellers who register at exchanges. Furthermore, many hope to secure jobs through direct access to employers. The position in 1969 and 1970 worsened. It is now estimated that the total number of people who join the ranks of the unemployed annually are in the region of about 40,000. Of this, the proportion of educated persons has

---

*At the census of 1963, to be classed as unemployed a person had to satisfy two conditions: he should be without employment or work and should be seeking or looking for work. This definition is very restrictive and underestimates the true position. Strict comparison of the data above is not possible because the definition of unemployment was different at each of the surveys.

increased appreciably.* If these figures are added to the 400,000 unemployed in 1965, a correct estimate of the number unemployed would be in the region of 600,000. Table 22 shows the number of registrants at the employment exchanges in the island in the period 1946-1969.

An analysis of the figures shows that the largest number of unemployed persons is in the unskilled categories. It is believed that the problem of unskilled workers is really one of underemployment and seasonal unemployment rather than a total lack of employment opportunities. As mentioned earlier, this is a feature of the rural agricultural economy where subsidiary employment opportunities are restricted.

Registrants in the semi-skilled category are next in importance. Those who have registered under this category are mostly persons under twenty years of age who are partially educated; they have not received training in agricultural skills. The type of employment sought by them would be in the minor employment categories, such as peons, office boys, messengers, and hospital attendants.

The third largest group are those who have registered for technical and clerical jobs. They consist mostly of those who have left school after completing the eight grade or the General Certificate of Education (Ordinary level) and who have not had facilities to continue with their studies beyond this point or acquire technical skills. Their education generally qualifies them for clerical jobs. Because of the

---

*The available information shows that 29 per cent of the unemployed are women. The highest number of unemployed (about 25 per cent) are those who have completed the General Certificate of Education (Ordinary) level. The next largest group is of those who have completed eight years of schooling (about 24 per cent). Among the rural unemployed, about 25 per cent were looking for clerical or teaching jobs.

TABLE 22

Number of Registrants at
Employment Exchanges

End of period	Total[a]	Technical & Clerical	Skilled	Semi-skilled	Un-skilled
1946	36,544	5,636	10,012	7,527	13,396
1947	34,477	2,883	7,325	8,113	16,423
1948	66,656	4,474	13,027	12,443	36,712
1949	69,732	5,132	11,994	13,591	39,015
1950	65,122	5,627	10,525	13,523	35,447
1951	52,707	5,515	8,186	12,520	26,486
1952	53,029	6,883	77,522	13,795	24,823
1953	51,546	8,374	6,462	13,676	23,034
1954	62,304	11,728	7,919	16,287	27,370
1955	71,010	14,498	8,544	20,142	27,826
1956	85,952	16,091	9,794	25,808	34,259
1957	110,856	18,532	13,429	30,864	47,971
1958	117,796	19,803	13,674	32,973	51,346
1959	128,018	20,869	13,859	33,723	59,567
1960	151,092	26,252	16,928	34,887	73,025
1961	151,265	27,629	18,201	34,212	71,223
1962	152,209	33,825	17,352	35,593	65,439
1963	151,922	35,924	16,384	36,255	63,159
1964	165,456	41,208	17,942	38,165	68,141
1965	199,655	55,238	20,051	48,907	75,459
1966	238,901	65,924	21,739	60,126	91,112
1967	257,070	72,400	23,684	66,651	94,335
1968	276,339	75,725	25,229	71,021	104,424
1969	341,286	85,184	31,147	86,492	137,833

[a]The figures listed are those of persons whose names remained on the registers of the employment exchanges at the end of each period. They include persons who were unemployed at the time of registration as well as persons who were employed on a full-time basis but wanted other employment.

Source: Department of Labor

large numbers leaving school annually and the very limited employment opportunities available to them, the problem of employment of school leavers is becoming more and more acute each year. Approximately 400,000 candidates sit for the General Certificate of Education (Ordinary level) examination each year, and about 75,000 are successful. Of this number not more than 25 per cent get jobs in the first year. According to independent estimates of the number of unemployed graduates, the minimum figure is in the region of 9,000 in 1970.

Table 22 also shows that the registration of workers in the skilled category is quite high. The really skilled and technically qualified person would not find it difficult to secure employment with attractive salaries because of the dearth of personnel in this field. But the numbers have continued to increase because many persons have registered themselves in the hope of securing better and permanent jobs, even though their qualifications may not give them access to jobs that require highly specialized skills.

There are probably three reasons for the increasing unemployment in Ceylon in recent years; the pressure of population, the migration from rural to urban areas, and the tendency for mechanization of new industry. With regard to the first, since 1965 the rate of increase of population has come down from about 32 per thousand in the early 1950's to about 27 per thousand in the middle 1960's. But this decrease has not made an impact on the unemployment problem as a whole. However, many have benefited from free education and are now seeking jobs in the towns. The educated nonurban dweller is not seeking a job that will provide his basic needs but employment that is consistent with his educational attainments. The exodus from the rural areas to the towns has been greatest in the 1960's, with increasing numbers of students from the villages entering the universities. Most of them have not gone back to the villages but have remained in the towns and looked for employment.

TABLE 23

Number of Persons Placed in Employment and Its
Relative Importance to Total Registrants in Each Category

Year	Technical and Clerical		Skilled		Semi-skilled		Unskilled		Total	
	Number placed	Per cent of total registr- ants in the category	Number placed	Per cent of total registr- ants in the category	Number placed	Per cent of total registr- ants in the category	Number placed	Per cent of total registr- ants in the category	Number placed	Per cent of total registr- ants
1960	1,400	5.3	771	4.6	1,247	3.6	4,744	6.5	8,162	5.4
1961	1,259	4.6	631	3.5	964	2.8	2,794	3.9	5,648	3.7
1962	1,263	3.7	468	2.7	809	2.3	2,315	3.5	4,857	3.2
1963	1,322	3.7	502	3.0	836	2.3	2,466	3.9	5,129	3.4
1964	1,722	4.4	535	3.2	945	2.5	3,599	5.5	6,801	4.3
1965	1,495	2.7	846	4.2	1,035	2.1	3,753	5.0	7,129	3.6
1966	1,056	1.6	740	3.4	917	1.5	4,089	4.5	6,802	2.9
1967	1,018	1.4	588	2.5	712	1.1	1,936	2.1	4,254	1.7
1968	680	0.9	780	3.1	794	1.1	2,696	2.6	4,950	1.8
1969[a]	865	1.0	710	2.3	800	0.9	2,908	2.1	5,283	1.5

[a]Provisional

Source: Department of Labor

The migration towards the towns has to some extent resulted from the lack of planning in the location of industry. When industries were first established between 1960 and 1963, the bulk were located in the Colombo district or along the western coastline. Therefore, there was no incentive for people to remain in the rural districts. A solution to this would have been to locate new industries as far as possible in rural areas. But this has not been possible because of infrastructure facilities like power, water, and transportation being unavailable to new industries in the nonurban regions. This has been overcome to some extent with plans to set up industrial estates and locate new industries away from the towns. A more serious problem is the tendency for new industries to use technologies which are capital intensive.

In 1969 the total number of employees in the nontraditional industries or the new industries was 103,726. The corresponding figure for 1968 was 101,348 and for 1966, 61,418. At present, more than 2,000 new industries have been approved, and the possibilities of increasing the number of industries in the near future are limited because approvals have been granted for the production of practically 90 per cent of the products that people in Ceylon consume. In view of this, the prospects of finding more employment in new industry is very limited, unless of course export markets are found. If a projection is made of employment in new industry by 1975, employment might rise by another 20,000, but this indeed is an exaggerated estimate, for there is a preference among new industrialists to use machinery instead of labor where possible. There is a good reason for this. In the past few years most new industries have been plagued with labor disputes and work stoppages that have seriously affected the profitability of the enterprise. The tendency to substitute machinery for labor has not been checked and regulated by the Ministry of Industries, which has been in overall charge of industrial development. Efforts have also not been made to ensure that, where a task could be done effectively by labor, machines are not used. For the procurement of machinery, foreign exchange seems to have been made available to new industries without much restriction. Now that the trend is quite clear, it will be impossible to reverse it; and the tendency for labor to be displaced by machines will continue. The avenues which offer greater prospects of employment in the future are the service industries such as tourism, marketing, advertising, transport, retailing, hotels, and catering. With the recent development of tourism, there have been increasing employment prospects. But it is most unlikely that more than 20 to 25,000 jobs would be available in the tourist service sector even after the construction of all the large and medium size hotels in Ceylon.

The difficulties may also be attributed to the defects in the present policy towards employment and the development of manpower resources before 1970. The manpower unit in the Ministry of Planning and Economic Affairs under the previous government was concerned primarily with academic exercises on employment and manpower resources. The strategy has revolved round the preparation of an input/output table and the possibility of obtaining some results for the formulation of policy on the basis of relationships in the table. There has been little or no attention paid to the practical problem of exploring avenues for utilizing idle manpower and of providing more employment opportunities. Reports on unemployment that have been submitted by committees in the Ministry of Planning and Economic Affairs only have given very academic solutions to the problem. One such report was concerned primarily with the number of vacancies in the government sector, particularly in the state corporations. There was no constructive analysis of the ways and means that could be adopted to increase the avenues of employment in the immediate future. What is required most urgently is a manpower policy with a more practically oriented approach to the problem. An analysis will have to be made of the manpower requirements of different sectors, particularly the industrial and services sector, and what potentialities there would be to increase the use of manpower. Furthermore, the overall question of appropriate technologies in new industry will have to be reviewed, and investments, both infrastructure and noninfrastructure, will have to be determined in terms of increasing use of labor.

The United Front Government that took office in May, 1970, is paying considerable attention to employment. The former Ministry of Planning and Economic Affairs has been replaced by a Ministry of Planning and Employment. Details of its employment program will be referred to in the last chapter.

NOTES

1. United Nations. Demographic Aspects of Manpower, Report I: Sex and Age Patterns of Participation in Economic Activities (Population Studies No. 33), New York, 1962.

2. National Planning Council, Ten-Year Plan (Colombo: Planning Secretariat , 1959), p. 46.

3. Ibid., p. 47.

4. Report of the Planning Committee on Education, Health, Housing and Manpower (Colombo: Ministry of Planning and Economic Affairs, May, 1967).

5. "Report of the Technical Working Group on Skills," in Reports of Committees and Technical Working Groups (Colombo: Planning Secretariat, 1959).

6. See Rao Sundram and S. Selvaratnam, "Manpower Resources of Ceylon 1956-1981" (Colombo: Planning Secretariat, 1959).

7. R. Bose and A.K. Das Gupta, Survey of Employment, Unemployment, and Underemployment (Colombo: Department of Labor, 1959-60).

CHAPTER 8
THE DRIVE TOWARD INDUSTRIALIZATION AFTER 1959

If a very broad meaning is attached to the word industrialization, Ceylon could be referred to as an industrial country even before the advent of the drive towards industrialization roughly after 1959. Frequent references have been made in literature to the rubber industry and the tea industry over a long period of time. Unlike many of the African countries, Ceylon had manufacturing units associated with primary production. For about sixty years, factories in Ceylon have been processing tea, rubber, and coconut. These small manufacturing units were principally concerned with the processing of primary products for export. Some of these commodities could be classified as final products because they are not inputs for other industries. But in a strict sense, tea for instance is not a primary product because when it leaves the factory it is practically ready for consumption. The only further processing is the blending of different grades of tea to meet particular consumer preferences and packing it. The total number of tea, rubber, and coconut processing factories, presumably, exceeded 2,000; and these were widely scattered throughout the central and southwestern provinces of the island where they still predominate. Apart from these, large-scale power-operated industries had hardly developed. There were, however, a few factories of importance in the private sector established before 1939 such as a cotton mill, a tile works, two match factories, two distilleries, and a few engineering works.

THE BALANCE OF PAYMENTS CRISIS AND INDUSTRIAL DEVELOPMENT

The period from 1950 to 1959 could be characterized as the least eventful in Ceylon's drive towards industrial development. This was the outcome of several factors. After the end of the Korean War boom, foreign exchange earnings reached a very high level, and these earnings enabled Ceylon to sustain economic activity and maintain a reasonably high standard of living. Ceylon enjoyed another spell of prosperity during the tea boom of 1956; and external assets, which decreased in the intervening years, rose again. This appears to have been the very last spell of prosperity that Ceylon enjoyed from primary production. Up to 1958, although Ceylon drew upon her foreign exchange earnings to maintain the level of imports to which she had been accustomed in the preceding five-year period, the trend thereafter was not so favorable. Deficits in the balance of payments had appeared from 1957 onward but were not noticeable until 1959 when the government became alive to the need for corrective action to deal with the impending crisis. Though in 1959 external assets were adequate in terms of current import policy, with a view to stemming the onset of a graver crisis in the years ahead, action had to be initiated as early as 1959 to reverse the balance of payments trend. In 1959, monetary methods of import control were used to minimize imports, but they were not very effective; and in 1960 and 1961 positive steps had to be taken to restrict imports. These included licensing, quotas, higher tariffs, and a complete ban on a large number of items that were classified as nonessentials.

The two factors that helped industrial expansion after 1959 were the controls on imports and the tax concessions given to approved new industries. Of these, it is a little difficult to say which has been more important in promoting industrial development in the private sector. Once import restrictions were imposed, Ceylonese businessmen became more optimistic of the possibilities of manufacturing goods for the home market. As early as 1960, there were indications that Ceylon was going to face for sometime to come a balance of payments crisis and that substantial relaxations in the controls would not be made in the future. Moreover, after 1960, the government was firmly committed to a policy of progressive industrialization, and industrialists accepted the fact that even if relaxations were possible in the future, the government would not in principle relax controls. Furthermore, the government was committed to a policy of diversifying the economy and of giving protection to domestic industries.

Import restrictions appear to have been more effective in giving confidence to businessmen than the tax concessions. These tax concessions are summarized below:

Tax holiday for new industries

The profits of new industrial undertakings were exempt from income tax for a period of five years from the date of production or manufacture. The conditions necessary are (1) it must be an undertaking for the production or manufacture in Ceylon of goods or commodities; (2) the undertaking must not be formed by the splitting up or reconstruction of an existing business; (3) the undertaking must employ more than 25 persons; (4) the goods or commodities produced or manufactured by the undertaking must be certified to be of satisfactory quality by an authority if and when an authority is prescribed for this purpose; and (5) the prices at which the goods or commodities are sold must be certified to be reasonable by an authority if and when an authority is prescribed for this purpose.

The dividends paid to the shareholders during this period are also exempt from income tax.

Lump Sum Depreciation

A once-and-for-all lump sum allowance for depreciation is granted in respect of plant, machinery, fixtures, and certain types of buildings like factories, lines, and staff welfare buildings. The rates are as follows:

Short-lived equipment	-	80% of the cost
Normal machinery	-	66 2/3% of the cost
Durable plant and machinery	-	50% of the cost
Industrial buildings	-	33 1/3% of the cost

Where the depreciation allowance exceeds the income, the excess can be set-off against the income of future years by being carried forward year by year. When this is done, the amount of unabsorbed depreciation available for set-off each year is increased by 4 per cent.

Development Rebate

A development rebate of 20 per cent is granted in respect of new plant, machinery, and fixtures to be used in the commencement of a business. The rebate is enhanced to 40 per cent if the business is an approved project.

Exemption of Export Trade Profits

The profits derived from the export trade of industrial undertakings that are approved by the Minister of Finance are exempt from income tax for a period of three years.

The full cost of advertising outside Ceylon incurred solely in connection with the export trade of these approved industrial undertakings is deductible in full.

Other Incentives

> Raw materials and machinery, equipment, and spares required by approved industries are permitted to be imported at concessionary rates of duties, while the export of raw materials required for local industries is banned by the government. Industrialists who export locally produced articles are entitled to a refund of duties paid on the imported raw materials used for such manufacture.

Tax incentives can contribute towards the retention of a greater part of profits, but they are not likely to help if the industrialist cannot sell his products in the home market. He is assured of a home market only if foreign competition is eliminated. It is difficult to make a clear assessment of the impact of these two factors on the private sector. There have been a few instances where the tax incentive has been more powerful than a protected internal market. In fact, there is reason to think that some of the bigger industries were set up because the tax incentives were more attractive. It appears that the profits from tax incentives were greater for the bigger industrialist than for his smaller counterpart.

Apart from these two factors, industrialization made headway because credit was relatively cheap. The borrowing rates from banks and financial institutions up to 1963 did not exceed 6 to 7 per cent. The establishment of the People's Bank in 1961 helped a number of small industrialists who had hitherto found it difficult to obtain finance from other commercial banks.

Tax concessions applied to all approved and registered industries. Industries in the private sector were approved only by the Development Division of the Ministry of Industries. Between 1959 and 1963, over 1,000 industries were approved by the Ministry while there were about 800 other industries in operation. Among these were some pioneering industries that had been set up earlier.

The criteria applied to approve industries has varied from time to time. In 1959 and 1960, almost any industry was approved. There is little evidence that a careful and systematic appraisal had been made of all applications. Haphazard development of industry in the period up to 1963 could be traced to the nonapplication of meaningful criteria in the evaluation of proposals to set up new industries. An appropriate economic policy on approving industries should have been utilized as an instrument of planning and coordinating development.

Between 1960 and 1963, new industrialists established their enterprises without direct foreign participation but with technical know-how from abroad. Few of these ventures had foreign equity participation and only a limited number issued shares to the public. Many were private limited liability companies with the bulk of the shares in the hands of the promoters. Capital was found locally, and foreign exchange costs were met out of the country's foreign exchange resources. The establishment of new industries, initially, was a heavy drain not only on foreign exchange earnings, but also reserves had to be diverted to procure equipment and know-how from abroad. In a country with a dearth of technically trained personnel and very little know-how in industrial management, active foreign participation in the initial stages would have been helpful in building a viable industrial base. Moreover had there been direct foreign equity participation in these projects, there would have been a substantial foreign exchange saving that would have helped to ease the balance of payments difficulties. But against this, foreign participation would have meant that dividends and profits would have been remitted abroad annually, and the net foreign exchange saving may not have been quite so substantial.

The establishment of industries without foreign participation was advantageous from a purely long term foreign exchange standpoint because there were no further commitments after the equipment was obtained from abroad. There would have been no problem if most of the industries were producing not merely for the domestic market but also for export, in which case the export earnings could have been used to meet foreign exchange commitments such as repatriation of profits and dividends. On the other hand, the lack of foreign participation was costly in other respects. There was the enormous waste of equipment, raw materials, and foreign exchange because of experimentation, the lack of know-how, and the inability to utilize the new machinery properly. The rejection rate of products was abnormally high because local personnel were inexperienced in handling machinery, and a great deal of time had to be spent on training persons on the job. This was true of a large number of industries although there were a few exceptions. Products that appeared in the first few years of industrialization were shoddy and largely substandard. Even today a good many of the products will not compare well with their imported counterparts. In most industries, where there has been active foreign participation, controlling the quality of products, eliminating waste, proper organization, efficient management, and the use of the most appropriate techniques have come naturally. Furthermore, in a country where there is considerable brand consciousness, the preference for a brand product is something that cannot be entirely ignored. This factor was overlooked to some extent in the period before 1963. Had sufficient attention been paid to this aspect, the consumer would have been guaranteed a quality product.

The inflow of foreign capital itself depends on the political and economic climate of the country. Even if there are inducements, foreign capital will not flow in unless certain assurances are given with regard to nationalization, taxation, employment of foreign personnel, repatriation of profits, dividends, and capital. Between 1959 and 1964, the door seems to have been open for foreign capital to come in; but the uncertain political and economic conditions, the lack of any form of specific guarantees on nationalization, taxation, and repatriation of dividends seem to have discouraged the inflow of foreign capital.

INDUSTRIAL POLICY IN THE FIRST FEW YEARS

Industries that were set up between 1959 and 1964 appear to have suffered from many defects. Industrial policy in this period appears to have been bristling with several inconsistencies. The most obvious of these was the decision to encourage the production of commodities locally, soon after they were banned, on the premise that they were not essential, mere luxury items. This was particularly true of cosmetics, floor coverings, and electric fans. In some cases imported products were subject to quotas or banned only after quantity production had been reached at home. Almost all applications made by industrialists, irrespective of the nature of the product, its quality, and its usefulness, either as a final good or as an input for another industrial enterprise, were approved. The haphazard nature of planning is reflected in the large number of industries with substantial surplus capacities that produced a wide variety of nonessential goods. These were referred to as "seeni bola" (sugar confectionery) industries because of the predominance of firms making chocolate and confectionery. Whereas one or two units would have been sufficient to meet the requirements of the domestic market, several industries were approved. This resulted ultimately in waste and misdirection of resources. Had there been a plan in terms of clearly defined priorities, attention would have been directed to the production of basic essential goods.

In determining priorities, goods which loom large in the import bill should be dealt with first. Items such as textiles, cement, ceramic ware, and building materials, which are basically vital to meet everyday requirements, were not given priority in the early stages; and plans for their expansion were delayed. Had decisions been taken to set up these industries, it would have helped to cut down foreign expenditure and enabled the conservation of foreign exchange for other industrial projects and the import of essential goods that could not be produced locally in the immediate future. Furthermore, the production of some of the items mentioned would have encouraged the utilization of domestic raw materials thus minimizing foreign exchange outlays on raw materials and stimulating activity in a large number of domestic enterprises concerned with the supply of raw materials.

The primary object of both import control and industrialization was to conserve foreign exchnage, but the lack of planning and clearly defined priorities actually resulted in increasing the country's foreign exchange outlays. Foreign exchange was expended on importing technical know-how and equipment, and in the long run it was more useful than importing essential consumer goods in the form of food, clothing, and basic requirements. But in actual practice, the high cost of raw materials, capital equipment, and expenditure on royalty payments meant that the cost of producing imported goods locally was far in excess of the foreign exchange cost of importing the same product from abroad.*

The first attempt at providing facilities for industries in the private sector was the establishment under the Industrial Estates Corporation, which was set up in 1959, of an industrial estate at Ekala, which occupies a land area of approximately 70 acres. This pioneering venture follows the pattern of similar estates in other countries, notably India, Malaysia, and Singapore, where the object has been to provide industrial units with basic amenities such as buildings, water, power, communications, and sewerage. The estate itself has been divided into four main zones. Two zones are designed to provide facilities for small and medium-scale industrial units, another for larger

---

*The loss appears to be significant because foreign exchange is in short supply, and in estimating the real loss we must compute the loss of foreign exchange in terms of shadow or accounting prices. On this basis, it is easily seen that the real loss is considerably more than the loss normally computed at the official rate of exchange.

industries, and yet another for noncompatible industries such as tanneries, manufacture of cement goods, and other similar enterprises that have to be isolated because of excessive noise, dust, or other hazards.

The industries located in the Ekala industrial estate are all private enterprises. The overall management of the site was originally in the hands of the Industrial Estates Corporation, whose chief function was to diversify the industrial pattern while ensuring a degree of complementarity and interdependence. The economies arising therefrom are, of course, one of the main advantages. Industries established on the estate are those that have been approved by the Ministry of Industries. In the small industries sector of the estate, space has been allocated for the manufacture or assembly of a fairly wide range of simple products; these include the manufacture of fruit cordials, jams and jellies, radio components, fiber suitcases, plastic goods, brushes, and tea chest fittings. The organization of the industrial estate has not shown any complementarity among the different industries. The final products manufactured do not depend for their raw materials on other units located on the estate. This apparent lack of complementarity has been due to the decision of the Industrial Estate Corporation to relax the original criteria of selection for the range of applications to manufacture products was limited.

INDUSTRIAL PROGRESS, 1959-63

An assessment of the progress made in industrialization, is difficult because up-to-date information from all the industrial firms is not easily available. There is also the problem of comparability of data and their aggregation, which is due chiefly to the lack of uniformity in the financial accounts of firms in the private sector. Furthermore, the rapid emergence of a large number of enterprises has also made it difficult to assemble data, partly because of the weak response of such enterprises to statistical inquiries. Lately, however, the position has improved because the Ministry of Industries has been collecting data from industrial firms annually for the purpose of determining the allocation of raw materials. To ensure uninterrupted allocations of raw materials, most industries have responded to the request for information. The Ministry of Industries published in 1968 a series of data on industrial production for the years 1965, 1966, and 1967. This data will be examined later.

Comprehsnsive statistics on industrial development in Ceylon in a systematic form were first prepared by the Central Bank.* Since 1962, the Bank has published in its annual report an account of the progress made in industry in the private and public sectors. Other than the Ministry of Industries survey referred to above, the Central Bank survey is the only other that gives an account of industrial progress in the private sector in the period 1960 to 1965. For the purpose of obtaining information, industrial projects were classified into the main branches of industry on lines similar to the International Standard Industrial Classification. The industries covered have been mainly those that have been approved by the Development Division of the Ministry of Industries and others which have been registered.

A scheme of assistance was initiated in May, 1961, for approved industries, which included concessionary rates of duty on capital equipment and spares imported for the use of these enterprises during the first five years and tax concessions. In the eighteen months that followed, a wide range of

---

*Apart from this the Department of Census and Statistics had carried out a census of industry. In the census of industry, 1952, private large-scale industry was reported to consist of some 700 establishments providing employment for 53,000 persons and producing value added of $46 million. These industrial units were in engineering, oil milling, printing, coir goods, soft drinks, soap, tobacco, matches, and confectionery.

industries, totalling approximately 396, were approved. Of these, nearly one-third were medium and large-scale projects. The estimated size of the capital investment in projects showed that there was a tendency for private industrial enterprises to engage initially in projects that required relatively small amounts of capital.

Of the industries approved between May, 1961, and December, 1962, 272 were small-scale industries. Three-fifths or 160 of them related to five branches of industry, i.e., textiles, garments, chemical products, metal products, food, drink, and tobacco. The total estimated capital in small-scale enterprises approved before 1963 was $3.0 million or $11,764 per enterprise, as compared with the figure of nearly $110,764 for the medium and large-scale sector. The relatively labor intensive nature of small industries is seen in the capital investment per worker being in the region of $453 as compared with $1,411 for the medium and large-scale industries. More than one-half of the small industries, or 144, were approved in the first half of 1962 while there was a sharp fall in the approvals in the second half.

Total industrial output from 315 reporting new industrial firms was $55.7 million in 1961, $65.2 million from 387 firms in 1962, and $72.6 million from 433 firms in 1963. On this basis the rate of industrial growth in 1962 was 16.9 per cent and in 1963, 11.3 per cent. Although these figures show a progressive rise in output, allowance should be made for underestimation of production because of the incomplete coverage of the surveys and the lack of full response from reporting firms.

Industrial employment expanded rapidly between 1961 and 1963. The total number of employees engaged in industries in 1963 increased by 6,300 to 26,304, or by nearly 30 per cent over the figure for 1961. Nearly two-thirds of this increase in employment was due to the expansion in four industries--garments, miscellaneous food preparations, miscellaneous chemical products, and biscuits and confectionery. The largest intake of employees occurred in 1962 when

3,900 vacancies were filled. This represented an increase of 19.4 per cent as compared with 10.2 per cent in 1963. The classification of industrial production into the major industrial categories showed that in 1963 consumer goods represented 63.7 per cent of the total industrial production, intermediate goods 29.3 per cent, and investment goods 7.0 per cent. In the period 1960-63, output of consumer goods increased by 62 per cent and intermediate goods by 6 per cent.

Up to 1963, much of the consumer goods manufactured consisted of food, drink, and tobacco; miscellaneous chemical products such as pharmaceuticals, soaps, matches, and cosmetics; garments and footwear and leather products. These items accounted for nearly 85 per cent of the value of consumer goods in 1963. Of the increase in industrial production of $17 million between 1961 and 1963, these products contributed $12.2 million. A little less than one-half of the increase of $7.5 million over the figure for 1962, in the total value of industrial production in 1963, was due to the expansion of three groups of industries--garments, biscuits and confectionery, and miscellaneous chemical products. Four other in-industries, tobacco, metal products, footwear and leather products, and paper, increased by $2.3 million in 1963. The substantial increases in production are the result of a phenomenal expansion in the capacity of a few established firms. Furthermore, the bulk of the value increase was confined to a small number of products. Between 1961 and 1963, the manufacture of soap increased by $1.0 million, biscuits by $0.9 million, confectionery by $0.9 million, and shirts by $2.3 million.

INDUSTRIAL PROGRESS AFTER 1964

A convenient method of indicating the growth of industry is to express output from manufacturing industry as a ratio of the GNP. But like all other methods, it has its limitations as it may not always reflect absolute increases in output. This would be true if the sectoral contributions of other fields

TABLE 24

Contributions of Manufacturing to GNP

	1960	1961	1962	1963	1964	1965	1966	1967	1968	1969
Manufacture[a] ($ million)	119.6	119.2	125.9	131.7	137.7	142.4	142.9	160.4	235.1	273.4
Gross National Product ($ million)	1056.6	1061.1	1092.9	1142.3	1225.3	1257.7	1293.9	1382.2	1648.5	1818.2
Manufacturing as a percentage of Gross National Product	11.3	11.2	11.5	11.5	11.2	11.4	11.1	11.0	14.3	14.0

[a]Includes old industries as well, hence the difference between the figures in this table and earlier ones in this chapter.

Source: Central Bank of Ceylon, Annual Reports.

of economic activity have increased at a relatively faster rate, although both the GNP and the value of industrial output have risen. Table 24 shows the contribution of all manufacturing industry to the GNP.

Table 24 indicates that industrial production has averaged about 11 per cent of the GNP from 1960 to 1967 but rose to about 14 per cent in 1968 and 1969. The stability in the percentage share of manufacturing industry is not due to a decrease in the absolute value of industrial production but rather to the rise in relative shares of other sectors, particularly agricultural production, that helped to step up the GNP from $1293.9 million in 1966 to $1382.2 million in 1967. In 1968, with the increasing availability of raw materials, industrial production rose sharply, increasing the share of manufacturing in the GNP.

Latest returns on the value of industrial production relate to the year 1969, but statistics on industrial progress have been available from 1962. In this study, Central Bank data will be used for the period 1965 to 1969. As indicated earlier, a comparison of the performance of industry between one year and another has to be made with certain reservations. Industrial activity in Ceylon has been dependent on the availability of raw materials while the availability of raw materials again rested on the availability of foreign exchange resources. In 1964 and 1965, industrial activity has been considerably curtailed owing to shortages of raw materials. In 1967, the supply position of raw materials improved and by 1968 there were hardly any shortages. Even so, the sharp increase recorded in the value of industrial production could in part be due to the better coverage of industrial units and might also reflect an increase in prices of both imported raw materials and final goods to consumers.

The Ministry of Industries and Fisheries has also collected statistics of industrial production for the years 1965, 1966, and 1967, but data for 1968 and 1969 are available only from the Central

Bank surveys. According to the Central Bank survey, the total number of reporting units has increased from 1,381 in 1965 to 1,962 in 1969. In 1969, of the 2,150 approved and registered industries, the Central Bank received returns from 1962. The total value of industrial production was $142.4 million in 1965, $160.4 million in 1967, and $273.4 million in 1969. These figures illustrate that within five years the value of indus rial production has nearly doubled, showing a fairly high rate of growth. The annual growth rates are given below:

	Value of Industrial Production ($ million)	Percentage Increase
1962	65.2	17.0
1963	72.7	11.4
1964	90.3	24.3
1965	142.4	57.6
1966	142.9	0.4
1967	160.4	12.2
1968	235.1	46.6
1969	273.4	16.3

Source: Central Bank of Ceylon, Annual Reports.

The rise in production between 1964 and 1965 was due to the availability of increasing supplies of raw materials and the efforts made by the new government to revitalize nontraditional industries. The slight increase in output in 1966 was due to unprecedented balance of payments problems that the country had to face and the restrictions that had to be enforced on the utilization of foreign exchange for industrial purposes.

An analysis of production figures for the nine industrial categories shows that the largest contribution has been made by the category fabricated metal products machinery and equipment where production has risen by nearly four times from $9.9 million in 1965 to $38.0 million in 1969. Sharp increases in output were recorded in 1968 and 1969, as a result of relatively free imports of raw materials. Industries in this group depend heavily on imported inputs such as ferrous and non-ferrous metals and semi-machined components. Substantial gains were noticeable in group chemical, petroleum, coal, rubber, and plastic products where output rose from $21.1 million in 1965 to $42 million in 1969 and in non-metallic mineral products, except petroleum and coal where the corresponding increase was from $6.8 million to $20.7 million. In the first group chemical, petroleum, coal, rubber, and plastic products, the largest increases were in miscellaneous chemical products where output rose from $15.3 million in 1965 to $26.2 million in 1969. This was due to increased production of insecticides and weedicides required for agricultural development, mostly in the nonplantation sector.

In non-metallic mineral products, except petroleum and coal, output rose from $6.8 million in 1965 to $20.7 million in 1969, which is treble the level in 1965. This increase has been due to the stepping up of production of cement and cement products from $9.0 million in 1967 to $15.0 million in 1969. The output of bricks and tiles also doubled between 1968 and 1969, increasing from $1.2 million to $2.5 million. In the group textiles, wearing apparel, and leather industries, there was a fair increase although it was not very marked. Output rose from $28.8 million in 1965 to $44.9 million in 1969. A good part of this increase was due to a rise in the output of spinning, weaving, and finishing of textiles where production rose from $15.3 million in 1965 to $22.9 million in 1968 and $28.9 million in 1969. The manufacture of food, beverages, and tobacco also increased, though not as much as the other categories. Output increased from $69.8 million in 1965 to $107.9 million in 1969. In this group, the increase was in the category beverages and spirits, which rose from the level of $3.4 million in 1967 to $13.0 million in 1969; production of arrack has been the largest contribution to this. On the other hand, output of tobacco products fell from $18.6 million in 1968 to $17.8 million in 1969.

In the five-year period beginning 1965, employment opportunities in the industrial sector have almost doubled, the total number of employees rising by about 90 per cent from 56,835 in 1965 to 103,726 in 1969. This was due to the expansion of new industries, which took advantage of market opportunities, and the establishment of several new large enterprises after 1965. The largest number of employees have been engaged throughout in the manufacture of food, beverages, and tobacco. Industries in this group require relatively less capital intensive techniques and employ a number of workers in tasks that are very often better done by hand than by machine. More than 40 per cent of the workers are employed in small-scale enterprises, particularly in beedi wrapping, which is a widespread industry in Ceylon. Despite the establishment of a number of large units utilizing power looms, employment opportunities in the group textiles, wearing apparel and leather industries have remained at a fairly high level. This has been due primarily to the preponderance of handloom units that provide more than 75 percent of the employment in this group. The two major groups, food, beverages, and tobacco and textiles, wearing apparel, and leather provide more than 50 per cent of the employment in new industry. The other seven categories are relatively capital intensive areas and employment is somewhat limited. In these categories, although employment opportunities have increased in the five-year period, they have not been very substantial in comparison to the total capital investment and value of output. The only exception is the category fabricated metal products, machinery, and equipment, where employment has risen from 4,491 in 1965 to 16,119 in 1969. There has also been a moderate increase in employment in the group chemical, petroleum, coal, rubber, and plastic products from 7,697 in 1965 to 12,414 in 1969.

Several industrial categories show output in excess of $16.8 million. The production of vegetable oils and fats is in a class by itself because its total output has exceeded $37.8 million both in 1968 and 1969. In the category textiles, wearing apparel, and leather, the value of output of spinning, weaving, and finishing of textiles has been $28.9 million. The output of tobacco, which averaged $8.7 million in 1965 and 1966, rose to $17.8 million in

1969. In the group chemical, petroleum, coal, rubber, and plastic products, only miscellaneous chemicals indicates an output in excess of $16.8 million, at $26.2 million. In the rest, output is appreciably less than $16.8 million.

With the total value of industrial production at the end of 1969 at $273.4 million, employment opportunities were only 103,726.* The increase in employment opportunities does not show a corresponding rise in production. For instance, between 1967 and 1969, production rose by $113.0 million, whereas employment rose by 29,771. An interesting feature is that productivity has been higher in industries that use a considerable amount of machinery and equipment rather than those in the labor intensive fields. Moreover, industries have concentrated on capital using technologies and as far as possible tried to avoid the employment of more labor because of the fear that labor unrest will be a recurrent problem. In the sectors that use a considerable amount of labor, particularly in the manufacture of food,

---

*Joan Robinson in her paper on "Economic Possibilities of Ceylon" in Papers by Visiting Economists (Colombo: Planning Secretariat, 1959), states that the "amount of direct employment that can be offered by organized industry is not great" and the "most we can expect from organized industry is to employ about 100,000 workers with another 50,000 in transport." This has well turned out to be true, as the figures above show. As against this, Oskar Lange in his paper on "The Tasks of Economic Planning in Ceylon" in the same publication states, "Further economic development rests on industrialization. Industrialization is the factor which alone has the dynamic force of carrying forward the island's economy by increasing national output and providing the necessary outlets for employment." Oskar Lange seems to have overlooked the potential for agricultural development. He wrote this in 1959 in the pre-industrial phase.

beverages, and tobacco, in view of the limited scope for expansion, employment opportunities have remained almost static.

In actual practice there are only a few units producing any one commodity. However, the largest number of units are in the manufacture of tobacco and beedis. In 1969, there were 382 units in the industry providing employment for 18,800 persons. But these are relatively small concerns. As against this, in the cotton, spinning, weaving, and finishing industry there were five firms employing 6,176 persons. In the synthetic, textile, weaving, and finishing industry there were eleven firms employing 3,863. These are industries with a relatively high capital output ratio. In the basic industrial chemicals group, more than one firm produced the commodity. In the manufacture of miscellaneous chemical products the number of firms varied from 1 to 25, depending on the nature of the product. For instance, in the cosmetics and perfume industry there were 19 units, in pharmaceuticals 20, and 10 for soap. It has been possible for so many firms to survive because the products manufactured are in everyday use, with high individual preferences and a large turnover. In the manufacture of leather products, there were 57 firms and in tire rebuilding 20 firms. In the category articles of paper and paperboard, 26 units produce corrugated cartons, while 23 firms make paper bags and 13 make exercise and drawing books. The lowest number of firms was found in the manufacture of glass and glass products, the manufacture of pottery, chinaware, cement products, and non-metallic mineral products. In the group metal products, the average number of producers in 1969 for each product was approximately 4, but for the manufacture of aluminium hollowware there were 12 firms, 3 for barbed wire, 23 for galvanized buckets, and 9 for wire nails. For these products, there are one or two producers who dominate the market and continue in business because of the large turnover.

The largest wage bills in 1969 were associated with the firms that engaged the largest number of employees. Since the tobacco industry has the largest number of employees, the wage bill exceeded $5.4 million. In the textile industries the wage bill totaled $4.0 million approximately, and in the miscellaneous food preparations group the wage bill was a little over $3.0 million. In industries operating only one unit, the wage bills tended to be relatively high. For instance, in the cement and cement products industry there were three firms with 2,096 employees and the wage bill was $1.2 million. Similarly, in the plywood industry, there was only one unit with 1,134 employees and a wage bill of $0.3 million.

Subject to the reservations made earlier, the wage bill in the industrial sector has increased from $14.9 million in 1965 to $33.5 million in 1969. The industries that are under consideration now are new, and the wage bill indicates the extent to which incomes have increased as a result of activity in the nontraditional industrial sector of the economy. Similarly, the employment figures too relate to new industries. In comparison to the total number of employees in the country, those engaged in the new industries are small. If the total work force is estimated at 2 1/2 million, the nontraditional industries employ only 103,726 people; but in relation to this, the total wage bill and the value of production have been high. All new industries pay more attractive wages than the plantations and service sectors. The value of production has increased from $90.3 million in 1964 to $273.4 million in 1969. In relation to the number of employees, these figures show that productivity in the nontraditional industry has been considerably higher than in the traditional sector. It would be useful as an exercise to estimate the number of employees needed to produce an output valued at over $273.4 million in the traditional sectors--that is, in the tea, rubber, coconut, and other industries. The wage payments to produce this output of $273.4 million has been approximately one-eighth, or $33.5 million. These rough indices of productivity are a measure of the extent to which growth in nontraditional industries have contributed to increase the GNP. Thus, the application of labor in nontraditional industries has resulted in a high ratio of value added than in traditional industrial groups.

The size distribution of manufacturing firms in 1969, on the basis of data collected by the Central Bank, showed that 73.3 per cent of the firms were small firms with an individual annual output of less than $42,016, 20.0 per cent were in the output range of $42,016 to $0.3 million, and only 6.7 per cent of the firms were in the large category with an output exceeding 0.3 million. One or a few firms controlled a substantial proportion of total output in a number of industrial groups. In soft drinks and carbonated waters, one firm provided 66.4 per cent of output; in biscuits and cocoa chocolate and sugar confectionery, five firms provided 66.3 per cent of the supplies; in the beer and stout industry there were two firms, one of which supplied 85.9 per cent. In footwear and leather products, rubber products excluding footwear, miscellaneous chemical products, machinery and transport equipment, and cement, cement products and asbestos products, a few large firms controlled the domestic market. Despite the existence of a large number of small firms, a high concentration in terms of output prevailed in the garments industry, if its principal products, _i.e._, shirts, banians, and umbrellas are considered individually. In 1969, production of banians was confined to two firms and almost the entire production of umbrellas to another. In the shirt manufacturing group, 44 per cent of the output was shared by five firms out of a total of 269, while two firms accounted for 30 per cent of the output.

SMALL INDUSTRIES

Table 25 sets out the principal data on small industries.

Of some 2,150 new industries that are in existence today, more than half are actually small-scale enterprises. These form the core of the industrial structure of Ceylon. Though the small industries analyzed here are said to employ less than 100 workers, in practice the majority employ 150 to 200. For purposes of analysis, these industries could be grouped by products into certain broad categories, and the data

TABLE 25

Selected Data on Small Industries,[a] 1968

Industrial Category	Range of Products	No. of Units	Situated in Colombo No.	Outside No.	Total No. of Employees	Capital	Raw materials used Local ($ 000)	Foreign ($ 000)
1. Knitted fabrics and made-up garments	Shirts, shorts children's garments, blouses, brassieres, banians, trousers, sweaters, sarongs, and socks	179	69	45	4106	1,184	1,280	1,146
2. Food preparations	Animal and poultry goods, ice cream, curry powders, papadams, and cordials	24	9	10	648	260	1,071	325
3. Cement and Asbestos products	Bricks, tiles, pipes, slates, roofing sheets, grills, and posts	19	9	8	352	65	61	100
4. Glass products	Glass mirrors	7	6	1	135	68	2	80
5. Beverage Industries	Arrack, beer, and aerated waters	12	6	6	510	2,387	705	133
6. Manufactures of wood	Furniture, tea, chests, doors and windows, and cane goods	15	9	3	330	64	94	41
7. Bricks and Tiles	Tiles	8	1	7	515	16	83	1
8. Rubber Products	Rubber goods, tire rebuilding, tire soles, rubber solution	17	7	8	706	401	219	232
9. Machinery (except Electrical Machinery) and Transport Equipment	Motor spares, tractor parts, industrial machines, trailers, tricycles, truck bodies, water pumps, cycles, and shafts	32	10	17	1431	496	280	870
10. Paper and paper products	Envelopes, boxes and cartons, paper bags, playing cards, exercise books, fiber suitcases	62	29	15	1840	1,405	1,028	1,540
11. Spinning and Weaving	Saris, sarongs, bed sheets, towels, gray cloth	61	19	33	1655	1,964	1,049	1,833

[a]Each with less than 100 employees

Source: Central Bank of Ceylon.

given is based on the industrial survey conducted by the Central Bank for the year 1968. Only few will be dealt with in order to illustrate their major characteristics.

In the group cement and asbestos products, there were 19 small units and of these 13 are in the Colombo district. Employees range from 6 in the smallest unit to 61 in the largest unit, while the value of output varied from $1,663 to $122,689. In the group paper and paper products there were 61 reporting small units manufacturing a variety of products such as paper bags, cartons, envelopes, boxes, fiber suit-cases, and sandpaper. More than 50 of these industries are located within a radius of 6 miles from Colombo and engage an average of 25 employees; the largest unit employs approximately 87 persons. Most of the raw materials required by this category, such as kraft paper and carton-making board are imported. In the group textile spinning and weaving, there were 60 reporting units producing a variety of goods including printed textiles, towels, gray cloth, garment labels, and thread. Here again, more than 75 per cent of the industries were situated in and around Colombo. Employment varied from five persons in the smallest unit to 96 persons in the largest unit. The value of output in the large units was in excess of $117,647; several units reported production in excess of $0.17 million per annum. In this category too the bulk of the raw materials was imported, and capital investment was higher than in the industries discussed earlier. Many of them had investments of over $84,033. There were 25 reporting small industries making various food preparations. With one exception, all were situated in or near Colombo. Employment provided by each of these industries varied from 11 to 62 in the largest unit. The capital investment of the unit with the highest output was $50,420, while the other units had a considerably lower investment. There were 16 units turning out various manufactures of wood, and 14 were located in Colombo. The value of their output varied from $1,848 for the small units to $53,781 for the largest unit; employment varied from 5 to 42.

Most small industries in Ceylon consist of unit enterprises without branches, although many of them have decentralized sales organizations to promote products in the nonurban areas. No branches have been opened because of the limited size of the market. Many of the small industries depend on imported raw materials, and the quantum of value added is limited to the labor that is required either in processing or assembling the components. Although several units have vigorously pursued the prospects of finding export markets, they have not met with much success. This is not because the products are inferior in quality and their prices are too high but because of increasing competition from foreign countries. Units producing shoes, batteries, shirts, and electrical components have, however, though not sizable, secured orders from markets overseas.

With regard to management and ownership, very few small industries are broad-based public companies. Possibly about 50 per cent of them are sole proprietorships or partnerships while a few of them are public companies with a limited number of shareholders. On the average, the number of shareholders does not exceed 15 to 20. This is also true of a number of larger industries that have sizable markets in the country. Working conditions of employees in small industries have been carefully regulated by labor legislation that has progressively been extended to all new industries. Trade unions for better working conditions have been formed in most industrial undertakings, and there is evidence to show that salaries of employees in many small new industries are appreciably higher than those in the country's traditional industries.

Small industries are ideally suited to the economic requirements of this country. They tend to provide more employment opportunities, are less capital intensive, and have contributed eventually towards the diffusion of wealth and development of technical and managerial skills. Most small industrialists, who have not had ready access to capital and technical resources available to the larger units, still have been able to secure maximum returns. Industrialists who were not able to get licenses to import machinery have been able to improvise and fabricate their own machinery.* This has provided more employment opportunities in other industrial units and also developed local skills. Because of competition from larger units, which are equipped with technical know-how and managerial skills from abroad, the small industrialists have been compelled to produce articles as superior as those manufactures by the larger units. Small industries have also paid as much attention to quality and consumer preference as their larger counterparts.

In the present context, there is considerable scope to provide more organized assistance to small industries and to give them financial aid with a view to making them viable in the long run. Many small industrialists have not housed their units in suitable buildings. Some of them do not even have an adequate or dependable supply of power and water, often resulting in prolonged stoppages of work adding to the financial burden that small industrialists have to shoulder. Assistance should be given to procure from abroad equipment which cannot be fabricated locally. It is a common complaint among the small industrialists that the Ministry of Industries has not issued licenses to import some vital piece of machinery for their units. Such drawbacks have compelled these industrialists to postpone their programs of turning out new products and improving quality. The policy adopted by the Ministry has been influenced by the view that as there are already several large units in production, it is uneconomical to provide incentives to the small industrialist. This is indeed a short-sighted policy. The social costs of promoting a large enterprise is heavy,

---

*In practice, the Development Division of the Ministry of Industries has been liberal with foreign exchange allocations for import of machinery by the big industrialists. Small industrialists have found it difficult to get import permits and foreign exchange. These are the findings of a personal survey undertaken by the writer.

whereas smaller industries will provide greater employment opportunities.

When industrialization was first given recognition, there were no specific policies designed to help small industrialists. Steps were taken in this direction only after the Industrial Development Board was set up in 1966. Prior to this, there was the Small Industries Service Institute just outside Colombo, but this had not proved to be very successful either in helping small industrialists or promoting new industries.* In 1965, steps were taken to transfer the Small Industries Service Institute from the Ministry of Home Affairs to the Ministry of Industries. With the establishment of the Industrial Development Board, the function of developing and promoting small industries was taken over by the board, and several subdepartments were set up within it to assist small industrialists. One department was specially allocated to provide information to small industrialists on the choice, feasibility, and planning of projects. Financial assistance was to be provided to procure essential pieces of machinery and capital equipment, tools, and raw materials; advice on sales promotion was also available. Training courses were inaugurated locally, and managers and technicians from new industries were given opportunities of going abroad for training and study courses not available in Ceylon. In addition, other facilities for industrial promotion such as an Investment Bureau and an Export Promotion Center were provided. The Industrial Development Board was strengthened further and widened on the basis of a new bill enacted in December,

---

*The Small Industries Institute now functions under the Industrial Development Board. The writer visited the institution in the latter part of 1969 and found that little or no work was done to help small industries. Most of the Institute's equipment and specialists were idling much of the time. Its charges for the limited services to small industrialists were excessive.

1969.* Now that the tax holiday scheme has been withdrawn, it is very likely that entrepreneurs will treat small industries not as a device to make money quickly but as a source that ultimately could contribute towards the development of the economy.** The government elected in May, 1970, is paying considerable attention to the promotion and development of small labor intensive industries.

PLANNING AND POLICY ON INDUSTRY, 1965-69

In the budget speech for 1964-65, the Minister of Finance outlined a new industrial policy:

1. There was to be a scheme of national priorities under which some of the existing industries were to be encouraged while some others were to be discouraged. Due consideration was to be given to such factors as the present or potential availability of local raw materials, the cost of production, and the relative contribution to economic growth.

2. The industrialization program was to be geared to a conscious plan of reducing the imported raw material content over a period of years. Industries producing a surplus of nonessential consumer goods were to be discouraged.

3. Immediate steps were to be taken to set

---

*The role of the Industrial Development Board has been re-examined by the new government. The Committee which issued its report in September, 1970, recommended that the powers of the bank should be curtailed and the new Ministry of Industries and Scientific Affairs should be responsible for the formulation and implementation of industrial policy.

**The tax holiday for new industries was withdrawn in 1968 on the basis of recommendations made by the Taxation Commission of 1967.

up machinery for adequate quality control of local products. Similarly, the question of excess profit margins on local products was to be scrutinized.

4. A program of implementation was considered an integral part of the new industrial policy. For this purpose, all private industries were required to furnish monthly targets of production, and the Ministries of Industries and of Planning were to keep a constant watch to ensure that these targets were achieved. The grant of import quotas was to geared to the implementation of these targets, and firms functioning more efficiently and selling goods at cheaper prices were to be given preference in the allocation of raw material quotas.

In September, 1965, an official committee was appointed to examine the progress made in the preceding five-year period in implementing the program of industrial development outlined in the Ten-Year Plan. The committee reported that the achievements in the sphere of investment should have been more substantial. It pointed out further that the investment targets laid down in the Ten-Year Plan had not been attained although industrial expansion had, to some extent, helped to fill the void created by import restrictions.

In 1965, the Ministry of Industries set up a planning committee in the Ministry with the object of preparing a comprehensive plan to rationalize the course of industrial development in the public and private sectors. The committee realized the importance of ensuring close coordination with the pace of development in other sectors of the economy, especially those sectors that constituted major suppliers of inputs to the industrial sector. These were, among others, the supply of electric power required by new industries, availability of adequate construction capacities, and the supply of vital raw materials for public sector industries. At the same time, long term programs were being drawn up for the development of specific industries such as cement, paper, and salt. For the textile and chemical industries, a program of development had been prepared by a team of experts from the German Democratic Republic. Public corporations in the industrial sector were also required to formulate their programs for further expansion and development in the period ahead.

With regard to private enterprise, the Ministry of Industries did not approve during 1965 and 1966 any new industries because of the shortage of foreign exchange resulting from an increasingly adverse balance of payments position. Even in the case of industries that had already been approved, it had not been possible to allocate sufficient exchange for their full raw material requirements. However, steps were taken to identify investments according to a scheme of national priorities and apportion scare exchange resources to obtain maximum results. At that time the Ministry of Industries had called for a comprehensive estimate of the foreign exchange requirements to keep all existing as well as approved industries working at full capacity. It was the intention to provide foreign exchange needs on a regular basis both for the procurement of raw materials and for additional machinery to existing industries. An island-wide survey of manufacturing industries was carried out, after an official notification, for estimating the foreign exchange requirements.

With the establishment of a planning unit in the Ministry of Industries to cover the regulation, control, and supervision of new industries and another to evaluate new projects, the entire responsibility of selection and approval of new industries in the private sector rested with the Ministry. For the approval of new industries, the Ministry has established a committee with representatives from the Ministry of Planning and Economic Affairs and the Department of National Planning. This committee has been concerned mainly with the appraisal of applications to establish new industries. There has been room for this committee to expand its functions in a more positive way. But because several thousands of applications had been received for new industries, a considerable amount of time has been spent on evaluation rather than advising and offering alternative proposals that are more feasible and dovetailing development from the point of view of the economy as a whole.

NEW INDUSTRIES AND THE EXCHANGE LIBERALIZATION OF 1968

Throughout the five years (1964-68) there was an abundance of applications for new industries. But the progress of industrial development was hampered, as there was no clear indication of the amount of foreign exchange that would be available from year to year, particularly to meet raw material and capital costs. However, with the introduction of the Foreign Exchange Entitlement Certification (FEEC) scheme in May, 1968, raw materials for industries have been classified into categories A and B. Small industries with a turnover of less than $16,806 per annum can purchase raw materials at the official rate, and bigger business units will be able to buy raw materials at the premium rate under category B without any restrictions.

As a result of the Foreign Echange Entitlement Certificate scheme the small industrialist with a turnover of less than $ 16,806 is at an advantage over his competitor who has a turnover of more than $ 16,806 per annum because the cost of imported raw materials to the latter will rise by about 45 per cent.* If two firms are producing the same article, two interesting features can be discerned. The small industrialist may sell at the price of bigger manufacturer making a profit of at least 56 per cent while the latter makes a smaller profit. If the market is very competitive and is dominated by many small producers, the large producer may have to sell

---

*The FEEC rate in 1968 was 45 per cent, in November, 1969, it was raised to 56 per cent; this is the prevailing rate. The new government has so far not modified the FEEC scheme.

at the price determined by the small manufacturer, in which case the former will find it difficult to survive unless the profit margins in the industry as a whole are over 60 per cent. In actual practice, most new industries make profits in excess of 60 per cent, and therefore, there is no likelihood of the FEEC scheme putting any industries out of production. In the captive market of Ceylon, industrialists will not find it difficult to pass on higher costs to consumers. This is relatively easy because in most industries there is very little competition from either other domestic industries or from imports.

The advantage of the FEEC scheme, as it operated up to May, 1970, was that the bigger industrialists were able to obtain their requirements of raw materials under Open General License without restriction.* Under the earlier quota system, industrialists had to depend on licenses issued by the Ministry of Industries, and manufacturers were not always assured of adequate supplies because of the limited availability of foreign exchange. The quota system often tended to push up the price of finished goods because output fluctuated. The Open General License scheme enabled manufacturers to obtain their full raw material requirements for maximum production. It also had a salutory effect on the price level, eliminated shortages, sustained optimum levels of production, and helped to keep the industrial labor force fully employed.

Before the implementation of the FEEC scheme, all industries were given allocations of raw materials according to a scheme of priorities worked out by the Ministry of Industries. Industries that were producing vitally essential consumer goods were given larger allocations of raw materials while others had their quotas reduced appreciably. By using this instrument, the Industrial Regulation Division of the Ministry was able to control production and industrial

---

*The Open General License scheme was discontinued from June, 1970.

expansion according to national priorities and to maximize benefits to the economy.* Under the arrangement up to June, 1970, any industry could establish itself without either approval or registration with the Ministry because it was free to obtain raw materials. With regard to machinery and capital equipment, new industrialists were able to obtain machinery through imports, because some items of machinery were on Open General License, or fabricate it locally.

One of the less favorable effects of the FEEC scheme is that it might stimulate the growth of a number of mushroom industries that may not make a substantial contribution to economic growth by producing commodities that are not absolutely essential. There will also be waste in these sense that new industries may procure capital equipment and machinery merely to duplicate manufacturing units that are already in existence and are able to meet the domestic demand. It may not be possible to use the redundant machinery for other purposes. Although competition might eventually help to weed out the less efficient units, the foreign exchange costs of this principle of survival of the fittest is likely to be very high. A country like Ceylon cannot afford to expend foreign exchange on uncontrolled and unregulated growth of industrial units. The alternative uses to which this foreign exchange may be put to increase productivity in other sectors, particularly in domestic agriculture, must be taken into account.

INSTITUTIONAL ARRANGEMENTS

In early 1968, the Ministry of Industries

---

*Before June, 1970, the Ministry of Industries allocated raw materials on quotas only to small industries in Category A who could pay for imports at the official rate. Industries in Category B could obtain raw materials on Open General License without restriction in quantity.

directed the Industrial Development Board to set up industrial panels for different industrial groups and sectors with a view to advising and making recommendations to the Ministry on the techno-economic problems of the various industrial sectors. Hence seven industrial panels for food and drink, industrial fiber including man-made fibers, chemicals, including drugs and pharmaceuticals, timber products, rubber products, non-metallic minerals, and light engineering industries were set up.

These industrial panels consisted of scientists from the Ceylon Institute for Scientific and Industrial Research (CISIR) university professors in the special fields, other persons with specialist qualifications, and technically qualified men in private industry. The panels were serviced by the Industrial Development Board secretariat, which consists of several research officers. The following aspects of industrial development were required to be examined and studied by the panels:

1. The utilization of raw material, import substitution identification of possible domestic resources, introduction of quality standards, and research and development in this field;

2. The development of ancillary industries and the coordination of production activities in the public and private sectors;

3. The development of simple machinery to mechanize smaller industries;

4. Problems of production, pricing, quality control, and distribution of industrial products in the domestic market;

5. Problems of export of industrial products;

6. Assessment of required skills and the formulation of training programs;

7. Formulation of industrial research programs;

8. Other matters relating to the development of the industrial sector.

These industrial panels have been concerned with rationalizing industry and making units interdependent. They have also assisted the Ministry in demarcating certain sectors where growth should be promoted, and targets have been laid out for each of them. The Regulation Division of the Ministry of Industries has been responsible for implementing the Ministry's policies on the basis of advice given by the industrial panels or other groups.

Several other agencies have been established to promote industrial development under the auspices of the Industrial Development Board. A Management Development and Productivity Center has been established with the object of promoting managerial skills so that productivity in the existing industries could reach a maximum. Another agency, the Industrial Credit and Supplies Agency, has also been established, and its function is to make loans available to small scale industrialists. An Investment Information Center has been set up to provide prospective investors with data and information relating to specific investment projects in the private sector. The Marketing and Export Promotion Unit performed the vital function of promoting the export of new industrial products. Another unit functioning under the Industrial Development Board is the Technical Services Center which provides new industrialists with the know-how on production techniques and management of industries.

The Ministry of Industries in 1968 set up a Bureau of Standards that lays down standards for domestic industrial products. The bureau is manned by technical personnel and has a consulting service of specialists from the Ceylon Institute for Scientific and Industrial Research. Up to the end of 1968, standards had been set up for fifteen important industries including blades, wire and barbed wire, tiles, matches, asbestos, and nails. The standards set up by the bureau will be enforced through the Regulations Division of the MInistry of Industries mainly by building up consumer resistance to products. Since certain agencies like the government may be large buyers, the Ministry can instruct them not to purchase particular commodities because they do not conform to the required standards.

The turnover tax on industrial products has been a further instrument that has been used selectively to discourage some types of industries. The present tax is levied on all industries with a turnover in excess of $16,806. A rate of 3 per cent is applied on essential industries, 5 per cent on basic industries, and 10 to 20 per cent on luxury items. Selectively some items carry higher rates. The differences in the rates have been instrumental in discouraging the production of certain varieties of luxury goods. But in a protected market and in the absence of much competition, the tax can easily be passed on to the consumer.

THE INDUSTRIAL DEVELOPMENT ACT OF 1969

The Industrial Development Act was passed in December,1969. It provided authority to reconstitute the Industrial Development Board, to set up an Industrial Advisory Council, industrial panels, and an Industrial Development Fund. The function of the Industrial Advisory Council was to advise the Ministry on matters connected with the development of industries. The Industrial Development Fund was set up for the encouragement, promotion, and development of industries. The resources in the fund could come from several sources, including a tax levied on industry, proceeds of license fees, the business turnover tax, and monies voted by Parliament. The membership of the Industrial Development Board was increased to nine and its functions were widened. The latter included the proper coordination and interrelated growth of all industrial undertakings in the private and public sectors to foster industrial research utilizing the natural resources of Ceylon, developing appropriate technologies, promotion of exports of local industrial products, and providing for services and facilities of every description for industry including capital, credit, marketing, managerial and technical facilities, and legal advice.*

PRIVATE SECTOR AND FOREIGN INVESTMENT, 1966-69

In March, 1966, the government made a fairly comprehensive statement of policy on private foreign investment.** The government was of the view that a steady flow of capital and technological and managerial skills were necessary for the country's development effort. Furthermore, it indicated that domestic savings were inadequate to meet the full requirements of the economic development program. An official declaration was made that the government would welcome foreign private investment on terms and conditions that were advantageous both to Ceylon and to the overseas investor. The White Paper stated that once an investment was approved, a foreign investor would be entitled to a number of benefits that included the free remittance of the proceeds of the sale on liquidation of investments after local liabilities have been met. Interest owing to non-residents and borrowings and proceeds of debentures, preference shares, and overdrafts were also freely remittable. Investors were to be permitted to bring in foreign machinery and technical personnel on

---

*The new government has curtailed considerably the powers and duties of the Industrial Development Board by the act of 1969.

***Government Policy on Private Foreign Investment* (Colombo: Ministry of Planning and Economic Affairs, 1966).

Earlier pronouncements on foreign investment were made in the budget speeches. See for example, Budget Speech for 1960-61.

condition that Ceylonese would be progressively trained to replace them. A guarantee was also given that reasonable royalty payments and technical service fees will be remittable.

The government stated that it had no intention of nationalizing any of the private undertakings and that foreign investors will be secure from any form of discriminatory treatment or expropriation. Where nationalization had to take place in the overall interest of the public, the White Paper guaranteed effective and adequate payments to compensate investors for losses. The White Paper also specified the areas that were reserved essentially for government operation of industries. These industries were cement, ceramics, paper, mineral sands, caustic soda, chlorine, plywoods, steel, tires and tubes, fertilizers, and petroleum. Furthermore, it was stated that foreign investment in these industries, although primarily reserved for government operation, would be welcome if they were geared to production for export and were "advantageous from the national point of view." Investment proposal that will receive greatest consideration would be those ensuring a relatively high value added in the course of domestic production and which would progressively reduce the import content of raw materials. The emphasis was on production for export. Wherever feasible, foreign investments were to be made in collaboration with local capital, although the White Paper did not rigidly stipulate the proportions in which local and foreign capital are to be combined. Where the initial investment was largely or exclusively foreign, it was indicated that it would be desirable to provide for a progressive transfer of the major part of the ownership to local interests.

The White Paper summarized the various tax concessions available to foreign investors, and in the appendicies to the paper a list of the existing industries in the private sector was given under broad headings so as to enable the private foreign investor to locate fields where there was sufficient potential for new investment.

Following the announcement of government policy on private foreign investment, an official committee consisting of representatives from the Central Bank, the Treasury, Ministry of Planning and Economic Affairs, and the Minsitry of Commerce, with the Director of Industrial Development as chairman, was set up under the Ministry of Planning and Economic Affairs to examine and report on applications for establishing new industries exclusively by foreign investors or by the latter in participation with Ceylonese business interests. The primary function of this committee, known as the Foreign Investment Approvals Committee, was to recommend to the Ministry of Industries the feasibility of specific investment proposals. In addition, it was empowered to deal with other questions arising from foreign investment such as the payment of royalties, technical service fees, and increases in the existing share capital of new industrial companies with foreign participation. In the first instance, the committee examined applications by reference to the primary information on the general nature of the project. If this showed that the project is likely to be viable and to make a contribution to economic growth, the committee would call for further detailed information on the project. This is in the form of an exhaustive questionnaire that seeks answers to about thirty-five to forty questions. Among the information sought is the foreign exchange saving potential of the project, the techniques of production, the employment it will create, the export possibilities of the product, provision for the use of local raw materials, and the progressive manufacture of components in Ceylon.

Since the committee's appointment and by the middle of 1970, it has recommended for approval over 100 new industries with foreign participation. These include the assembly and progressive manufacture of motor cars, spinning and weaving of cotton and synthetic textiles, making of galvanized sheets and other items of hardware, the manufacture of radios and electronic components, pharmaceuticals, and several other small industrial lines. Some of the projects are among the biggest that have been undertaken in the private sector; in the latter category are the spinning and weaving mills for textiles. In some cases, the total cost of each project has exceeded $ 9.0 million and approximately half of this capital has been contributed by foreign investors, either directly in the form of equity participation or in the form of supplier's credits for machinery or a combination of both.

PROBLEMS OF NEW INDUSTRY

One of the less salutary aspects of industrial growth in Ceylon has been the increasing dependence on imported raw materials. To some extent this is inevitable in an economy with a short history of nine to ten years of industrial growth in the private sector. For instance, in the survey of industry conducted by the Central Bank in 1969, data on the use of raw materials were available only from 1,385 out of a total of 1,962 reporting firms. Firms have been hesitant in divulging information on the use and availability of raw materials while many of them have had difficulties in identifying the source, especially when it comes to making a distinction between imported and local raw materials. It has been the practice for Ceylonese industrialists to purchase imported raw materials from wholesalers and importers and classify them as local raw materials.

Most of the raw materials utilized in industries are of foreign origin. In food preparations, the percentage of local raw materials used was 53 per cent while imported raw materials was 47 per cent. Foreign inputs for the beer and stout industry amounted to 100 per cent. In the spinning, weaving, and finishing of textiles, 85 per cent of the raw materials as imported; in the footwear and leather products industry 47 per cent; in the rubber products 54 per cent; and in the metal products 93 per cent of the raw materials as imported. Statistics also show the heavy dependence on imported materials in industries that involve the fabrication of metal or allied products where the import content is about 80 per cent. A study of the various industrial groups would show that the actual import content of raw materials is much higher than is given by these figures.

When industries were first approved, industrialists were not required to plan production on the basis of progressive use of local raw materials, although many of the industries could have substituted local raw materials for imports. But most of them have not attempted to do so. Perhaps this may be due to the fact that smaller firms do not have the resources and the trained personnel required to carry out research to find the appropriate substitutes. A few of the larger firms, however, have been successful in finding suitable substitutes. Although local raw materials are sometimes readily available, industrialists prefer to use imported components because they require very little processing. Certain difficulties are likely to be encountered in devising procedures for the progressive use of local raw materials in industries. The allocation of foreign exchange for the procurement of raw materials from abroad could be reduced. This may not be very successful in all cases because of the reasons already given. The other alternative would be to encourage the development of raw material supplying industries. But this will require the growth of basic metal, petrochemical, and other industries.

The quality of final products of local industries has been poor. This has been so despite the fact that much of the inputs have been imported products. Furthermore, the lack of appropriate skills and the almost total absence of quality control in many of these industries has resulted in poor products. This is true particularly of the smaller units, but increasing attention has now been given to quality control in the larger units. The need to maintain high quality has not arisen because the Ceylon market is a protected market, and the consumer has no option but to purchase whatever is available in the market. Had there been even limited imports, the producer would not have been able to pass on substandard products to the consumer. If imports are liberalized in instances where the quality of the local product is definitely inferior, the producer will be faced with the option either of improving quality or closing down the plant.

An associated problem is the high cost of manufactured products. This again seems to flow from the lack of competitive imports, where the producer has been at liberty to determine the prices irrespective of the cost and a reasonable margin of profit. In the plastics, metal products, and electrical goods industries, profits margins have been unconscionably high, as much as 200 per cent. Of course, it might be argued that the high prices and high profit margins may be due to the scarcities in the market. But what has been overlooked is the lack of competition in the domestic market resulting from import restrictions. It has also been argued that the local industrialist cannot get sufficient raw materials to increase his output, in which case he can bring down the prices. But there is no such evidence even in cases where allocations have been liberalized to ensure production at high levels. Another contributory factor seems to be the absence, until recently, of effective machinery to control prices. (About twelve new industrial products, including flashlight batteries, shirts, pencils, slates, toothpaste, and soap were brought under price control between October and December, 1970.)

Price control, in certain cases, has resulted only in reducing the profit margin from 200 to 100 per cent. What is even more significant is that these high profit margins have remained static despite the added attraction of the five-year tax holiday. If there were no tax holiday, there would have been some justification to allow industrialists to make very large profits because they could be taxed by government. These proceeds could then be utilized for purposes of industrial development in the public sector or for schemes of social welfare. The privileges enjoyed by new industries in Ceylon have little comparison in other countries. The withdrawal of the tax holiday scheme in the budget for 1968-69 is unlikely to act as a serious disincentive in the case of established industries because of the protected market where producers assume the role of monopolists.

INDUSTRIAL PRODUCTS AND EXPORTS

In view of the limited size of the domestic market, the expansion of industrial production will largely depend on promoting sales abroad. In most industries, new firms can spring up if markets can be found. However, as a large number of new industries are dependent on imported raw materials, these enterprises will be able to expand without being a burden on the economy only if they can earn enough foreign exchange to pay for increased raw material requirements. More recently, the government has focused its attention on export promotion and steps have been taken to provide incentives.

Before 1968, the export bonus scheme was the main incentive for exports. Exporters of a number of nontraditional products were entitled to a voucher that could be utilized to import raw materials or other items that were not available under license, or in the alternative they could sell the bonus voucher at a premium in the open market. With the operation of the FEEC scheme the export bonus was withdrawn.

At present there are a number of incentives for industrial export. A 100 per cent rebate of customs duty is permitted on imported raw materials used for the production of export commodities. Export industries are allowed the facility of removing raw materials without the payment of customs duty on furnishing a bank guarantee. Exemption from the turnover tax and excise duties have been granted for nontraditional exports. Foreign exchange allocations for raw materials are issued on a priority basis on the production of firm export orders. Industrial exports listed under Section 7 of the Inland Revenue Act No.4 of 1963 are exempted from income tax for a period of three years from the date of the first export, while 5 per cent of the FOB value of industrial exports is allowed as an

TABLE 26

INDUSTRIAL GROWTH AND EXPORTS

	1960	1963	1966	1967	1968	1969
Industrial Production (at constant prices) ($ million)	122.4	143.4	169.4	176.8	193.9	205.2
Growth rate over previous year	-	7.1	7.6	9.7	7.7	5.8
Industrial Exports (at constant prices) ($ million)	12.3	12.3	11.3	12.9	13.9	13.8
Per cent of domestic exports (at constant prices)	4.1	3.8	3.5	3.9	4.0	4.2
Employment Index	100	131	284	364	506	518

Source: Central Bank of Ceylon Annual Reports.

income tax rebate, and all development expenses incurred in promoting new exports are set off against assessable income.

The effectiveness of these rebates has been negligible. Though the customs duty rebate was officially published as early as 1964, because of administrative difficulties only one exporter finally qualified after a period of four years. Similarly, the facility of removal of raw materials from customs on funishing a bank guarantee had been availed of by only one exporter. The turnover tax and the excise duties have been in operation for some time, and the priority issues of foreign exchange allocations are working satisfactorily. It will be observed that a good many of the incentives are indirect concessions. For instance, an industrialist has to wait for nearly one year before he is entitled to the tax rebate. In this respect, the export bonus voucher, though limited to 20 per cent and 30 per cent of the value of exports, was more advantageous than the FEEC scheme; the bonus voucher fetched a much higher premium, sometimes as much as 350 per cent. Furthermore, bonus vouchers were transferable. On the other hand, the FEEC voucher, though it is for 100 per cent FOB value, could be sold only to the Bank at a fixed premium of 56 per cent. The exporters, therefore, are net losers of approximately 25 per cent of the FOB value. In addition, industrialists have to pay 56 per cent more on industrial raw materials because of Foreign Exchange Entitlement Certificates. It will be seen then that the FEEC scheme has enhanced the cost of industrial raw materials, especially for the producer with a turnover of over $ 16,806.

THE FUTURE

Traditionally, although Ceylon has not had an industrial sector during the last ten years, substantial progress in industrial development has been achieved. While increasing production and adding about 14 per cent to the gross national product, new industries have trained many persons in advanced technology and diffused skills which could be used with considerable advantage in industries yet to be set up. Several new management and technical consulting firms have sprung up in the private sector to give advice and evaluate projects. At the same time, managerial and entrepreneurial skills have been developed. The private sector has conducted training courses for middle and higher management personnel. In addition, the government itself has taken steps to train people for managerial tasks in the public sector through the Academy of Administrative Studies. The universities have geared themselves to the task of training people by introducing courses in business administration, management studies, and economic development.

One of the greatest limitations that the country is likely to face in its progress towards further industrial development is the inadequacy of natural resources. Ceylon lacks the vital ingredients for industrialization such as coal, oil, and a large variety of essential minerals like aluminium, high grade iron ore, tin, and copper. This means that industries will continue to depend on foreign sources for these essential raw materials. But despite this, a certain amount of substitution of local raw materials is possible provided considerable research is undertaken. To achieve this objective, it may be necessary to reorient the work of the the CISIR towards purely industrial research. It may also be necessary for the institute to work in closer collaboration with industry than hitherto.

There are certain areas where the industrial policy may have to be reexamined and reoriented. These could be conveniently summarized as follows:

1. Although the Ministry of Industries is now taking steps to make industries more interdependent, sufficient research has not been done on the use of local raw materials and on the development of substitutes for imports. It is equally important to carry out a comprehensive survey of mineral and other industrial raw material resources that are found in the country. A separate industrial research

and advisory unit might be useful for this purpose if the present research and advisory services are inadequate.

2. Implementation of industrial policy seems to require more machinery than is now available. Several industries have been given approval on various conditions, such as progressive manufacture of components in Ceylon and ceilings on prices. To ensure that industries conform to these stipulations, an industrial policy implementation division may be necessary, or in the alternative, the Regulations Divisions that presently handles this work will have to be strengthened.

3. Scant attention has been paid to the location of new industries. At present, almost 80 per cent of the industries in the private sector are located in the Western Province, and of this a great many are in or just outside Colombo. As discussed earlier, the economic and social effects of this are not very favorable. Industrial development has done very little to solve unemployment and underemployment in the rural districts where the problem is very acute. The location of industries in the rural areas may help to solve the problem of population pressure in the urban areas, promote development of nonurban areas and reduce the increasing influx of people from the rural areas of the cities. It would act as a nucleus for the promotion of skills in the rural areas and also develop smaller industries that could provide inputs for the bigger industries. Remedial action would be to set up industrial estates well away from the cities and provide them with basic amenities such as power, roads, and water.

4. Wherever possible, the Ministry or private industrialists should sponsor the establishment of training schools for various industries, e.g., textiles, metal products and chemicals. Such schools should be associated closely with big industries that could provide the practical training; the technical schools and colleges now being established may be handicapped in this respect. A specialized credit agency such as an industrial development bank

would also be useful to cater exclusively to the financial requirements of industrialists who have found it increasingly difficult to get accommodation from the Development Finance Corporation, commercial banks, and other specialized credit agencies. An industrial development bank, properly constituted, would be in a position to undertake risks that at present cannot be taken by the existing credit institutions. Ceylon is among the very few countries in the Asian region that does not have either a development bank or an industrial bank.

5. A task of singular importance is the coordination of industrial development with agricultural development. It is well known that industrial development is largely dependent on agricultural development. Furthermore, agriculture could supply some part of the raw materials for industry. For instance, in Ceylon the progress of the textile, spinning, and weaving industry depends mainly on the availability of cotton. The expansion in the cotton weaving and spinning industry should be tied up with an extensive program of cotton cultivation. For the expansion of industry, there should be a growing market in the country, and such a market can emerge only if incomes rise progressively in the rural areas. The present market limitations are largely due to the relatively slow rate of progess in agriculture in the last two decades.

At the same time, there is a growing awareness in the country that the diversification of the economy does not mean industrialization alone. The economy can be diversified by growing new and non-traditional agricultural products and developing export markets. The problem of unemployment and underemployment will have to be tackled through agriculture, and the development of service industries as industry alone cannot provide much employment. Attention is now being directed to developing non-traditional agricultural exports and new agricultural pursuits such as dairy farming and the livestock industry.

CHAPTER

9

INDUSTRIAL EXPANSION IN THE PUBLIC SECTOR

THE DAWN OF AN ERA OF STATE PARTICIPATION IN INDUSTRY

The first report on prospects for industrial development in Ceylon was published in 1921-22.[1] But provision was made for a separate Ministry for Industry and Commerce, which was to undertake industrialization, under the Donoughmore Constitution in the early 1930's. This can be considered as the most significant step taken by the administration in the early years towards industrial development in the public sector. The new Ministry's most important task was the determination of the country's industrial potential. Thereafter, it drew up a plan for the development of industries. Unfortunately, in the 1930's the world had to face a depression and soon after the threat of war in the West. About the same time, there was also considerable unemployment in the country, and conditions were not very favorable to implement the plan. The government had to devote all its time to the more urgent task of providing employment through means that required relatively small capital outlays.

Furthermore, because of difficulties in raising sufficient funds for capital work and the absence of technical skills, the government did not find it possible to embark on highly sophisticated industrial development schemes; those selected for consideration were relatively simple projects. With the outbreak of the war, several new problems confronted the administration. One of these was the immediate demand for a variety of essential consumer goods that could not be imported. Hence the administration decided to rush through several industrial projects in the war years. Plants, which had been intended to function only as pilot projects, were thrown into the production of far larger quantities of goods than their capacity warranted. Factories were set up for the manufacture of plywood, quinine, and drugs, leather and tanning, coir yarn, paper, ceramics, acetic acid, glass, and for steel rolling. They were financed by an allocation of $0.5 million for industrial development under the 1937 loan scheme. These factories were set up primarily for the supply of scarce consumer goods rather than ushering in an era of industrial development. Despite the inferior quality of goods produced at these factories, there was a ready market as the consumer had no alternative but to buy them. Up to about 1946, most of these government factories ran at a profit.

But with increasing competition from imports in 1950, producers found that they were no longer able to sell the inferior goods, and total losses incurred by these amounted to $0.9 million as compared with the net profit of $69,243 at the end of 1946. On the ground of losses alone, the Commission on Government Commercial Undertakings recommended that some of the factories should be closed down. This recommendation was put into effect and several thousands lost employment. The closing down of factories and the liberalization of imports, from a standpoint of development, was a retrograde step; it pushed back the progress of industrial development by at least one decade. The solution would have been to reorganize the factories and afford them some measure of protection in the home market.

The government had at that time set up a Committee of the State Council to report on the industrial policy of the government. The report of this committee, published as Sessional Paper No. 23 of 1947, urged that the government adopt a positive policy for setting up a number of basic industries that it should, on principle, reserve for the public sector. In the meantime, the plywood, leather, ceramics, and glass factories continued to function under the direction of the Department of Industries. But as they were subject to bureaucratic controls and management was weak, they could not function as viable commercial enterprises. The committee recommended that these factories should be reorganized and seven other new units should be set up in the public sector to produce the following items: cement, textiles, refined vegetable oils, caustic soda, steel, paper, and fertilizer. State participation in industry could be traced to the interest that the government evinced in setting up factories for these products. The government believed that investments for the production of the items mentioned would have to be on a large scale, and it was unlikely that private businessmen would venture into these areas with the necessary capital.

In 1947, before the report could have been tabled, the State Council was dissolved to give way to parliamentary institutions under the new constitution. The recommendations contained in the report, however, had considerable influence on government policy in the years to follow. Between 1950 and 1958, although several new industries were set up in the public sector, a systematic program was not followed. If priority had been given to essential consumer goods, the obvious firsts in the list would have been products like textiles, hardware, fertilizer, and cement. Of these only cement was singled out for development and a factory established in Jaffna to meet about one-third of the country's requirements. The location of the cement factory may have been politically motivated because the minister in charge of industries happened to represent a constituency in the Jaffna Peninsula. This reflected the bases on which decisions to establish industries were taken in the 1950's. Cement, refined oil, and paper factories were established in the early 1950's. But circumstances changed when a recession followed close upon the collapse of the Korean War boom of 1950-51. The immediate victims of the economic situation that followed were the textile, steel, and fertilizer projects. The crisis postponed interest in these projects for a considerable time, and they had to be revived eventually by a later government.

In the industrial development of the public sector, a most noteworthy factor was the lack of planning. This affected not only the system of priorities on which public sector investments should be made but also the actual implementation of projects with the least possible delay and expense. Some of the results were bad location, ill-conceived planning and execution, bad management, and production capacities that were unrelated to the country's requirements. With the exception of the cement plant, other factories were severely handicapped in earlier years. It was in this context that the report of the IBRD mission of September, 1952, and the report of the Commission on Government Commercial Undertakings, November, 1953, were prepared and published. Both reports were extremely critical of the organization and management of public enterprises. The World Bank mission was specific in its condemnation of these industries and suggested the abandonment of most industrial projects envisaged in the public sector.

Up to 1950, Ceylon's public enterprises, functioning under government departments, were financed by the advanced account system. Experience showed that the very restrictive nature of financial regulations and Treasury circulars hampered the proper functioning of commercial ventures. It did not permit a commercial undertaking the degree of freedom of action necessary for a dynamic approach and efficient and successful working. Therefore, the establishment of the public corporation was a means of combining the advantage of private enterprise with publis responsibility and to escape the danger of bureaucracy by introducing the principal of flexibility of commercial operation. Once there was general agreement that public corporations were most suited to manage state industrial ventures, the government proceeded to enact further legislation for this purpose. Two acts were passed that helped the corporation to free itself of ministerial responsibility for the day-to-day administration of the undertaking and financial independence from Treasury regulations.

During the 1950's, the government was thinking in terms of an overall plan. In an earlier chapter the first experiment of the Six-Year Plan has been referred to. This plan included no new proposals for industry. It merely dealt with projects that had been individually planned earlier. From 1957 onwards, the concept of industrial development through public corporations was accepted in principle. This was influenced largely by the view that in most underdeveloped countries it was not possible for considerable industrial progress to be achieved without state participation in industries. Reference has also been made to the Ten-Year Plan, prepared in 1959, in which some of the more important public sector projects, which were carried out in the late 1960's, were first conceived and steps taken to line them up in some orderly fashion to enable their final execution.

THE INDUSTRIAL CORPORATIONS ACT

Prior to 1955, the state industrial ventures were under the Department of Industries as purely government concerns. In 1955, the state introduced the government-sponsored Corporations Act No. 19 of 1955. The purpose of this act was to incorporate industrial undertakings that were being run by government departments. The act gave powers mainly to incorporate existing industrial undertakings. To open a new industry, however, the government had to amend either the act or introduce a new bill. In 1957, the latter problem was overcome when State Industrial Corporation Act No. 49 with much wider scope was passed and empowered, inter alia, (1) the setting up and carrying on of any industrial undertaking; (2) taking over of any industrial undertaking carried on by any corporation that was established under the government-sponsored Corporations Act No. 19 of 1955. Under the act, the government also ensured that the accounts of corporations would be audited annually by an auditor appointed by the Minister. It also ensured that there would be parliamentary control over the capital of the corporations and in their efficient working by means of discussions and debates in the Houses of Parliament on their annual statements, reports, and accounts.

Upon transition to a corporation status, the enterprise was granted a substantial amount of autonomy in matters relating to management and finance. By the time the new act came into operation, several important state-owned industrial enterprises had already started functioning, such as cement, paper, ceramics, and footwear. The government had laid down specifically that certain industries would be confined to the public sector only, whereas in other areas private investment would be welcome.[2] The fields government had reserved for itself were cement, steel, paper, tires, mineral sands, salt, flour milling, plywood, petroleum refining, and the manufacture of fertilizer.

In some industries, where government interest predominates, private enterprise has also been encouraged. For instance in textiles, the government set up a factory for spinning and weaving when a privately owned factory already existed. There were several other units that started to function in the 1960's. Ceramics is another industry which was opened to private enterprise. Ceramic industries in the private sector are small units producing mostly ornaments and souvenirs. None in this field have ventured into the production of domestic crockery and sanitary ware. Articles being produced by the State Hardware Corporation, such as cutlery, builders' hardware, and metal fittings, are also being made by several private concerns. The Leather Products Corporation has had to face increasing competition from at least three large producers of footwear in the private sector. Similarly, bricks and tiles produced by the National Small Industries Corporation are sold in the market along with the products of more than one hundred units of various sizes in the private sector.

The government has chosen to have a monopoly in industries where the capital investment has been of some magnitude. There are very few new industries in the private sector with a capital outlay of over $8.4 million. State enterprises of cement, tires, paper, steel, and plywood have been established with a capital investment of well over $8.4 million. Even where private participation has been permitted, the public sector units have virtually dwarfed the privately owned plants. The National Textile Corporation spinning and weaving mill at Thulhiriya is the largest in the country. Similarly, the tannery and footwear factories of the Leather Products Corporation are larger than their counterparts in the private sector.

By 1963, there were fourteen industrial corporations in production, among these were cement, national textiles, sugar, paper, chemicals, fats and oils, ceramics, mineral sands, leather. At the end of 1966, the number in production had increased to fifteen while three others, the Ceylon State Flour Milling Corporation, Ceylon Steel Corporation, and the Ceylon Tires Corporation were about to commence production.

The greatest expansion in public sector industry took place between 1962 and 1966. At the end of 1967, the number of industrial corporations had increased to twenty-one, although four of them, the State Flour Milling Corporation, State Fertilizer, National Milk Board Condensary, and the Oil Refinery had not yet commenced production. After 1967 the government extended its industrial activities to several other fields. The Ceylon Fiber Board and the State Timber Corporation were established in 1968, and the Lanka Leyland Company with government participation for the assembly and manufacture of bus chassises was set up in 1969. (The new government is reviewing the Lanka Leyland Project.) By the end of 1968, many of the corporations that had previously not made much headway were functioning as relatively efficient units. This was chiefly due to the efforts made by the new administration in 1965 to improve the organization, management, and profitability of government-owned enterprises.

It has been estimated that the total capital invested in the twenty one state industrial corporations at the end of 1968 was in the region of $296.2 million. In the financial year 1968-69, a further investment of 43.0 million was contemplated. These new investments were primarily for major industrial plants such as the cement factory at Puttalam, the Thulhiriya Textile Mill of the National Textile Corporation, and the plywood complex of the Ceylon Plywoods Corporation at Avissawella. These outlays would bring the total investment in the industrial corporations in 1969 to an estimated figure of $322.4 million.

ASPECTS OF STATE-RUN ENTERPRISES

This section refers to the organization and activities of the more important industrial corporations in the public sector. One of the first industrial enterprises of the government, which is still in existence, is the tannery and shoe factory established in 1941 and incorporated as the Ceylon Leather Products Corporation under the State Industrial Corporations Act of 1957. Since then the factory has expanded and modernized its equipment and buildings. The corporation at present produces shoes, chrome and bark leather, and other miscellaneous leather goods. The value of output has risen from $0.8 million in 1965-66 to $1.2 million in 1968-69. In 1968-69 the production of chrome leather was 661,000 sq. ft. and the total output of shoes 275,000 pairs. The corporation provided employment in 1969 to 688 employees. As mentioned earlier, there are at least three large private firms making footwear, and because of heavy expenditure on advertising and sales promotion, these firms have been able to make substantial inroads into the profits of the corporation. This accounts for the relatively low profitability of the enterprise; profits have generally not exceeded $50,420 over the last few years. The Leather Products Corporation happens to be one of the few state-owned industrial enterprises that has had to face very severe competition from other private footwear manufacturers. Despite these handicaps, the corporation has been able to expand its sales because of the quality of its products and the moderate prices at which they have been offered to the public.

The development plans of the corporation include the establishment of a new tannery, which began production in March, 1970. A good proportion of these hides now finds an export market in India as kips, or unprocessed hides. One of the problems of the industry is the inadequacy of quality hides. It is known that quality hides find their way abroad through fraudulent means, although only rejected hides are given a license for export. The smuggling of superior hides should be prevented. The total investment on the tannery would be approximately $0.7 million. It will have a capacity of processing 1.25 million sq. ft. of chrome leather and 413,000 pounds of vegetable leather.

The ceramics industry sprang up during World War II. A pilot factory for the manufacture of crockery was set up in Negombo in 1942. This factory, however, had troubles at the beginning. It lacked sufficient equipment and skilled workmen. Furthermore, after the war, the factory had to close down as it could not compete with imports that were freely available. In 1955, a new factory was established by the Department of Industries as a pilot project with an annual capacity of 400,000 pounds of domestic crockery. In the same year, the unit was incorporated as Ceylon Ceramics under the government-sponsored Corporations Act of 1955 and was reincorporated as the Ceylon Ceramics Corporation on August 1, 1958, under the State Industrial Corporations Act of 1957.

As a result of progressive expansion, the corporation now operates two ceramics factories, one at Negombo with a capacity of 940 tons and the other at Piliyandala, which began in 1968, with a capacity of 1,600 tons. In addition, in close proximity to the Piliyandala factory there is a kaolin refinery with a capacity of 5,000 tons supplying raw materials to both factories. The total investment by the corporation has been $3.4 million; of this, $2.0 million has been apportioned to the Piliyandala factory, which has been equipped with modern plant and machinery. The output of ceramic ware has more than trebled from 852 tons in 1965-66 to 2,871 tons in 1968-69. The substantial increase in output was due to the manufacture of ceramic wall tiles and a wide variety of decorated crockery and sanitary ware by the new factory at Piliyandala. Although the kaolin refinery has increased its output consistently to meet the increasing need for raw materials, its output is still below its rated capacity; total output in 1968-69 was 2,900 tons.

Total sales of the corporation have risen from $0.6 million in 1965-66 to $2.2 million in 1968-69. The corporation enjoys a protected market for its products. Every item it now produces in quantity has been banned from import; it is still in the process of meeting the tremendous backlog in demand that appeared as a result of import restrictions introduced in the early 1960's. There has also been a notable improvement in the quality of products, which has been achieved through better glazing and by decreasing to a desirable proportion the average weight of clay per unit of output. The consumer at home has developed a gradual liking for the local product. Three expansion projects for the ceramics industry were approved by the government in 1968. The Negombo expansion scheme is designed to increase further the capacity of the factory to 1,000 tons per annum to enable sanatiry ware to be produced, and the electrical insulator project was due to come into production by the end of 1970. The wall tile expansion project was expected to be implemented in two stages--the first by the end of 1969, while the second, when completed, will result in the production of about 1,000 tons of wall and bathroom tiles per annum.

The ceramics plants have consistently operated at a profit, and since 1967 profits have exceeded $0.2 million, rising to $0.7 million in 1968-69. From the point of view of the consumer, the paucity of the sales outlets for ceramic ware at prices fixed by the management has led to some inconvenience.

Until 1969, the bulk of the products of the corporation found its way to the open market and were sold to the consumer at exorbitant prices, sometimes twice as much as the maximum price fixed by the corporation. With regard to the quality of the products, there is yet considerable scope for further improvement because the finish is not quite comparable with the very superior grades of foreign ceramic ware. There is also evidence that the designing and color schemes lack imagination; they have been mostly reproductions of cheaper and inferior wares found abroad. Efforts are now being made to rectify these defects and some progress has been achieved.

In the postwar period, the first large scale industrial enterprise was the government cement factory at Kankesanturai. The manufacture of Portland cement commenced in October, 1950. The rated capacity of the kiln was 80,000 tons, and each of the two grinding plants had a capacity of 85,000 tons per year. The plant experienced initial technical and managerial difficulties, but these were overcome a short while later. The government cement factory was transferred to the Kankesan Cement Works Corporation in November, 1956, and thereafter, in January, 1959, to the Ceylon Cement Corporation set up under the State Industrial Corporations Act. The functions of the latter were to develop the cement industry on an island-wide basis, and it was also entrusted with the monopoly of cement imports since 1963.

Although the output of the Kankesanturai plant was rated at 80,000 tons, it fell short of capacity production until very recently. Between 1951 and 1966, output has fluctuated between 65,000 tons and 80,000 tons. The consumption of cement in 1968 was estimated to be about 400,000 tons, with consumption rising at the rate of about 50,000 tons per year. The single cement factory that functioned from 1950 to 1967 was able to provide only about 20 per cent of the country's requirements. In June, 1967, a clinker grinding plant with a capacity of 100,000 tons was set up in Galle to utilize imported clinker or excess production from other factories in Ceylon. The economics of the cement grinding plant in plant was linked with the development of the Kankesanturai harbor and the transportation of clinker at relatively low cost by sea. The proposal to develop the Kankesanturai harbor, however, has not materialized, and clinker has had to be transported to Galle by rail at a much higher cost than originally anticipated.

Economically, cement is one of the products that could be produced in Ceylon on a large scale with minimum imported inputs because plenty of raw materials, limestone and clay, are available in several parts of the island. Plans to step up production of cement by the establishment of a new plant at Puttalam were ready some time ago. But the project was delayed and the country has had to maintain imports at a high level. The output of cement rose sharply from 79,000 tons in 1965-67 to 246,709 tons in 1968-69 with improvements to the plant at Kankesanturai and 100,000 tons of new capacity at the Galle terminal grinding plant. The first stage of the development program for the Kankesanturai factory was the installation in 1966 of a new kiln with a rated capacity of 165,000 tons of clinker. Thereafter, the old kiln was modernized and its capacity increased from 80,000 tons to 110,000 tons. These improvements stepped up the clinker production capacity of the plant to 270,000 tons. The first stage of the cement factory at Puttalam with a rated capacity of 220,000 tons was completed in March, 1970, and the second stage with a similar capacity is due for commissioning in mid-1971. The aggregate capacity of these three units is 350 tons, which is less than the anticipated requirements of cement for 1970. With the installation of a grinding plant with larger capacity at Kankesanturai and the completion of Stage II of the Puttalam project, the total capacity of the cement industry in Ceylon will reach 850,000 tons per annum.

The total capital investment of the Cement Corporation has risen from $16.8 million in 1966-67 to $40.8 million in 1969-70. This has been distributed in the proportions $13.4 million for the Kankesanturai factory, $3.4 million for the Galle terminal grinding plant, and $23.9 million for the Puttalam project. The value of production rose from $2.8 million in 1966-67 to $10.0 million in 1969-70. In the same period, profits rose from $1.3 million to $3.9 million.

This corporation has enjoyed a monopoly of sales in the country because it is not only the sole producer but also the sole importer, and the demand for cement always has exceeded supply, with the result that frequent shortages due to delays in imports, strikes, or breakdown of machinery at the factories have caused prices to move up very sharply. The selling price of cement, both wholesale and retail, is almost twice as high as the cost of imported cement. At present, a hundredweight of cement costs about $2.10, but it is possible to import cement from Japan or from India at a cost of less than $1.00, even after the payment of customs duty. The profitability of the corporation has been due largely to the high prices at which the product is retailed in the local market. With the commissioning of several new plants, it is possible that cost of production will decline sharply. But the question remains whether the corporation would be willing to pass on the benefit to the consumer. Pricing policies of public corporations are decided in consultation with the government because the bulk of the revenue goes into the consolidated fund.

The present pricing policy of the Cement Corporation has had fairly severe repercussions on the building industry in Ceylon. At a time when the housing problem is very acute, building costs have risen. Cement is a very vital item in house construction; if the price of cement is halved, it would be possible for prospective house builders to cut down costs by as much as 40 per cent. The corporation at the moment is concerned mainly with supplying the domestic market. Since plenty of raw material is available and if production could be stepped up and costs reduced to competitive levels, there is every reason to believe that cement could be exported in large quantities to the neighboring countries.

The factory of the Ceylon Oils and Fats Corporation on the west coast, at Seeduwa, was originally designed and installed in 1955 by the Department of Industries as part of an integrated chemical complex to be established in the area. However, the economics of the project as a whole, which were based on market conditions prevailing in the 1940's, did not outlast the war years and a decision was subsequently made to locate the caustic soda plant and the chlorine factory at Paranthan in the Northern Province. The oils and fats factory, thereupon, had to limit its activities to the manufacturer of high quality coconut oil by solvent extraction and the manufacture of provender. Because of adverse conditions in the world market for oils and the difficulties in obtaining raw materials, the corporation gradually concentrated on the manufacture of animal feeds, glycerine, and fatty acids.

The management of the factory has been in the hands of a government-sponsored corporation since 1955. In 1967, a major reorganization of the entire factory was carried out on the advice of a specialist from the Economic Commission for Asia and the Far East. The initial capital of the corporation was $3.3 million. The capital investment has since increased to $4.7 million due to the addition of a new provender plant. The factory consists of a number of production units. The continuous solvent extraction plant extracts residual oil from poonac, from which oil has been previously extracted by other millers. The capacity of the plant is 120 tons of poonac per day. Lately, the operating efficiency of the solvent extraction plant has been greatly improved. There is also a batch solvent extraction plant with a capacity of 50 tons per day for the purpose of extracting oil from minor oil seeds. Up to now, sufficient supplies of oil seeds have not been available to make full use of the plant. The provender plant has a capacity of 100 tons per day using extracted meal as the main ingredient. With the development of the poultry and the cattle industries in the country, the plant is now working to full capacity because of the increased demand for animal feed. The oil refinery processes up to

30 tons of oil per day. The equipment in this unit consists of neutralizing, bleaching, and deodorizing machinery. The fats splitting plant, with a capacity of 17 tons per day, processes low grade coconut oils into fatty acids and glycerine. Commercial production of this unit began in 1967. The ability of the corporation to obtain supplies of both copra and poonac has depended on the relative difference between the local price and the world market price and also on the export licenses granted for copra. Because of these factors the corporation has not had sufficient raw material to keep its extraction plants working to capacity.

The corporation has in recent years been plagued with labor and management problems, but they appear to have been gradually overcome. In the early 1960's, much of the equipment remained idle because foreign specialists who visited the factory were of the opinion that partly due to the foregoing considerations it was wholly uneconomical to operate the solvent extraction plant and the fatty acid and glycerine units.[3] Furthermore, the supplier of the solvent extraction plant went into liquidation before deliveries were completed, and problems arose about maintenance and an adequate supply of spares. In fact, a proposal was made that these untis should be scrapped because there were no possibilities of utilizing in Ceylon the by-products, notably glycerine and fatty acids. Recently, however, substantial export markets have been found for these products, which have helped to increase production substantially. Since 1967, the corporation has run at a profit; in 1968-69 profits rose to $0.8 million and were due mainly to the earnings from the export of glycerine. The profits from the export of glycerine alone in 1968-69 was $0.5 million. The total value of all products has risen from $2.2 million in 1965-66 to $5.7 million in 1968-69.

This Corporation has to an increasing extent utilized large quantities of locally grown maize for processing into animal feeds. It has also pioneered the collection and processing of coconut refuse to produce industrial oils that on previous occasions had gone to waste. A comprehensive plan has also been drawn up to convert progressively the export of primary coconut products into industrial exports and to invest approximately $4.2 million over a three-year period to produce a wide range of products based on industrial oils derived from coconut. These include stearic acid, detergents, hydrogenated bakery fats, glycerine, and linoleic and oleic acids.

The plywood industry in Ceylon has been one of the first manufacturing enterprises to be set up in the public sector. In the late 1920's Ceylon imported approximately 4 million plywood chests for exporting tea. Attempts made by the government to evoke interest in the private sector to produce tea chests met with very little response. Hence the present plywood factory at Gintota on the southwest coast was set up in 1941 as a government-run institution. The factory was incorporated in 1955 to function as the Ceylon Plywoods Corporation, and thereafter, its capacity was increased to 25 million sq. ft. of 3-ply wood per annum. Apart from tea chests, the corporation manufactures a variety of items such as plywoods boards, block boards, doors, and veneers. Investment of the corporation, which was $12.6 million in 1965-66, had increased to $15.3 million in 1969. This increase was for the purpose of establishing an integrated complex consisting of a chipboard factory, a sawmill, and furniture plant estimated to cost $12.5 million and a mechanized timber exploitation project with an outlay of $2.3 million. The chipboard factory, plywood plant, and sawmill are expected to come into operation in 1971. Working three shifts, the output is estimated to be 34,720 cu. meters of plywood, 21,500 cu. meters of sawn timber, and 9,000 cu. meters of chipboard. It is anticipated that employment for 2,000 would be available and a foreign exchange saving of about $3.4 million per annum would be effected. The profits of the Plywoods Corporation have increased substantially in the last two years. In 1966-67, profits were a little over $84,033 and in 1969-70 was in excess of $0.4 million. The foreign exchange saving in the last two years was in the region of

$1.3 million. The present factory of the Plywoods Corporation produces only about one-seventh of the country's total requirements. The market is a captive one and raw material is freely available. In view of this, the question that is hard to answer is why was plywood production was not stepped up earlier by increasing plant capacity. This is one industry where the local input content is very high. Mr. G. W. Naylor who reported on the economics of the industry said that the foreign exchange cost of the new plant could be recovered in six months.[4]

Salt manufactured in Ceylon is obtained solely by the solar evaporation of sea water. There are at present three main salt-producing centers in the north, west, and in the south. The National Salt Corporation was initially established in 1957 for the development of salterns in the southern region, while the government Salt Department was in charge of the other salterns in the northern and western regions. The object of the corporation was to produce 50,000 tons of salt per annum for export, whereas the output from the salterns belonging to the Salt Department was to cater to the domestic market. After the abandonment of the southern scheme in 1963, it was decided to consolidate all salt production activities under the corporation. This decision was implemented.

The capital invested in the corporation in 1957 was $1.4 million. In 1969, the capital was increased by $3.4 million for the purpose of installing new mechanized equipment at the main salterns in Jaffna in the north. At present, the corporation owns eight salterns with a total capacity of 83,900 tons per annum, and it also purchases salt from seven privately owned concerns with an annual capacity of 13,500 tons. Production from the corporation's salterns was valued at $1.5 million in 1967-68 and $1.3 million in 1968-69. The island's requirements of salt at present is approximately 78,000 tons per annum and more than 90 per cent of this is used for human consumption. Between 1945 and 1955, the average annual production was 45,000 tons. The present output of the corporation's own salterns and other private salterns meets the country's requirements. Before 1968, the deficit was met by imports. In the last two years, the profits of the corporation have exceeded $0.3 million, resulting in a foreign exchange saving on the average of about $0.8 million per annum. The installation of new equipment at the Jaffna Lagoon scheme, due for completion in 1970, was expected to yield 115,000 tons when in full production. The development of the salt industry will enable the establishment of a chemical complex and other large-scale salt-based industries.

No other industrial enterprise in the public sector has come in for so much criticism as the chemicals factory at Paranthan belonging to the Parathan Chemicals Corporation. In 1951, a series of units were set up for the production of caustic soda, chlorine, DDT, and sulphuric acid. Work commenced on this project in 1952, and in 1955 it was also decided to install additional equipment to produce lauryl alcohol. Soon after, the plan for the manufacture of DDT was abandoned, and the equipment that was imported to manufacture DDT was sold finally to an overseas buyer. The main reason for this was the estimated high cost of production and the declining demand for the product at that time because of the island-wide decrease in the incidence of malaria. The Paranthan Chemicals factory came into production in 1957, and by that time, the proposal to manufacture lauryl alcohol had also been abandoned. The main products of the corporation today are caustic soda, chlorine, and table salt. In the production of all these items, except table salt, the corporation has throughout worked far below capacity. For instance, in 1967-68 there was a slight decrease in the production of caustic soda over the figure for the previous year. The latter was despite the fact that caustic soda has a ready market in Ceylon, and the corporation produces only about 30 per cent of Ceylon's needs. On the other hand, the chlorine produced is not readily salable and the corporation's ability to dispose of surplus chlorine determines the output of other chemicals. As there was only a gradual increase in the demand for chlorine, the corporation found it uneconomical to produce all the requirements of caustic soda. The main reason for the decline in caustic soda output has been the constraints imposed by the demand for chlorine, which is purely a by-product of caustic soda manufacture. The corporation has very often had to release the unsalable surplus chlorine gas into the air.*

The initial capital outlay of the corporation was $2.6 million. In December, 1962, after the cabinet decided to shut down several units, the initial capital was written down to $0.7 million, the latter being the estimated value of the DDT, lauryle alcohol, and stearic acid plants that the corporation had decided to abandon because their operation appeared to be uneconomical. In January, 1969, the capital was written down by a further sum of $87,058, which was the value of the buildings that had been erected to house the three abandoned plants. The corporation had improvised two plants for the manufacture of hydrochloric acid and potassium chlorate with an annual capacity of 600 and 25 tons respectively. This plant will utilize approximately 400 tons of chlorine. In the meantime, the corporation has undertaken feasibility studies for the manufacture of soda ash and ammonium chloride. It is thought that if the output of chlorine is stepped up, it would form the basis for a viable chemical complex that could feed ingredients to several other new industries. The additional 7,000 tons of chlorine would enable the production of about 2,000 tons of polyvinyl chloride, 1,000 tons of hydrochloric acid, 200 tons of potassium chlorate, and 250 tons of tropical chloride of lime.

---

*G. W. Naylor's recommendations on the Paranthan Chemicals plant were that the plant should be shut down unless the chlorine problem was solved by (a) converting hydrochloric acid to ammonium chloride fertilizer, which would also help to triple the output of caustic soda, (b) setting up a small unit to produce caustic bleach, bleaching powder, and liquid household bleach.

Troubles in this industry in the 1950's and early 1960's have been attributed to bad planning and lack of proper management. This industry too has a history of prolonged industrial disputes. An added disadvantage is the location of the plant in an area distant from Colombo and the unwillingness of managers to reside so far away. It has been increasingly difficult to effectively manage the plant from the head office in Colombo. Although technically qualified men have been available, they were reluctant to be associated with the plant because of the poor reputation it had earned from the very beginning. Moreover, in setting up the original plant, no program was envisaged for the utilization of by-products, notably chlorine, and emphasis was given to the manufacture of products like DDT whose long-term use could have limitations and which could be procured from sources outside at a lower price. As originally planned, the object was to set up a chemical complex close to Colombo in the Negombo district with the fats and oils plant as the nucleus. The transfer of the chemicals plant to Paranthan and its isolation from the industrial region around Colombo was presumably the decision of the minister in charge of industries at this time to locate the industry in a politically advantageous environment. The Parathan Chemicals Corporation has been the only major industrial venture in the public sector with a record of unbroken losses. Profits appeared for the first time only in 1966. The complete reorganization of the directorate and the recruitment of qualified senior managerial and technical staff enabled the corporation to function as a viable economic unit.

The first attempt to manufacture paper in Ceylon was made during World War II when the Department of Industries set up a semi-mechanized paper factory. The factory, which was designed to convert waste paper into wrapping paper, proved uneconomical and was closed down in the late 1940's. In 1952, a comprehensive study of the possibility of manufacturing paper from indigenous raw materials was made, and in 1956 the paper mill, which is located in the east at Valaichenai, was completed. The original capacity of the mill was 3,750 tons of paper per annum made out of 30 per cent imported fiber and 70 per cent paddy straw and illuk grass; the last two are raw materials available locally. The Eastern Paper Mills, established under the government-sponsored Corporations Act of 1955, operated the mill from 1956 to 1958. The Eastern Paper Mills was incorporated in its present form as the Eastern Paper Mills Corporation in July, 1958. Up to the early 1960's, the factory had some growing problems. These related to water supply, excess labor, and the failure to grow sufficient illuk grass, the main raw material. When the project was formulated, the mill was to be fed with illuk grass to be grown in the vicinity of the factory; this was one of the reasons for locating the factory at Valaichenai. But it was never possible to grow illuk in adequate quantities to supply the mill. So the problem was overcome with the substitution of paddy straw for illuk. This is freely available in the Eastern Province, which is a large rice-growing region.

After the reorganization of the factory in 1965 on the basis of foreign expert advice, the mill has operated in three shifts. Ever since, the paper mill has been running at full capacity. In 1966 and 1967, production actually outstripped installed capacity in terms of tonnage. The fall in production in 1968 and 1969 was due to the inclusion of a higher proportion of lightweight paper in the product mix to satisfy the local market. The utilization capacity increased from 91 per cent in 1966 to 95 per cent in 1967. In 1967-68 the total output of all grades of paper was 9,500 tons. Printing and writing paper were the largest items of production. The corporation is also the sole importer of various grades of superior writing and printing paper. In 1968-69, the corporation imported about 7,000 tons of paper.

The initial capital of the corporation was $3.7 million, but this has since been increased to $11.4 million. The increased outlays have been for improving the quality of its products, the installation of a second manufacturing unit for the production of 12,000 tons of paperboard and a further increase in paper-making capacity of the paper mill to 10,500 tons.* The paperboard mill is expected to commence operation in 1971; in the meantime the corporation has made feasibility studies for the construction of a paper pulp mill with a capacity of 15,000 tons. This has been found necessary because the annual demand for paper and paper products is expected to increase to 85,500 tons by 1975. Commercial profitability has been in excess of $0.6 million since 1965; a profit of $1.1 million was made in 1968-69, although the estimated profits for the following year was slightly less. The total foreign exchange savings in the past four-year period has been around $1.3 million per annum.

In 1945, immediately after the war, the goverment established carpentry workshops to provide employment to several workmen who were displaced after retrenchment. These were originally converted into carpentry societies on a cooperative basis and later incorporated as the Ceylon Carpentry Corporation, with a view to manufacturing furniture for government offices. This again was reconstituted in 1958 as the National Small Industries Corporation. Several additional functions were added to this corporation, including the manufacture of bricks, tiles, boats, and ayurvedic drugs. It is, at present, concerned with the manufacture of all these products with the exception of boats, which were entrusted to the Fisheries Corporation in 1968. The corporation has carpentry workshops in seven towns and six brick and tile factories. Manufacture of ayurvedic drugs began in 1966 in a single factory. The production of tiles and bricks started in 1964-65. Despite the increase in the value of production from $1.0 million in 1964-65 to $1.9 million in 1969-70, the enterprise as a whole has had substantial losses yearly. But there has been a tendency for losses to decrease from $0.3 million in 1964-65 to a little over $109,243

---

*Naylor in his report urged the establishment without further delay of a paperboard mill.

in 1969-70. The reason for the losses is that the industry has faced severe competition from private brick and tile making concerns. Since products of the corporation are somewhat specialized, the demand is limited in comparison to products marketed by private enterprise.

The textile industry in Ceylon is characterised by the coexistence of a widely distributed traditional handloom industry and rapidly developing modern large-scale textile plants. At the turn of 1970, there were two large textile plants in the public sector and about six plants in the private sector manufacturing cotton and synthetic textiles. In addition, several privately owned plants were in the course of being set up. Total installed weaving c capacity in April, 1969, was 92 million yards in cotton and 23 million in synthetics. There was capacity for 5.8 million pounds of cotton yarn and cor finishing 75 million yards of cotton and 46 million yards of synthetics. The state-owned textile plants are managed by the National Textile Corporation, which was established in January, 1958, to undertake initially the installation of a spinning mill at Veyangoda with 11,200 spindles and an annual capacity of 3.4 million pounds of yarn. The mill was completed in 1963; since then capacity has been increased to 26,000 spindles with a yarn intake of 3.4 million pounds. A weaving and finishing mill with an annual capacity of 14 million yards and finishing equipment to handle 40 million yards was added in 1965. The total number of looms in the establishment is now 504.

At the Veyangoda spinning mill output has fluctuated during the last five-year period and has been considerably below capacity because of the uneven supplies of raw cotton from abroad, absenteeism, and labor disputes. The output of the weaving mill has also been about 50 per cent below installed capacity, partly due to industrial strikes and partly due to the shortage of skilled operators to work the looms in three shifts. In addition to finishing textiles produced at the mill, the plant also undertakes work for other private weaving mills. Despite the difficulties in management and operating the plant, the project has been commercially profitable since 1967. The estimated profits for the year 1969-70 were in excess of $0.8 million.

After the completion of the Veyangoda mill, the corporation incurred some expenditure on another textile mill to be set up at Pugoda; but this was later abandoned, and in 1967-68 construction began on an integrated textile mill at Tulhiriya. The designed capacity of the Tulhiriya mill in three shifts is 17.4 million lbs. of cotton yarn, 14 million yards of fabrics, and 40 million yard of finished, dyed, and printed cloth. The total capital invested in the Veyangoda textile complex is $9.0 million. Although the estimated cost of the integrated textile mill at Tulhiriya was $26.9 million, the costs already incurred have exceeded $40.3 million. This is attributable to very poor estimating procedures of capital works, excluding imported machinery, and the inability of the construction company, the State Engineering Corporation, to keep to the time schedules that were specified when programs were first prepared, and the intervening rise in the cost of both labor and materials.

In 1968-69, the textile industry of the public sector received a severe setback because of the delay in completing the integrated textile mill at Tulhiriya. The costs resulting from this delay have been twofold. First, textiles that could have been woven and finished in Ceylon had to be imported from abroad; and second, the German Democratic Republic, who is the principal supplier of machinery, stated that because of bad storage of the equipment, some machinery had deteriorated and that they were unable to afford the usual guarantee on the machinery. Another setback was the very sharp increase in building and installation costs. Current projections would seem to indicate that the final expenditure on the project would be about three times what was originally estimated. Therefore, the overall profitability of the venture is likely to be very much less because the mill will take a considerably longer period to pay for itself.

With the operation of the Tulhiriya mill, sufficient capacity has been provided for cotton weaving in the public and private sectors. Deficiencies, however, exist in spinning capacity, and efforts are being made to encourage the establishment of more spinning mills in the private sector. The most fundamental breakthrough in the development of the textile industry could come if the island meets a larger proportion of its own requirements of cotton.

Since 1966, active steps were taken to encourage the cultivation of cotton, and the National Textile Corporation took over the 2000-acre cotton farm at Hambantota belonging to the Department of Agriculture. So far the success of this cotton project has been negligible. At present, the cotton produced by the National Textile Corporation, which is possibly less than 2 per cent of the country's requirements, is processed prior to spinning at a private mill, the Wellawatte Spinning and Weaving Mills, because the corporation has no ginning plant. The local cotton is mixed with the superior imported long staples and used for spinning different kinds of yarn. Substantial foreign exchange savings will accrue if the country could grow a much larger percentage of its cotton. At present cotton imports do not cause a considerable drain on foreign exchange because much is imported under barter agreements with countries in the Middle East, notably Egypt. Nevertheless, it would be comparatively easy to increase cotton production as ideal climatic and environmental factors are found in more than one region of Ceylon. Under the Walawe Development scheme, which was completed in 1967-68, over 3,000 acres have been set apart for the cultivation of cotton. Since November, 1964, the corporation has been the sole importer of cotton yarn, which is sold mainly to the local handloom weaving industry.

Some of the heavier industries in the public sector emerged after the 1960's. There was much controversy as to whether Ceylon should go in for industrial products such as steel, hardware, petroleum refining, fertilizer, and tires. Institutions like the World Bank believed that there was no economic basis for Ceylon to set up these industries. Considerable pressure on government was also brought to bear by importing interests. But government policy was determined independently of these pressure groups, and active steps were taken to set up heavier industries. The State Hardware Corporation was established in 1963 for the manufacture of hardware, small tools, agricultural implements, and miscellaneous items from ferrous and nonferrous metals. In 1963, the government entered into a contract with a Polish firm for the supply of technical equipment and assistance to set up a hardware factory. Originally the cost of the machinery amounted to $1.1 million. But the final cost was far in excess of this amount, totaling $2.7 million. The main feature of the plant is that the machinery is geared to the manufacture of a range of diverse products. They include mammoties and other agricultural equipment, builders' hardware, cutlery, carpentry tools, and light engineering equipment. Commercial production in the factory began in October, 1965. The corporation has also established a cast iron foundry financed partly from a loan from the Federal Republic of Germany. The foundry, utilizing scrap metal, has a capacity of 6,000 tons of castings on a single shift per day; its estmated cost is $3.6 million. Approval has been granted to the corporation to undertake the construction of an agricultural implements factory together with a heat treatment plant and die casting unit at an estimated cost of $1.1 million. The work on this project has not yet begun.

The hardware factory initially had to face some difficulties, such as errors in planning production and producing articles that were not specifically suited to the country's requirements. The technical assistance from Poland resulted in the production of certain articles that were more suited to requirements in the West than in Ceylon. The corporation for instance took considerable time to perfect a suitable mammoty for the Ceylon farmer because copies of specimens brought from elsewhere were of little use. At present the factory is running without foreign technical assistance and is managed by Ceylonese technicians. A good part of the equipment now installed is being fully utilized, despite the fact that some of the equipment cannot be used as it would not produce articles that are most in demand. Much headway has been made in producing utility items such as cutlery, water service fittings, hinges, tower bolts, engineering tools, anvils, and bench vices of very high quality. The factory's initial troubles have been overcome and products are in considerable demand. A common problem with many corporations is the lack of a properly organized sales policy and a series of sales outlets to market products. In this instance too only a few retailers sell the corporation's products; the main outlet is the head office, which is engaged primarily in administrative matters.

The establishment of a steel plant was specified in the Technical and Economic Cooperation Agreement between Ceylon and the U.S.S.R. signed in 1958. Preliminary studies on this project were completed; and a detailed project report for the establishment of an integrated iron and steel works, comprising a charcoal blast furnace for pig iron production an open hearth furnace for steel making, and a rolling mill with an output of 35,000 tons of mild steel and wire rods, was received from the U.S.S.R. in 1960. The project was designed in three stages, commencing with the rolling mill. After taking into account the size of the local market and after advice had been received from several Indian experts, it was decided to increase the initial capacity of the rolling mill to 60,000 tons on two shifts. In addition, a decision was taken to establish a wire mill with a capacity of 12,000 tons. Preliminary work at the site commenced in 1962, and construction and installation was completed by the end of 1966. The rolling mill began production in January, 1967, and the wire mill a few months later. The initial capital outlay on the project was estimated to be $13.4 million, but the projected increased capacity resulted in the capital investment going up to $14.7 million. The authorized capital was later increased to $19.5 million and finally to $20.3 million in 1967, to take into account the outlays on a steel foundry, a structural shop, and a galvanizing plant.

Although the rolled steel and wire products mills continue to operate well below capacity, production has progressively increased. The ratio of capacity utilization is 44.2 per cent for rolled steel and 40.2 per cent for the wire mill. This has been due principally to the fact that the corporation proposes to achieve capacity production gradually, taking into account the relatively slow increase in demand for its products. The corporation's profits rose from $0.3 million in 1967-68 to $1.3 million in 1968-69. The Steel Corporation has also taken preliminary steps to establish a machine tool plant in technical collaboration with Hindustan Machine Tools Ltd. of India. Initially, it hopes to assemble machine tools and then start progressive manufacture. Preliminary work on stage two of the project, which includes the manufacture of steel out of imported pig iron and local scrap steel, is now in progress. The third stage comprises the utilization of local iron ore deposits in the manufacture of iron and steel.

The rolling mill uses as its raw material imported mild steel billets. The billets are heated in an oil-fired furnace and rolled into rods of various thickness. In addition to rods, the mill makes other merchant sections such as angles and tees. It does not do any rolling of steel plates and sheets because the machinery is not equipped for this. The mill has a barbed wire plant and a welding unit for wire mesh. The corporation has experienced difficulty in selling its products because of the limited size of the domestic market. Wire, which is a raw material for making iron nails, is also imported by wire nail manufacturers, although the corporation can supply their full requirements. Sales have also been affected by the lack of coordination between industrial policy and import control policy.

With the introduction of the Foreign Exchange Entitlement Certificate scheme and the inclusion of some items of hardware under Open General License, (between June, 1968, and May, 1970,) the corporation's sales suffered a setback. Earlier, the corporation, together with two units in the private sector, manufactured the country's entire requirements of barbed wire. With the introduction of the OGL scheme, free imports of barbed wire were allowed. This resulted in tremendous stocks of barbed wire accumulating in the corporation's stores; in fact, the accumulated stocks were sufficient to meet the country's requirements for one whole year.

Also included in the Technical and Economic Cooperation Agreement between Ceylon and the U.S.S.R. in 1958 was the establishment of a motor car and truck, tire, and tube factory. Preliminary studies were conducted by a team of Soviet specialists in 1958 and 1959; thereafter, a project report was issued for the establishment of a factory with a minimum annual capacity of 360,000 pneumatic tires and a corresponding number of tubes. The construction of the factory was planned in two stages. The first was with an initial capacity of 250,000 tires and tubes; in the second stage, output was to be brought up to 360,000 units. The capital cost of the project was $11.3 million. The factory began production in April, 1967, and in the first year 57,622 tires and 62,062 tubes were produced. In 1969-70 the projected output was 146,000 tires and 130,000 tubes. Throughout, production has been well below the plant's rated capacity. Performance was only 44 per cent in the case of tires and approximately 25 per cent in the case of tubes. The low capacity utilization of the plant was due primarily to restricting production to six tire sizes.

The policy of the corporation is to gradually extend production to other tire sizes as well. Since a large variety of tire sizes are still imported, the corporation has been handicapped because an alternative imported size could be fitted on some cars, and this has tended to reduce sales of locally made tires. The Tire Corporation budgeted for a profit of $3.4 million in 1968-69 on an output of 135,000 tires. But because of the delay in the arrival of tire moulds, actual production was reduced to half the budgeted production. As against the estimated profit, actual profit during that year was approximately $0.5 million. The corporation has not succeeded in getting export markets for its products. The success of stage two, which proposes to increase the annual output of tires to 360,000 units and 350,000 tubes, will depend almost entirely on whether export markets can be secured. Even if all sizes of tires required in the country are produced, it unlikely that the corporation could market its products unless there is a substantial increase in the total number of vehicles on the road.

Tires are made wholly of Ceylon rubber. Imported tires are made of synthetic rubber or are partly mixed with natural rubber; the quality of those made of synthetic rubber has been found to be superior. Because the corporation produces tires out of natural rubber certain defects are noticeable. In view of this, if the corporation is to produce a superior tire, as well as other rubber motor car accessories that require an oil resistant quality, it would have to think of using a certain amount of synthetic rubber. With the opening of the refinery, it may not be difficult to produce synthetics in limited quantities for specialized requirements in the tire and associated industries.

The Ceylon Mineral Sands Corporation was established in December, 1957, to exploit an estimated 4 million tons of heavy mineral-bearing beach sands on the northeast coast of Ceylon. The minerals, consisting of ilmenite, rutile, and zircon, are found as deposits of beach sand and probably have the highest concentration of any mineral deposit in the world. The ilmenite separating plant, with a capacity of processing 100,000 tons of raw sand per year, has been in operation since 1961. In 1969, the installation of a 20-ton dryer to ensure uninterrupted operations during the monsoon rains increased the annual capacity to 120,000 tons. A factory for the further processing of the residue, after the separation of ilmenite to produce rutile and zircon, commenced production in 1968. Approximately 2,000 tons of commercial grade rutile were produced at this factory up to the end of 1968. The production of ilmenite has tended to fluctuate over the years. This is due partly to production being based on actual orders received from abroad. A firm order from Japan enabled the corporation to step up production in 1968-69. In spite of this, there was considerable underutilization of capacity. In 1968-69, the profit of the corporation was $0.2 million, but future profitability is likely to rise with the manufacture and sale of higher priced rutile and zircon. The operations of the ilmenite plant consist of separating the ilmenite and other ores. There is considerable scope to process the raw material further into products such as titanium oxide, which could be used directly in the paint and aircraft industry. Further foreign exchange earnings could accrue if these aspects of the industry are explored.

With increasing emphasis on agricultural productivity, fertilizer consumption in the island has risen sharply during the last five to six years. In 1969, total fertilizer requirements were in the region of 215,000 tons, and fertilizer consumption is expected to rise to 350,000 tons by 1975. The establishment of a fertilizer plant was envisaged more than ten years ago.* Originally, it was expected to be part of the chemical complex that was to be set up in the Negombo district, but this did not materialize until after plans were finalized for the construction of the oil refinery. At present the oil refinery exports the bulk of the naptha that is a basic raw material for the fertilizer industry. The proposal to establish a fertilizer plant was

---

*In Industrial Policy of the Ministry of Industries (Colombo: Ministry of Industry, 1954), Sir Kanthiah Vaithianathan stated: "On the fertilizer project . . . I only wish to mention that we have by no means abandoned all hopes of producing our own requirements within Ceylon. The preliminary investigations, costing several lakhs, have been more the rough than in any other scheme. But we are baulked by its costs. The factory would be in the $25 million bracket, and even though we do spend $41 million every year on foreign fertilizers, it just doesn't seem to be possible to find the capital funds for this factory."

largely influenced by the availability of raw material and other inputs which are by-products of the petroleum refinery. The fertilizer factory is to be located next to the petroleum refinery, which is located some ten miles outside Colombo. This would seem to be the most feasible arrangement because of the availability of power for the fertilizer plant from the refinery and the grid, and also, raw material inputs. Distribution will also be facilitated because the agricultural regions and plantation districts are within easy reach of the plant. The new plant is expected to manufacture 220,000 tons of ammonium sulphate and 44,000 tons of urea. Its cost would be $45.4 million.

The Ceylon Fertilizer Corporation was established in January, 1964, and deals primarily with the improtation, processing, sale, and distribution of fertilizer; it does not manufacture fertilizer at present. The supplies made available by the corporation are mainly for the government's fertilizer subsidy scheme for coconut, paddy, tea, and rubber cultivation. The imports of raw materials and the mixing and distribution of fertilizer by the corporation has shown a steady increase during the last five years. This was due to increased requirements for the government's agricultural development program.

The State Flour Milling Corporation was set up in 1964 for the establishment and operation of a flour mill, with aid received from the U.S.S.R. under the economic agreement between Ceylon and the U.S.S.R. The mill can annually process 70,500 tons of wheat, working three shifts per day. The initial projected capital outlay on the project was $2.7 million, but this had to be increased later to $4.9 million. The increase in the cost was due to defects in the engineering work executed by the State Engineering Corporation, which constructed the buildings and installed the machinery. Since commencement of production in January, 1969, utilization capacity has increased from 42.5 per cent to about 80 per cent by the end of the year. A feature of the mill is that its capacity cannot be expanded and the plant cannot be utilized for milling of any grain other than wheat. Working at full capacity, the mill can produce only about one-sixth of the country's total requirements of wheat flour, which amounts to about 450,000 tons per annum. The output of the mill consists of 72 per cent flour, 23 per cent bran, and 3 per cent feed meal. Much of the wheat is imported under the Australian Commodity Aid Program. Bran and other by-products of the mill are used by the Oils and Fats Corporation in its provender plant.

Several industries engaged in the manufacture of foodstuffs and consumer goods do not come under the purview of the Ministry of Industries. One such enterprise is the National Milk Board, an undertaking of the Ministry of Agriculture; it was set up in 1954 with the object of operating an efficient unit and ensuring a cheap supply of milk to consumers. The Milk Board has several plants now functioning. The first of these was set up for the purpose of processing and bottling fresh milk. More recently it has established a condensed milk factory at Polonnaruwa and a powdered milk packing plant at Welisara. These two projects have been carried out with the foreign collaboration of Unigate Ltd. of the United Kingdom. Milk production has increased during the last two years owing to an incentive in the form of a higher minimum price being paid, from January, 1967, to suppliers of milk.

The milk packing plant now entirely uses milk powder imported in bulk from Australia and New Zealand. Up to now, even the containers have been imported from India, but steps are being taken to place orders with a local manufacturing firm for the containers. The viability of this project will depend solely on the early operation of the spray drying plant that is being set up at Ambawela to use local milk for for the production of milk powder. The condensary utilizes imported milk powder as well as small quantity of local milk. Foreign exchange savings could be maximized only if more milk is produced in the country; this will involve revolutionizing the present animal husbandry techniques in Ceylon. The steps taken so far to increase the production of milk, other than raising the guaranteed price, have not been very effective in increasing supplies. In the present context, it is most unlikely that the country will be able to produce a sufficient quantity of milk in the foreseeable future to feed the condensary and the spray drying plant.

Imports of sugar into Ceylon have increased steadily; one of the first import saving measures which was considered by the government was to produce sugar at home. Records show that Ceylon has had a history of producing a good part of its requirements of sugar in early times. In 1957, the government established the Kantalai Sugar Corporation to produce 21,000 tons of sugar and to use the by-products in a distillery to make 600,000 gallons of alcohol. About the same time, another sugar factory with an annual capacity of 19,000 tons of sugar cane and a distillery with a capacity of 750,000 gallons of alcohol was established in Gal Oya under the control of the Gal Oya Development Board. Both factories opened up their own sugar cane plantations for the supply of cane. In 1966, the government decided to vest the operation of all state-owned sugar factories and plantations under one management and, the Kantalai and Gal Oya projects were placed under a new corporation, the Sri Lanka Sugar Corporation.

Problems connected with the sugar industry in the island are numerous and have been the subject of several reports. The most recent report appeared in 1970.[5] Both the Kantalai and Gal Oya sugar factories have operated well below capacity due to the lack of regular and adequate supplies of sugar cane for crushing. This problem has arisen primarily because of the lack of coordination between cane cultivation and sugar production and the shortage of labor for cultivating and harvesting. In 1967-68, the output of the Kantalai factory fell by more than 50 per cent of the previous year's output because of an acute shortage of water, while in the same year, because of a better supply of water in Gal Oya, the output of the Gal Oya factory rose by more than five times. The Sugar Corporation has sold its entire output of sugar to the government. The average imported cost of sugar in 1966-68 was around 4 cents, but the cost of production at Kantalai was 10 cent in 1966-67 and nearly 17 cents in 1967-68. Both sugar factories have been total failures because of the high cost of production. The inability of the two enterprises to grow sufficient cane to keep the factories running at optimum capacity throughout the year has been the cause of high production costs. Despite the losses made on the manufacture of sugar, the production of spirits has been very profitable, and the overall position is that the enterprise has been running at a profit.

The foregoing review of public sector industries shows that most of these enterprises started functioning in the last fifteen years and that within this short period they have had a fairly impressive record of achievement. The present efficiency of these industries should be examined in the light of difficulties that they faced in the first few years. The early difficulties are attributable largely to the lack of proper organization, technical know-how, and managerial skills. In 1969, almost all the industrial corporations were running at a profit as against the situation in 1960 when only some three to four of these showed a profit. Programs have been drawn up for expansion and diversification of products in most factories, and many others are in the process of preparing plans for further expansion.

What is heartening to note is that most of these public sector industries, unlike those in the private sector, are dependant on local raw materials. The Oils and Fats Corporation utilizes copra and coconut meal as raw materials; the Cement Corporation, limestone and clay; the Leather Corporation, local hides; the Plywood Corporation, Ceylon timber; the Paper Corporation, paddy straw; and the Tire Corporation, Ceylon rubber. The only exceptions are the petroleum refinery, the hardware, and steel corporations that are dependant primarily on imported inputs. For this reason, future prospects for growth are extremely favorable because they are based on

TABLE 27

State Industrial Corporations:
Capital, Profits/Losses, and Return on Investment

Corporation	Capital Employed in Production[b] 1967-68 (in $ '000)	Profit[a]/Loss (in $ '000) 1964-65	1965-66	1966-67	1967-68	1968-69 (budgeted)	Return on Investment before Tax 1967-68 %	Estimated Return[c] 1968-69 %
National Textile Corporation	6,302.5	n.a.	n.a.	112.1	260.5	638.7	4.1	10.1
Ceylon Cement Corporation	12,996.5	1,181.5	1,302.5	1,392.4	2,331.9	2,777.8	17.9	21.4
Ceylon Ceramics Corporation	2,888.2	53.3	n.a.	128.6	504.2	672.3	17.2	23.3
Ceylon Steel Corporation	16,340.5	-	-	-	58.5	2,689.1	0.37	16.5
National Small Industries Corporation	3,199.7	(211.1)	(209.9)	(110.9)	(108.4)	(104.4)	loss	loss
Eastern Paper Mills	5,197.1	235.0	384.4	600.2	867.6	1,075.6	16.6	20.7
Ceylon Tire Corporation	11,348.7	-	-	-	135.3	3,429.2	1.2	30.2
Ceylon State Hardware Corporation	2,777.5	-	-	(176.8)	3.4	542.2	0.12	19.5
Paranthan Chemicals Corporation	2,070.8	(103.2)	(44.5)	34.1	112.1	145.4	loss	n.a.
Ceylon Mineral Sands Corporation	1,943.2	(123.2)	(34.1)	9.1	32.3	182.9	1.6	9.4
Ceylon Leather Products Corporation	1,049.6	36.3	49.2	65.7	31.4	69.4	2.9	6.6
Ceylon Oils and Fats Corporation	2,666.9	36.1	93.9	41.7	(89.7)	339.0	loss	12.7
National Salt Corporation	982.9	n.a.	n.a.	144.5	287.9	301.3	29.0	30.7
Ceylon Plywood Corporation	470.6	63.5	2.4	100.8	93.6	269.4	19.9	57.3
Ceylon Fisheries Corporation	3,949.6	-	216.0	(774.8)	(605.0)	(800.4)	loss	loss
Total	74,184.3	1,168.2	1,327.9	1,566.7	3,915.6	12,197.5	3.2	16.4

[a]Profits from purely trading activities are excluded in most cases; figures given are before deduction of tax.
[b]Capital referred to is capital actually employed in production.
[c]Budgeted profit/loss over capital employed in production in 1967/68. Actual return in 1968/69 may in some cases be lower than figures given here since additional capital will then be employed.

Source: Ministry of Industries & Fisheries. Review of the Activities of Corporations in 1967-68.

the utilization of local raw materials. And further expansion would result in very substantial foreign exchange savings.

Several public sector industries have exported products. These have included fatty acids, glycerine, ilmenite, chlorine, and tires and tubes. The Ceylon Mineral Sands Corporation exports it entire output of ilmenite and rutile. The overall success of these industries has, in general terms, proved that the public sector enterprises could play a vital role in further economic development. This would be true particularly of enterprises with heavy capital outlays that are likely to be of little interest to the private sector.

NOTES

1. *Sessional Paper*, No. 1 of 1922 (Colombo: Government Printing Press, 1922).

2. See *Government Policy on Private Foreign Investment* (Colombo: Ministry of Planning and Economic Affairs, 1966), pp. 2-3.

3. See G. W. Naylor, *Report of Reconnaissance Mission to Ceylon in connection with State Industrial* Corporations (Colombo: Ministry of Planning and Economic Affairs, 1966), pp. 37-40.

4. G.W. Naylor, *op. cit.*, pp. 41-42.

5. See *Report of the Gal Oya Project Evaluation Committee*, Chapter 7. *Sessional Paper*. No. 1 of 1970 (Colombo: Department of Government Printing, 1970).

CHAPTER

10

THE INSTITUTIONAL FRAMEWORK FOR PLANNING AND PROJECT IMPLEMENTATION

MINISTRY OF PLANNING AND ECONOMIC AFFAIRS

Within the institutional framework created to carry out planning and implementation, a new ministry known as the Ministry of Planning and Economic Affairs was set up in 1965 (designated Ministry of Planning and Employment since May, 1970). Prior to this, the function of planning had been assigned to the National Planning Council, which was serviced by a fairly small department, the Planning Secretariat. This secretariat operated independently of the planning activities of individual government departments. The National Planning Council was set up in 1956 to formulate a development policy for Ceylon. In actual practice, it turned out to be a purely advisory body without executive functions. The new Ministry absorbed the Planning Secretariat and in addition established several other departments and divisions to handle specialized functions. Furthermore, the work of the National Planning Council was entrusted to the Cabinet Planning Committee, which consisted of three ministers, the ministers of finance and state, and was presided over by the Prime Minister.

Once these units started functioning, the strategy of economic planning underwent considerable change. In the fifteen-year period after followed 1950, considerable time was spent on the preparation of the five-year, six-year, ten-year, and two-year plans. The Planning Secretariat devoted a great deal of its time on the preparation of these macroeconomic plans rather than formulating a program of high priority projects with procedures and machinery geared to their effective implementation. After 1965, the administration realized that the planning techniques hitherto adopted were not having a significant impact on growth.

Therefore, strategy henceforth was to formulate concrete programs for key sectors of the economy, where growth was found to be most desirable both from the welfare and foreign exchange standpoint. Another objective of the new approach to planning was the identification of specific projects suitable for early implementation and those that required external financing. It was felt that if these two objectives were given emphasis, a comprehensive overall plan would emerge in due course.

In January, 1966, when the government of Ceylon made a request to the United Nations Special Fund for technical and other assistance to carry out development programs; it said: "It is not the immediate objective of the new planning organization to devote all its energies at the initial stage towards the preparation of a macro-economic plan and development of the conventional type, *i.e.*, a five-year or ten-year aggregative plan. Such overall plans have been prepared for Ceylon in the past but have been in some respects of too abstract a nature to provide a base for action. The diversion of the planning organization towards a fresh effort on similar lines would involve a lot of time that would be ill-afforded at the present time. It is expected that various elements of a comprehensive overall plan would emerge from this work."[1] The Ministry of Planning and Economic Affairs emphasized that the broad strategy of development was designed to achieve a substantial breakthrough in domestic agriculture, to step up the tempo of industrial development, to improve the economic infrastructure--meaning development of roads, railways, and power systems--and training and orienting human resources towards development.

To deal with these aspects of development on systematic lines, four committees consisting of permanent secretaries were appointed, each with a secretariat consisting of officials of the Department of Planning and of the Ministry of Planning and Economic Affairs. By the middle of 1966, the four committees on industry, economic overheads, domestic agriculture and manpower, and education, respectively, had finalized their reports. The task of these committees was to indicate very broadly the fields that most urgently required development. As these reports were of a preliminary nature, a good many of them had to be studied in detail before they could be dovetailed into a joint program and their viability assessed in terms of the broad objectives stated earlier. The committees made a good beginning in sectoral programing, but much work had to be done before these programs could be shaped into an overall five-year plan. The planning authorities were faced with the problem that this time ministries, departments, and state organizations did not have technically qualified and competent men who were best able to prepare sectoral programs. Of the officers in the Department of National Planning, very few had experience in the broad aspects of planning to work out the overall impact of the sectoral programs on the balance of payments and the gross domestic product. Most of the officers in the planning organization had been engaged in the task of preparing development budgets, and they had also been entrusted with the task of reviewing individual projects for the various ministries directly connected with development.

The Ministry of Planning and Economic Affairs was charged, among other duties, primarily with the formulation and appraisal of economic and financial policy. It was also required to carry out the implementation of national plans and to secure foreign aid for national development. The ministry came directly under the Prime Minister, who was also in charge of planning, and in addition its parliamentary secretary was a cabinet minister. Like all other ministries, the Ministry of Planning and Economic Affairs had a permanent secretary who was in overall charge of the various departments and divisions. Breaking away from earlier practice, for the first time the government appointed a trained economist as the permanent secretary to the ministry. Most other permanent secretaries in other ministries were administrators who belonged to the defunct Ceylon Civil Service, a relict of British colonial administration. Within the ministry, five divisions were established dealing with perspective planning, plan implementation, external resources, private sector affairs, and general economic affairs.

PERSPECTIVE PLANNING

The Division of Perspective Planning was responsible for the preparation of plans for successive planning periods, indicating the magnitudes of investment that were required in each of the major sectors. It was also expected to verify the internal consistency of plans with overall national objectives. It further deals with the international aspects of perspective planning that arise out of work of international organizations, such as the United Nations Conference on Trade and Development UNCTAD and with questions of regional cooperation and harmonization of regional development plans. Since its inception, the duties of the division have been confined largely to fitting sectoral programs into the framework of an aggregative long-term plan. For many sectors, particularly the government sector, the first drafts of the sectoral programs have been prepared by various committees that have been set up under each of the ministries. Apart from these, the division has been preoccupied with several rather complex and academic exercises, such as the preparation of an input output table for the country. In a country like Ceylon, the usefulness of a table of this kind is very limited. The primary difficulty is the nonavailability of data on inputs and the fact that the coefficients that ultimately emerge are quite unrealistic. So far the division has not put out a long-term plan.

PLAN IMPLEMENTATION

The Division of Plan Implementation deals mainly with the project content of plans, and it is also responsible to some extent for project evaluation, although its full time function is plan implementation.* The overall work of the Division comes under the Plan Implementation Committee consisting of key officials from the Ministry of Planning and other important government departments. This division has reviewed only project proposals from implementing agencies in the public sector and has very little to do with implementation of projects in the private sector.

As a first exercise, projects are examined by teams of officers, including those in the Department of Plan Implementation and in the sponsoring agencies. Once a project has been accepted by the Cabinet Planning Committee, which is primarily a ministerial body, it becomes a part of the government investment program. Thereafter, the task of the department has been to ensure that the capital expenditures are met during the financial year in terms of a schedule that has been laid down for the completion of the project. The division is expected to keep track of the projects by submitting quarterly reports on work undertaken. These reports are prepared in collaboration with the agency that is carrying out the project;

---

*Several World Bank reports have pointed out that previously projects had not been selected on the basis of their economic benefits and against a clearly defined set of economic priorities and assessment of resources. Particularly with regard to public investment, there have been delays in the award of contracts and undue delays in carrying out programs according to schedule.

See IBRD. Note on Recent Developments and the Exchange and Growth Outlook 1967-71 of Ceylon (Colombo: Ministry of Planning and Economic Affairs, 1967).

in most cases it is a government department or corporation. Its primary task has been to break down bottlenecks and to ensure that no obstacles appear in the path of progress. In the period before 1965, experience had shown that the lack of a proper plan implementation agency hindered the speedy completion of projects. Very often lack of controls and proper procedures of review have resulted in inferior workmanship, and difficulties have been experienced initially in getting the project started. Such weaknesses have been associated with public sector investments. Because of the same reasons, public sector projects have been badly formulated and are apt to have inordinately long gestation periods. Furthermore, the potential of the investment has not been exploited completely either because of deficiencies in planning and designing or because of the failure to take appropriate steps in this direction.

For the Plan Implementation Committee to undertake a regular review and evaluation of progress of all projects under the various ministries, a national operations room was set up in 1969. The departments and corporations under which the project comes periodically make their own evaluation of the progress achieved, while commenting briefly on the factors that may have impeded progress or have caused shortfalls in implementation. These progress reports are submitted to the Plan Implementation Division. The national operations room has a diagramatic panel for each ministry detailing progress achieved on each project. This panel indicates the targets for each project on a quarterly basis and the quarterly progress that has been achieved. Shortfalls in each project are immediately highlighted. The Plan Implementation Committee then isolates and studies the reasons for the shortfall, and appropriate remedial action is suggested at once. At one stage, the Ministry of Planning and Economic Affairs suggested that in order to ensure closer control of progress, each ministry should have an operations room of its own, containing all the relevant data relating to the ministry's implementation program and the progress achieved. However, this recommendation was not put into effect.

The Plan Implementation Division has pointed out that one of the major reasons for the failure of individual ministries to achieve their targets within the prescribed period has been the lack of proper programing. The completion of most projects has depended on the rendering of certain services by subsidiary agencies. If subsidiary agencies had not been consulted at the time when programs were drawn up, they cannot be made responsible for the completion of the project over the prescribed period. Delays on the part of the subsidiary agencies have resulted inevitably in inordinate delays in the completion of projects. To overcome these problems the ministries have been advised to identify the subsidiary agencies that are required to complete the different items in a project. These could be power supply, roads, acquisition of lands, and the supply of machinery. Since all these take considerable time, it is necessary to ensure that the work of these subsidiary agencies is carried out simultaneously according to a satisfactory schedule. In the operations room, network charts have been prepared outlining the consecutive stages necessary to carry out a project. These networks indicate the extent and the points of time at which different ministries or departments would have to participate in the project. The Implementation Department has to identify the contribution of each ministry and the time taken by each ministry to complete the work.

Regular reviews and evaluation of public sector programs have also been undertaken by the Plan Implementation Committee. This has been done by having a series of working sessions in the operations room to enable departments and corporations to take remedial action where delays or difficulties have emerged. Meetings have helped the Ministry of Planning and Economic Affairs to examine all items of expenditure that have been sanctioned in the capital budget, to ensure that the results from financial outlays are consistent with the quarterly targets, and to see that all equipment, material, and resources would be available within the period stipulated for the completion of the project. Moreover, the committee has examined the total program to which a department has been committed, the work that is on hand, and the capacities available to ensure that operational plans are realistic. Discussions at such meetings have enabled the committee to identify the subsidiary agencies participating in the project and to make certain that firm time schedules have been assigned to each of them. The most important function of the committee has been to examine and confirm the targets of output for public sector corporations in terms of availability of resources and improvements effected by management.

With regard to private sector activities, particularly domestic agriculture and plantations, the committee has prepared estimates of output targets for both raw material products and industrial commodities. Considerable time has also been spent on making definite organizational arrangements for a system of progress reporting and the supply of information to the national operations room.

EXTERNAL RESOURCES

The Division of External Resources (until 1968 it was known as the Department of Foreign Aid) now undertakes functions that had been assigned earlier to the Treasury and the Central Bank. The importance of this division has arisen out of the significance of foreign aid in the development program in the preceding five-year period. This department is expected not only to receive aid that is forthcoming, but also to take active steps to ensure that sufficient aid would be available to finance foreign exchange deficits in new investment proposals. Further, it examines various aid proposals and negotiates with donor countries to secure better terms. All foreign aid proposals are submitted to the monetary board of the Central Bank for approval before agreements are entered into in terms of statutory requirements in the Monetary Law Act. If the terms are not favorable the monetary board will advise that further negotiations are necessary on specific terms in the draft loan agreement. The aid negotiated since 1965 and discussed in the next chapter has been handled by the External Resources Division. In addition, it has coordinated technical assistance, training programs, and scholarships.

The Division of External Resources is also responsible for the formulation and administration of the foreign exchange budget. A foreign exchange budget was prepared for the first time in 1965-66. Its significance arose out of the growing scarcity of foreign exchange on the one hand and, on the other, that resources would be ensured for the completion of projects that have been given priority in the development programs. Experience had proved that in the earlier period many projects were delayed or could not be completed because adequate foreign resources were not forthcoming to meet the foreign exchange costs of projects. The Foreign Exchange Budget Committee has been entrusted with the allocation of foreign exchange for development and consumption. The Committee consists of the Permanent Secretary, Ministry of Planning and Employment (Chairman), the Secretary of the Treasury, permanent secretaries to the ministries of Internal and External Trade, Industries and Scientific Affairs, and a Central Bank representative. The foreign exchange budget is more or less an integral part of the general budget, which is presented by the Minister of Finance in July or August of each year.* The budget consists essentially of forecasts of the total earnings from exports and foreign aid that is expected in the coming financial year. On the basis of these resources the task of the Foreign Exchange Budget Committee is to examine requests for foreign exchange and to allocate them according to a scheme of priorities.** In these allocations, changes in import

---

*Under the present arrangements, in October every year. From 1971, the financial year will be the calendar year. Previously the financial year was from October to September.

**With the introduction of the Foreign Exchange Entitlement Certificate Scheme in May, 1968, and the

control policy have been taken into account. The committee has always approved requests for foreign exchange for high priority projects from various government departments and corporations. The main criteria in determining its allocations have been the priorities laid down in the budget and in policy announcements by government. In practice, although the exercise has been quite useful in ensuring adequate resources development, there has been great difficulty in making accurate forecasts of export receipts. In the preceding years the gaps in the Foreign Exchange Budget have been quite noticeable because of unexpected trends in export markets. These have made accurate forecasting almost impossible.

PRIVATE SECTOR AFFAIRS

Another important unit in the ministry is the Division of Private Sector Affairs. This is an entirely new unit. Before 1965, very little attention had been paid to initiating, formulating, and assisting investment in the private sector; it had been left to manage its own affairs for a long time. The importance of this division has arisen because the bulk of the investment and productive activity has been in the private sector. The main functions of this division are to study, prepare, and promote monetary, fiscal, and institutional measures that are necessary to achieve the targets of investment and output in the private sector within the overall targets provided for the economy. It also assesses the progress in implementation and makes recommendations, from time to time, for changes in policy that may be necessary to achieve the targets within stipulated periods.

---

appointment of the FEEC's Review Committee to consider the day-to-day problems arising out of the work of the FEEC scheme, the Foreign Exchange Budget Committee and the FEEC Review Committee have been working in liaison. In 1969, about one-third of all imports were financed on FEEC's.

One of its more important duties is to review, examine, and report on private foreign investment in Ceylon. For this purpose, a committee known as the Foreign Investment Approval Committee has been set up to examine and report on private sector investments before they are formally approved by the Ministry of Industries. Reference to the work of the committee has been made earlier. The committee has to determine whether a tie-up with a foreign firm would result in substantial foreign exchange saving to the country, bring in technical know-how, and also help in the production of high quality goods. On the question of foreign investment, the Ministry of Planning and Economic Affairs issued a document in 1966 stating the terms and conditions on which foreign investment would be welcome in Ceylon and the concessions foreign investors would be entitled to.[2] The committee has examined these various proposals primarily in the light of the guarantees given to prospective foreign investors.

The Division of General Economic Affairs of the Ministry of Planning is responsible for the study of economic aspects such as wages and fiscal and monetary policy. It also deals with matters relating to the United Nations and its agencies and the Commonwealth Regional Organization. The Ministry of Planning and Economic Affairs (now called the Ministry of Planning and Employment) has been designated the coordinating ministry for these organizations.

OVERALL PLANNING PROCEDURES

The procedures for drawing up investment programs in the period 1965 to 1969 have improved from year to year. Broadly, the work consists of preparing plans and programs for each department under a given ministry for a period of about five years. In this way, the proposals emerge from the bottom in the sense that each department is in contact with the public or the agencies actually handling the investment proposals. Once a department prepares a plan, further work on it involves a detailed techno-economic analysis before it can become part of a sectoral plan.

Not all projects put forward by different departments would be able to stand up to the rigorous evaluation. Furthermore, some may not conform to the government's scheme of priorities. The Ministry of Planning examines each project in relation to all others and selects those in the high priority category. To facilitate matters, ministries have been directed to submit all their major capital proposals before the middle of the year when the actual preparation of the budget takes place.

The budgetary framework within which the ministries would have to program their investments is prepared by the Ministry of Planning. Each ministry is required to manage its investments in relation to the estimated resources made available under the budgetary framework. The guidelines specified by the ministry for the preparation of capital programs by individual ministries include the following. Each ministry is expected to prepare a forecast of expenditure on all capital projects undertaken by departments, corporations, and other agencies under it. These forecasts should indicate the annual phasing of expenditure until the completion of the project and should be based on reliable estimates of expenditure related to realistic time schedules for the implementation of projects. They are intended to give an estimate of the capital funds that would be necessary during the financial year. Furthermore, each ministry is expected to re-examine the phasing of investments in the program with a view to securing the best returns on the investments as well as making room for new projects of high priority.

The ministries are expected to study the feasibility of deferring or phasing over a longer period of implementation those projects of relatively low priority, while projects likely to contribute to the output of the economy immediately are required to be completed in the shortest possible time. Investments under administration overheads fall within the category of projects where postponement or extended phasing may be possible. Ministries are required to identify elements within each project that may not be immediately essential and to find out whether these investments could not be deferred or substantial economies effected if they were undertaken on a modest scale. Wherever a corporation has undertaken a project, the ministry has to examine and report whether the project could be financed by the corporation's own resources. In recent years this aspect has been given considerable weight. The ministry is also expected to examine whether some of the new projects that are planned could not be undertaken in the private sector, either entirely or from private resources so that the burden on the government could be reduced, or in the alternative, whether or not joint participation is possible.

During 1969, efforts were made to set up programing units in each ministry so that the guidelines for planning indicated earlier could be effectively put into operation, thereby decentralizing the decision-making process and also entrusting duties to more specialized personnel in each ministry. In several ministries, notably the Ministry of Agriculture and the Ministry of Industry, programing units have been functioning for sometime and have worked in close liaison with the Ministry of Planning. From the point of view of organization, the programing units will be equal more or less to a decentralized sectoral planning agency. They have set standards and criteria for operating departments and other agencies associated with the preparation and implementation of projects. These units have participated in the formulation of the overall investment program and have made provision for recurrent expenditure in successive budgets until projects have been completed. The programs developed by these units are assembled into an overall plan by the Ministry of Planning after considering the volume of external and internal resources that may be available to finance projects. This is done by the Ministry of Planning in consultation with each of the ministries that originally submitted the proposals. Before the final decision is taken, the Plan Implementation Committee reviews these programs, and they are submitted to the Cabinet Planning Committee with their recommendations. The Cabinet Planning Committee then analyzes the programs in light of the recommendations made by the Plan Implementation Committee.

Finally, the cabinet approves the programs; once this is done, they become part and parcel of the budget for the following year.

NOTES

1. Albert Waterston, *Recommendations on Economic Planning in Ceylon* (Colombo: Ministry of Planning and Economic Affairs, 1966), p. 1.

2. *Government Policy on Private Foreign Investment* (Colombo: Ministry of Planning and Economic Affairs, March, 1966).

CHAPTER 11
FOREIGN AID

FOREIGN AID AND ECONOMIC DEVELOPMENT

Soon after the war, when plans were formulated to assist developing countries, the rationale of aid was expressed mainly in terms of a "savings gap" or a "resource gap," which is the gap between investment needs for a desired rate of growth and domestic savings. More recently, in the 1960's particularly in view of the balance of payments problems of the developing countries, attention has been focused on a "trade gap," which is the difference between export earnings and the minimum import requirements for a given rate of economic growth. If the gap between minimum import requirements and export earnings cannot be bridged by conscious international efforts to reverse adverse trends in the terms of trade, the deficit could be filled only by the transfer of capital from the richer to poorer countries. Ceylon has had to contend not with a savings gap but with an increasing trade gap from the early 1960's onwards. With concerted efforts made to achieve a high rate of growth, this trade or foreign exchange gap has perceptibly widened; and in order to maintain the rate of progress at a consistently high level, increasing recourse to foreign aid was necessary.

There is a significant difference between the aid received in the 1950's and that received today. Up to 1964, aid programs were geared specifically and closely to individual projects. There is considerable evidence to show that underutilization of aid receipts for specific projects was a common feature in the 1950's. This was the result of the lack of effective implementation procedures. Very often, although project aid was forthcoming, Ceylon had not taken effective steps to prepare the ground for the project and to utilize the proceeds with the least possible delay. Requests for aid were also made without sufficient investigation and evaluation of projects and how far these would fit into the development complex. A White Paper on foreign economic aid, published in 1962, stated, "During the early years of the period under review, offers of aid were accepted somewhat indiscriminately without any relation to any program of development. An offer of aid had only to be made for it to be accepted".[1]

Despite the fact that Ceylon has received aid from the early 1950's, the tempo of assistance from abroad rose only after 1965. Prior to 1964, the bulk of the aid received was for projects and technical assistance, whereas in the last five years the emphasis has been on commodity aid. In view of the change in character, composition, and utilization of aid, the impact of aid on economic development in Ceylon is reviewed in terms of two broad periods--1950 to 1964 and 1965 to 1970.

Foreign aid received by Ceylon has taken various forms such as grants, loans, soft loans, hard loans, project aid, program aid and bilateral and multilateral aid. Similarly, aid has been provided by international agencies, foreign governments, or private institutions. Of these sources, foreign government aid has been the most important.

In this section, the extent and nature of assistance Ceylon has received since 1950 will be reviewed. The year 1950 is significant because it saw more than one international effort to launch schemes of assistance for development. In 1950, U.S. President Truman inaugurated the Point IV Technical Assistance Program, and soon after the

Colombo Plan for economic cooperation was conceived at a meeting of Commonwealth prime ministers in Colombo. Since then, Ceylon has received aid in several forms, such as capital grants, loans, donations of equipment, and technical assistance.

THE COLOMBO PLAN

The Colombo Plan, or the plan for the cooperative economic development of South and Southeast Asia, was conceived for the improvement of living standards of the people of that region. After the ministerial meeting in Colombo, a consultative committee was appointed to survey the needs and resources of the countries in the region. The original members of the plan were Australia, Canada, Ceylon, India, New Zealand, Pakistan, and the United Kingdom. Presently the plan has a much wider membership and includes Afghanistan, Australia, Bhutan, Britain, Burma, Cambodia, Canada, Ceylon, India, Indonesia, Japan, Korea, Laos, Malaysia, Maldive Islands, Nepal, New Zealand, Pakistan, Philippines, Thailand, U.S.A. and Vietnam. The Colombo Plan was originally drawn up for a period of five years, but in 1955 it was decided to extend the period of the plan up to 1961. Since then, further extensions have been made from time to time because donors and beneficiaries have been appreciative of the work done. Aid under the plan has been made available in several forms, including plant and equipment, loans, technical training facilities, and assistance of experts. A council for technical cooperation was set up in Colombo for the purpose of coordinating and supervising the operations of the plan.

The Colombo Plan has provided countries not only within the Commonwealth but also several others in South and Southeast Asia with the necessary capital equipment, technical skills and, training needed to accelerate the rate of growth. Ceylon was one of the first beneficiaries under the program of assistance. In fact, in the early 1950's, the plan was one of the major sources of aid in kind as well as assistance for training Ceylonese abroad. In addition to the foreign aid that was channeled through the Colombo Plan since 1951, Ceylon has also concluded aid agreements with other countries and institutions including members of the Sino-Soviet bloc.

AID RECEIVED UP TO 1964

As mentioned earlier, a good deal of the aid has come under the Colombo Plan, particularly from countries within the Commonwealth. Aid from Australia commenced in 1951 and uninterrupted assistance has continued thereafter. Much of this assistance has come to Ceylon in the form of grants and technical assistance under the Colombo Plan Economic Development and Technical Assistance Programs. Capital aid grants have been received in the form of equipment and materials. Australia has given wheat flour, which is sold under the government's food purchase and distribution scheme. The rupee proceeds of such sales are apportioned on a grant basis for development expenditure by the government of Ceylon on purchases that have been agreed upon mutually by the governments of Australia and Ceylon. Up to 1964, the value of equipment and material received from Australia was $1.8 million and up to 1962-63 the value of sales of Australian flour $4.5 million. Rupee or counterpart funds from the sale of flour have been allocated for a variety of purposes. These include the establishment of an Agricultural Central Research Institute, which was primarily to undertake all aspects of rice research such as varietal improvement, planting methods, weed control, and water relations of the rice plant; the development of several ancient irrigation projects in the North and North Central Provinces; the establishment of chest clinics; and the purchase of anti-TB drugs. Training facilities have been provided for 285 Ceylonese in Australia in a number of fields with an emphasis on agriculture and dental health, and 56 experts were sent to Ceylon under the Colombo Plan technical assistance scheme.

Up to 1964, Britain has given aid to Ceylon in the form of gifts, materials, and technical assistance.

Besides this, a loan was made available to finance purchases from Britain. At the end of 1964, the total value of equipment and material given to Ceylon was $0.7 million. The largest gifts were made to the Ceylon Institute for Scientific and Industrial Research in the form of equipment and books and for the construction of secondary school workshops. Britain also made available to Ceylon a loan of $5.6 million for the purchase of telecommunication equipment for the Greater Colombo area telephone development scheme. The loan agreements were signed in 1960 and 1961, and the proceeds were utilized to meet payments in sterling for the supply of telecommunication equipment manufactured in Britain. This loan was more in the nature of a suppliers' credit because repayment was to be made in five installments from the date of drawing. With the completion of the Colombo area telephone development scheme in 1968, the total number of subscribers in this area increased from 20,000 to 30,000, and subscribers were able to dial directly more than twenty towns within a radius of 15 to 20 miles from the city. Under the Colombo Plan, technical assistance program, many scholarships were offered for the training of Ceylonese in the U.K.; by the end of June, 1963, 676 Ceylonese had availed themselves of the offer. Britain also released 126 experts in various fields who were attached to different development schemes.

The aid program from Canada began with an agreement signed between the two governments in 1952. Under this agreement, Canada has allocated substantial funds annually as economic assistance to Ceylon. It has included gifts of equipment and materials, allocation of counterpart funds on a grant basis, dollar loans, and technical assistance under the Colombo Plan. As in the case of Australian aid, the rupee counterpart funds have arisen from the gifts of wheat flour, which is distributed under the government's food purchases and distribution scheme. Up to 1964, dollar grants for equipment and materials totaled $10.7 million. The major items under this have been the Aerial Resources Survey (1955-60), $1.8 million; equipment for the Mutwal fish processing plant, \$0.6 million; Laxapana-Gal Oya power transmission link, \$2.8 million; diesel locomotives, \$1.4 million, equipment for the port of Colombo, \$0.5 million; and development of the Katunayake International Airport, \$1.8 million. The value of wheat flour supplied up to 1963 was \$9.2 million and the rupee counterpart funds were utilized for a number of projects such as rural road construction, powerlines, fisheries harbors, university buildings, rural development, purchase of equipment for the Colombo port, and construction of trades schools. In November, 1958, the government of Canada granted a loan of \$2 million to finance the purchase of 25,000 tons of wheat flour. The loan was repaid in seven annual installments beginning in 1961. Soon after, the Export Credit Insurance Corporation, on behalf of the Canadian government, agreed to make available a credit of \$8.0 million to finance the foreign exchange costs of the largest hydroelectric plant in Ceylon, the Maskeliya Oya Power Project, with a generating capacity of 75 megawatts. Technical assistance from Canada up to 1963 consisted of scholarships for the training of 125 Ceylonese and the assignment to Ceylon under the Colombo Plan of 110 experts in various fields.

Economic aid was forthcoming from the People's Republic of China under four agreements: one of these was signed in September, 1957, the other in October, 1958, and the other two in October, 1962, and June, 1964. In the agreement concluded in September, 1957, China offered Ceylon economic aid up to \$12.5 million at the rate of \$2.5 million annually for a period of five years, commencing in January, 1958, with provision for a further extension of five years. The aid was in the form of goods, and prices were negotiated between the two countries. The proceeds from the sale of these goods were to be utilized for the Rubber Replanting Subsidy Program. The third agreement, concluded in October, 1962, ensured the free supply of capital goods to the value of \$8.4 million in the form of agricultural implements and machinery. Up to September, 1963, grants from the People's Republic of China amounted to \$4.7 million, of which \$4.0 million was for rolling stock for the Ceylon government railway, and $0.3 worth of tires and tubes were supplied to the Ceylon Transport Board. The first loan agreement between China and Ceylon was concluded in December, 1958; the government of China agreed to give a five-year loan of $8.4 million for the purchase of goods from China, mainly in support of the flood relief and the rehabilitation program after the major flood of 1957. The bulk of the purchases under this loan consisted of rice. The loan was repayable in ten years in the currency of a third country mutually agreed upon. In June, 1964, China agreed to waive all interest on this loan, retrospectively, and to utilize the interest payments already made against repayments of capital.

The first economic cooperation agreement with Czechoslovakia was signed in August, 1950. Aid under this agreement was used to set up seven tile factories, the Kantalai sugar factory, and to modernize the shoe factory of the Ceylon Leather Products Corporation. Deferred payment facilities spread over four years were granted for machinery and equipment supplied to the shoe factory. With the re-equipping of the Ceylon Leather Products Corporation factory, production increased more than four times and employment increased by about 70 per cent. Czechoslovakia also supplied 504 automatic looms for the National Textile Corporation factory at Veyangoda. The mill has a capacity of three million pounds of cotton yarn, ten million yards of woven fabric, and a finishing capacity of thirty million yards.

Aid from the Federal Republic of Germany consisted of grants, loans and technical assistance. An economic agreement was signed between the government of Ceylon and the Federal Republic of Germany in October, 1958. Under this, Germany agreed to establish a training workshop at Werahera for the Ceylon Transport Board to train skilled workers in the repair and maintenance of buses. Soon after the major floods in 1967, Germany also provided assistance to repair some of the flood damage. The value of this assistance was $1.6 million. In the period up to 1964, two loans were obtained from the

Kreditanstalt Fur Wiederaufbau for $8.4 million. The first of these loans for $6.5 million was used to finance the expansion of the Kankesanturai Cement Works by the addition of a second kiln and the construction of a cement clinker grinding plant at Galle. The loan was repayable over a twelve-year period and carried interest at 5½ per cent. The second loan was for $1.6 million for the purchase of specific equipment for the port of Colombo. A technical assistance agreement was signed with Germany in November, 1963, whereby Germany agreed to assist the government of Ceylon in the establishment of technical training centers and to make available the services of German experts and consultants for specific projects. The German government, at its own expense, has made specialist studies, among others, of the Ceylon Transport Board, the processing of coconut fiber, the hardboard, fertilizer, and paper factories, and on the port of Trincomalee.

Up to 1964, Japan had not entered into a formal aid agreement with Ceylon but some assistance was available under the Colombo Plan. This included training facilities for eighty-two Ceylonese and assistance for the establishment of a fisheries training center designed to provide technical and practical training for fishermen. The scheme included the construction of buildings, the supply of necessary equipment and machinery, and training boats for fishermen.

From 1952 onwards, New Zealand provided economic aid primarily in the form of grants. The total aid up to September, 1963, was $2.1 million. Apart from scholarships and training facilities for Ceylonese in dentistry and health, the New Zealand government has also made available to Ceylon the services of technical experts. Aid in the form of grants was given for the restoration and augmentation of a breached tank in the Vavuniya district. An allocation of $0.4 million was made for the establishment of a central milk processing station in Colombo with a capacity of 51,000 pints for the National Milk Board. A further grant of $0.5 million was made for the provision of irrigation facilities in the dry zone to include assistance to the agricultural research station at Maha Illupalama.

Poland entered into an agreement with the government of Ceylon in 1963 for financing the foreign exchange costs of industrial plant and machinery for development projects. Under a separate agreement concluded in January, 1963, a line of credit was given to meet the foreign exchange costs of industrial equipment and machinery for the hardware factory of the Ceylon Hardware Corporation, which was set up for the manufacture of agricultural implements, builders tools, hardware, and cutlery. The total cost of Stage I of the project was estimated at $2.7 million while equipment and machinery were estimated at $1.0 million; of this, $0.6 million was to be available from Poland. The corporation was expected to manufacture 46 different items with an estimated output of 750 tons per annum valued at $1.5 million.

An economic and technical cooperation treaty was signed between Ceylon and the U.S.S.R. in 1958 whereby the U.S.S.R. undertook to carry out surveys and investigations through Soviet organizations, to render technical assistance, and to provide the necessary equipment for specific projects. The agreement provided for a loan of $24.0 million, with interest at 2.5 per cent repayable over a period of twelve years for the financing of 16 projects. This agreement was initially valid for a period of five years but could be further extended by mutual agreement. The major projects undertaken were the steel plant, the flour mill, and the tire factory. Plans for the iron and steel mill with a capacity for the manufacture of 60,000 tons of steel products per annum were drawn up with the assistance of Soviet specialists. The third stage of the project was completed first. The normal order of construction of the mill was reversed in view of the explorations that were being undertaken by the Department of Geological Surveys on the availability of iron ore. For this reason, the steel rolling mill was completed before the construction of the blast furnace. The flour mill was originally estimated to cost $3.0

million, of which $1.4 million was the foreign cost of equipment and material required for the erection of the flour mill, the costs of investigation, the preparation of designs, and the subsistence of several specialists and engineers. The Technical and Economic Cooperation Agreement between Ceylon and the U.S.S.R. provided for the establishment of a tire factory with an annual capacity of 250,000 tires in Stage I and 360,000 tires in Stage II. The Soviet Union was to provide the working drawings, plant, and machinery as well as construction equipment and materials and was also to train Ceylonese personnel for the factory. The cost of Stage I was $8.7 million, and $0.7 million was required for Stage II. Other assistance from the Soviet Union included the clearing of 6,000 acres of jungle land at Kantalai for a sugar cane plantation and assistance for the cotton plantation project at Hambantota, which required the clearing of 5,700 acres of land. Technical assistance was also provided for investigations into the Malwatu Oya project and the development of the Kelani Ganga basin.

One of the earliest aid agreements was signed between Ceylon and the United States in November, 1950, for the purpose of providing technical aid to Ceylon under the Point Four assistance program from the technical cooperation administration of the United States. In terms of this agreement, the two governments undertook "to cooperate with each other in the interchange of technical knowledge and skills and in related activites designed to contribute to the balanced and integrated development of economic resources and production capacities of Ceylon".[2] This was followed by a bilateral agreement signed between the United States and Ceylon in April, 1956, for the provision of development aid and the supply and sale of commodities in Ceylon. The total value of dollar grants made to Ceylon by the U.S.A. between 1956 and 1963 was $6.1 million. This covered a variety of projects such as agricultural extension services, water resources planning, minerals exploration, highway development, Colombo area railway services, malaria eradication, and science education. A good deal of the early rupee grants arose out of the sale of U.S. wheat flour for rupees under Section 402 of U.S. Public Law 665. From these sales, rupee funds amounting to $1.8 million were allocated for malaria eradication, public health administration, to the University of Ceylon, and to hydroelectric power surveys.

Under PL 480, rupee funds have been made available to Ceylon by the domestic sale of U.S. surplus agricultural commodities, particularly wheat and rice, in accordance with the provisions of the U.S. Agricultural Trade Development and Assistance Act of 1954 (U.S. Public Law 480). Rupee funds arising from these sales have been set apart for the use in Ceylon of the U.S. Government, such as U.S. embassy expenditure and for grants and loans to the government of Ceylon on agreed projects. Up to the end of 1964, four such agreements were entered into between Ceylon and the United States in March, 1958, March, 1959, September, 1960, and July, 1962. The objects of these agreements were "to extend trade in agricultural commodities between the two countries by purchasing for Ceylon rupees surplus agricultural commodities produced in the United States and utilizing the Ceylon rupees for purposes which are beneficial to both countries".[3] Under the four agreements, the value of rice available to Ceylon was $9.4 million, wheat flour $11.1 million, and freight $4.0 million, resulting in a total cost of $24.5 million. The rupees from transactions, including ocean transportation, under the four loans were used by the United States government in Ceylon in the following manner: $5.3 million or 26.4 per cent was for the United States embassy and other uses; $4.0 million or 17.3 per cent was made available as Cooley loans to the private sector;* $3.9 million or 19.8 per cent was

---

*Funds allocated under Section 104 (e) Cooley are handled by the Export/Import Bank and are utilized for granting loans to the private sector and to meet administrative expenses of this bank; very little of the monies earmarked were actually used as Cooley loans in Ceylon.

available as grants to the government of Ceylon; $8.1 million or 36.4 per cent was available as loans to the government of Ceylon. The total rupee funds allocated from the loans were $21.3 million.

Each PL 480 agreement has been followed by a loan agreement between the Export/Import Bank and the government of Ceylon in respect of the loan component of individual PL 480 agreements. These agreements stipulate the terms of repayment and the rate of interest. The rate of interest on the first four agreements with the Export/Import Bank has varied between 5 per cent and 3 1/2 per cent, depending on the maturity of the loan. Repayment periods ranged from 12 to 25 years.

Dollar loans were available from two sources, the Development Loan Fund and the International Cooperation Administration. Four loans were negotiated and agreements entered into with the Development Loan Fund. The first, dated June, 1958, was for $1.1 million to be used on a program of irrigation, land development, and reconstruction of flood damaged reservoirs. The loan was repayable in 20 years and interest was at 3 1/2 per cent; these same terms were applicable for the three subsequent loans. The second loan of July, 1958, for $0.8 million was specifically for the improved maintenance of roads, including roads damaged by the floods of 1957. The third loan of $0.6 million was to meet the foreign exchange costs of buying five diesel powered railway coaches from Germany. By an agreement signed in January, 1961, the Development Loan Fund also agreed to finance the foreign exchange cost of materials and equipment required for the development of the Katunayake airport into an international jet airport.

Up to 1964, agreements for four dollar loans from the International Cooperation Administration were concluded. The proceeds of $1.0 million of the first loan were utilized for irrigation and land development and the second loan of $1.0 million was used for a variety of small and medium projects including mechanization of fisheries, agricultural extension, and industrial estates. Up to 1964 the monies available under the last two ICA loans had not been drawn.

Aid received from the International Bank for Reconstruction and Development is in a different category altogether. IBRD loans were intended specifically for infrastructure investments in the country and in the period up to 1964 were restricted wholly to the development of electricity. Ceylon became a member of the IBRD in August, 1950. The first loan agreement was concluded in July, 1964, when the Bank agreed to extend a line of credit of $13.2 million to meet the foreign exchange costs of installing an additional 25 megawatt plant at the hydroelectric station at Laxapana and for the construction of associated transmission lines and substations to Colombo. This loan was repayable in 20 years and carried an interest rate of 3¾ per cent while a charge of ¾ per cent was levied on amounts not withdrawn. The second loan of $5.9 million was also for the development of electricity. It was sanctioned in September, 1958, some four years after the first loan was given. The proceeds of this were to be utilized for the installation of a thermal generating plant at Grandpass, Colombo, to supplement the power available from the hydroelectric stations. This loan was repayable in 17 years and carried a rate of interest of 5⅜ per cent. The third loan agreement with the IBRD for $12.0 million was signed in June, 1961, to meet the foreign exchange requirements of further development of the hydroelectric complex at Norton Bridge. It was utilized for the construction of a 50 megawatt power station and a second 25 megawatt thermal unit in Colombo. The loan also provided the foreign exchange costs for transmission lines and substations. The rate of interest on this loan was 5¾ per cent and was repable in 22 years. The total amount available for electricity development under these three loans was $31.1 million.

The background to these credits could be found in the views expressed in the report of the World Bank survey mission in 1953 wherein the mission indicated that the most urgent need for development financing would be in infrastructure projects. The bank took the view that the most feasible projects from its standpoint would be those in the field of power development, which would make an immediate impact on the country's industrialization program.

In addition to aid from the IBRD, several other organizations affiliated to the United Nations, such as United Nations Technical Assistance Administration (UNTAA), the International Labor Organisation, the the Food and Agriculture Organisation, the United Nation's Educational and Scientific Organization, and the World Health Organization have given aid by making available the services of experts, by initiating training programs, by organizing demonstration projects, by conducting seminars, by awarding scholarships and fellowships, by preparing and executing pilot projects and tests, and providing any other technical assistance that may be agreed upon mutually by the organization concerned and the government.

FOREIGN AID PROGRAM AFTER 1965

After 1965, the character of aid changed considerably. These features have been highlighted in a document issued by the Ministry of Planning and Economic Affairs entitled "Foreign Aid" in 1966. This official document pointed out that the need for foreign aid in Ceylon had increased because of the widening trade gap resulting from the comparatively slow growth of export receipts in relation to the growth of the country's import requirements. For instance, in the period 1948 to 1964, export volume had increased by 2.7 per cent, but because of the decline in the terms of trade, the purchasing power of exports had increased by 1.6 per cent per year. This rate of growth was very much lower than the rate of growth of population of approximately 3 per cent. Up to 1960, despite the fall in the per capita import capacity, imports had been maintained by a heavy run on the country's external assets. After 1960, the strain on external assets had increased so rapidly that restrictions had to be applied on a wide range of imports. But as the position was getting no better, the coverage of these restrictions also had to be increased progressively with a view to cutting down sharply import outlays. These controls had resulted in severe shortages of consumer goods, which became progressively worse between 1960 and 1964. In the context of this situation, when the new government took office in 1965, a concerted effort was made to mobilized substantial external resources to meet Ceylon's foreign exchange difficulties and to put into operation a program for economic recovery. These objectives were facilitated by several aid meetings organized by the World Bank in the period after 1965.

Total aid receipts up to 1965 were negligible in relation to the quantum of aid the other developing countries had received. In developing countries as a whole, capital and aid flows during the early 1960's had helped to finance about 25 per cent of the imports, while for Ceylon in the period 1960 to 1964, aid flows and foreign assistance had only helped imports to the extent of 4.2 per cent. In 1964, the ratio of net capital inflows to gross capital formation in all developing countries averaged about 25 per cent. The corresponding ratio for Ceylon was only 8 per cent.

Under the new arrangements, meetings of various donor countries were sponsored by the World Bank. As a preliminary step the Bank prepared fairly detailed reports on the state of the economy, the measures that had been taken to achieve stability and the quantum of aid that would be found necessary to ensure a reasonably high rate of growth. The first programs submitted by the World Bank were designed to effect a relatively rapid economic recovery and included a number of measures for monetary and fiscal stabilization, the strengthening of the planning organization, and harnessing resources through a variety of incentives and measures. As a preliminary step, to inspire confidence in the donors, the government took active and effective steps to settle the dispute over the payment of compensation to oil companies and to relax the moratorium on dividends and profits of foreign private capital in Ceylon. Since aid meetings were held under the auspices of the IBRD, the response from the donor countries was very favorable primarily because they were able to secure a fairly authoritative view on the prospects of economic growth in Ceylon in the future.

Early in 1965, after a special mission of the World Bank had submitted a report on the state of the Ceylon economy, the Bank convened a meeting in Washington of countries willing to assist Ceylon. The first aid consortium meeting held in July, 1965, was attended by Australia, Britain, Canada, Japan, and the U.S.A. with the Federal Republic of Germany and India as observers. At this meeting, the aid group accepted the World Bank assessment that Ceylon needed $50 million of assistance in the second half of 1965. Under this aid program, the government of Australia pledged $0.6 million to help Ceylon tide over her balance of payments problems. These monies were utilized to purchase Australian flour. At the same meeting, Britain agreed to grant a commodity loan of £3.75 million free of interest and repayable over a period of 25 years including a grace period of three years. Canada also agreed to give commodity aid in the form of a soft loan of $1 million in addition to an outright gift of wheat flour worth $300,000. The first commodity loan from Germany of $6.4 million was used to purchase goods from Germany for the development program. This was followed by a loan agreement in January, 1966, between the government of Ceylon and the Kreditanstalt fur Wiederaufbau under which commodities could be procured from Britain. In June, 1966, another agreement was signed between Ceylon and the Kreditanstalt fur Wiederaufbau for DM 18 million to be utilized on projects to be agreed upon between Ceylon and Germany. Japan extended a commodity loan of $4.8 million. This was to be used to procure goods from Japan.

As a result of the aid consortium meeting, the bulk of the aid available in the second half of 1965 consisted of commodity loans. The emphasis was placed on commodity aid because the World Bank and the donor countries took the view that Ceylon's immediate problem was to ensure adequate supplies of machinery and raw materials to sustain the industrial and agricultural development program and that it would be unwise to tie up resources in projects with a long gestation period. The immediate problem was to provide for capacity utilization and to step up the level of investment in industries making consumer goods. Moreover, commodity aid would help to clear the backlog of consumer demand for a large variety of essential and semi-essential goods. The progressive application of restrictions on imports, since the late 1950's, had created severe shortages in the market. In 1966 and 1967 too, the earlier pattern of assistance with the emphasis on commodity aid continued to be of significance.

By July, 1967, three aid meetings had been convened. The second meeting, in London, was held in May, 1966, and the third was held in Tokyo in April, 1967. Apart from the $50 million pledge at the first meeting, a sum of $37 million was made available at the second meeting and was allocated for the import of specific items. At the third meeting, donor countries had indicated their willingness to continue with their program of assistance to Ceylon on a scale similar to the first two programs. By June, 1967, of the $33.8 million pledged under the first program, $28.0 million had been utilized. In the second program, while total aid pledged was $37 million, arrivals were only $10.2 million, leaving a balance of $26.9 million available for 1967. Under the second program, Australia granted $0.8 million for financing imports of wheat flour; and under the third program a similar commitment was made. In the fourth program in 1968, a grant of $1 million was made available to finance the shipment of wheat flour, seed potatoes, motor vehicles, and equipment for the Sri Lanka Sugar Corporation. In 1969 the grant was raised to $1.1 million.

Britain extended in 1966 the second commodity loan of $8 million mainly for imports of fertilizer, commercial vehicles, tractors, industrial raw materials, and machinery. Under the third program, too, Britain made a further contribution of $8 million to finance basically the same categories of commodities imported under the second program. The total contribution of Britain in the fourth program was $8.4

million; of this $5.9 million was in the form of an interest-free loan for the import of machinery and equipment. Canada's commitments under the second, third, fourth, and fifth programs were very similar. In each of the years 1966 and 1967, aid in the form of food amounted to $1.5 million, while grants of industrial raw material and machinery in 1966 was $ .03 million and in 1967 $0.12 million. Industrial raw materials were also made available under a loan of $0.37 million in 1966, of $0.9 million in 1967, and $1.8 million in 1968 and 1969, respectively.

Germany's contribution in the second program was a loan of $5.0 million which was utilized to purchase from Germany goods such as tires and tubes, fertilizers, building materials, motor spares, commercial vehicles, industrial raw materials, and machinery. Of the loans sanctioned under the third and fourth programs, half was to be in the form of project aid and the other half as commodity aid for imports of fertilizer, motor spares, commercial vehicles, sanitaryware, and industrial raw materials. In 1966, France offered a commodity credit of $6.5 million at 6 per cent repayable in half-yearly installments in a period of 4 years. The proceeds were used mostly to purchase tractors, building materials, and motor spares. In 1968, a second credit for $8.1 million at 5.5 per cent was sanctioned. This had a longer maturity (8 years) than the first credit.

Credits from the Indian Government amounted to $11.8 million in the period up to 1968. The first line of credit of $2.1 million was used to import consumer goods and the second credit of $6.7 million was allocated wholly for the import of commercial vehicles, electrical equipment, industrial machinery, telephone equipment, and railway coaches. In June, 1969, a third credit, also for $6.7 million, was concluded for the purchase of Indian made capital goods. For the first time, in 1967, the government of Italy agreed to provide a line of credit of 2,500 million Italian _lire_ to be used to import Italian goods. The loan was repayable within a period of 14 years including a two-year period of grace. Under the third and fourth aid programs in 1967 and 1968, commodity aid to the value of approximately $5.0 million each year was made available from Japan; the items imported were mostly fertilizer, tractors, and commercial vehicles.

Contributions from the United States have consisted of commodity loans and the supply of surplus U.S. wheat flour under PL 480. Commodity aid under the first aid program was $9.6 million, and $6.0 million under the second. In each of these programs, assistance under PL 480 was $3.6 million in the first year and $9.1 million in 1966 in the second year. In the third, fourth, and fifth programs the contributions consisted of food aid of 150,000 tons of wheat flour in each year. Under the fifth program in 1969, a development loan of $5 million was given for the purchase of fertilizer. In addition 90,000 tons of PL 480 wheat flour was also to be made available in 1969-70.

In 1970 a development loan for $2 million was signed with Canada, along with a gift of wheat flour and a long term loan for a timber factory. A loan agreement was signed with the U.K. for £5 million for the purchase of commodities. Australia gave a credit of $1.6 million for the procurement of wheat flour.

Whereas commodity aid became the predominant form of foreign aid after 1965, the technical assistance program, which had been launched very much earlier by many of the donor countries, continued without interruption during the period. In fact, the number of scholarships offered under training programs by each country increased after 1965. Of the loans from international agencies concluded after 1965, those from the IBRD and the Asian Development Bank stand out. The World Bank provided its fourth loan to Ceylon in 1968 of $4 million. This loan was given to the Development Finance Corporation of Ceylon for financing the foreign exchange costs of imports of machinery required by the private sector. The loan was guaranteed by the government and was repayable in 15 years at the rate of interest of $6\frac{1}{4}$ per cent.* The IBRD provided a loan of $4.9 million and its affiliate, the International Development Association, extended a similar sum to finance the foreign exchange cost of a highway project. The latter is a three-year pilot program of mechanized road maintenance and rehabilitation of a pilot area. It includes provision of facilities for major repairs and overhaul of highway equipment. This loan is repayable in 30 years, including a grace period of 10 years with interest at $6\frac{1}{2}$ per cent. The international Development Association also granted a credit of $2 million for a lift irrigation project. This was repayable in 50 years including a grace period of 10 years and was free of interest. For the first time, in July, 1968, an agreement was signed between the Asian Development Bank and the Central Bank of Ceylon for financing the foreign exchange costs of the modernization of tea factories in Ceylon. Purchases of tea machinery and equipment were to be made from the member countries of the Asian Development Bank. The loan carried a rate of interest of $6\frac{7}{8}$ per cent and was repayable in 15 years, including a grace period of three years. In 1970 the Asian Development Bank extended another loan of $3.5 million for tea factory modernization.

Aspects of Foreign Aid: PL 480 Assistance

PL 480 transactions are handled by the Commodity Credit Corporation of the U.S.A. This corporation purchases from American farmers at subsidized prices agricultural commodities that are then sold to foreign countries at "prices consistant with the maximum market prices of like commodities for similar quality." If the selling price is less than the purchase price, the difference is financed by the

---

*Three project loans negotiated with the IBRD have been stopped since the general election of 1970. It is likely that new proposals modifying the loan agreements will be made shortly.

TABLE 28

Foreign Loans
(In millions of dollars)

	Withdrawals in 1968-69	Repayments in 1968-69	Increase in 1968-69	Liability as of September 30, 1969.
1. Sterling Loans	-	-	-	15.0
2. Project Loans	15.8	7.6	8.2	84.3
2.01 IBRD	-	1.4	-1.4	26.2
2.02 U.S.A.[a]	0.3	0.3	...	4.0
2.03 United Kingdom	0.1	0.8	-0.7	1.2
2.04 U.S.S.R.	-	1.6	-1.6	14.3
2.05 Federal Republic of Germany[b]	0.8	0.9	-0.1	8.9
2.06 German Democratic Republic	13.5	0.1	13.4	15.0
2.07 People's Republic of China	-	0.9	-0.9	5.8
2.08 Canada[c]	0.7	0.8	-0.1	6.3
2.09 National and Grindlays Bank	-	-	-	0.7
2.10 France[d]	-	0.3	-0.3	0.5
2.11 Yugoslavia	0.1	0.3	-0.2	0.5
2.12 Poland	-	0.1	0.1	0.7
2.13 Denmark	0.3	-	0.3	0.3
3. Non-Project (Commodity) Loans	47.6	4.3	43.3	131.9
3.01 U.S.A.[e]	25.1	0.1	25.0	54.8
3.02 Federal Republic of Germany[b]	3.0	-	3.0	17.7
3.03 United Kingdom	7.1	-	7.1	29.6
3.04 Canada	1.6	-	1.6	2.9
3.05 France	1.9	1.3	0.6	6.5
3.06 Japan	5.1	2.0	3.1	15.8
3.07 India	3.7	0.9	2.8	4.5
4. Grand Total	63.4	11.9	51.5	231.2

[a]Includes loans from International Cooperation Administration and Development Loan Fund.
[b]Kreditanstalt fur Wiederaufbau loans.
[c]Includes Export Credit Insurance Corporation credits.
[d]Societé Eau et Assainissement - Socomen (SOCEA) Credits.
[e]Includes loans from International Cooperation Administration, Agency for International Development, and PL 480 loans.

Source: Central Bank of Ceylon.

United States taxpayer in the form of a loss to be debited against Commodity Credit Corporation funds. PL 480 transactions between Ceylon and the U.S.A. commenced with the signing of the Agricultural Commodities Agreement in June, 1958, as amended by exchange of letters dated June 30, 1958. Under this agreement, the U.S. government agreed to sell rice and wheat flour for Ceylon rupees. The agreement was amended in June, 1958, with an additional stipulation to the effect that 50 per cent of the cargo covered by these transactions should be transported in U.S. vessels.

Examining the costs and value of PL 480 products, Theodore Schultz has observed, "The Commodity Credit Corporation costs are more than twice the value of these products to the recipient countries. Yet, in terms of marginal revenue foregone from foreign sales of the United States farm products, if we treat our farm program and production as given, the cost to us is much less than the value of these products to the countries receiving them; the cost to us, treated thus, may be zero".[4] In Ceylon, the rupee counterpart funds from the sale of agricultural commodities were first deposited with a few commercial banks in Ceylon. Later they were all transferred to the Central Bank. One of the problems Ceylon had to face was the accumulation of counterpart funds just before 1964. A sum of about $25.2 million had accrued from sales of United States commodities between 1958 and 1964 and had been credited to the United States disbursement officer's account at the Central Bank. Although this sum was expected to be allocated for various purposes in terms of agreements, in actual practice only a portion had been disposed of leaving a very large balance in the United States disbursement officer's account. The credit balances has since progressively increased. The main reason for the shortfall in disbursements was presumably the suspension of economic aid to Ceylon in March 1964, after the nationalization of foreign owned oil companies.

The fact that these funds had remained idle shows that projects suitable for financing were not immediately available and the extent to which development projects worthy of consideration would not have had access to finance.

United States Disbursement Officer's Account, 1958-65
(In millions of dollars)

Year	Amount (balance outstanding)
1958 end December	4.3
1959 "	11.3
1960 "	8.9
1961 "	10.0
1962 "	10.6
1963 "	11.5
1964 "	11.6
1965 "	11.8

Source: Central Bank of Ceylon.

Another aspect of transactions under PL 480 agreements concerns the selling price of commodities to the aid-receiving country. At times, American prices of flour and rice were substantially higher than world market prices. For example, in June, 1958, when the first commodity agreement with Ceylon was signed, the price of wheat flour under the PL 480 was approximately £28 per ton, whereas wheat flour was available from Australia at Sterling £26 per ton. This represents an 8 per cent difference between American and Australian prices. At the same time, wheat flour from European sources, particularly France and Germany, was available at an average price of about sterling £20 per ton. The premium, therefore, on American wheat flour as against wheat flour from Europe was about 40 per cent. Then again, under the 1958 agreement, 24,500 tons of rice were imported from the United States at a price of £52.5 sh. 6d. per ton when the ruling market price was £37. 5sh. 0d. per ton. This consignment cost the government $1.1 million more than if it were procured in the open market.

The PL 480 agreements have stipulated that 50 per cent of the cargo should be transported in U.S. flag vessels. Actual freight charges in the United States have been substantially higher than those from other countries. These provisions did not result in widening the price gap between United States and non-United States flour because Article 3 of the Agricultural Commodity Agreement stipulates that any excess costs resulting from the requirement that United States flag vessels be used could be charged to the United States government. Costs of commodities transported in American flag vessels under the first PL 480 Commodity Agreement were $262,506, but of this amount only $127,509 was charged to the government of Ceylon. The difference was borne by the American government through the Commodity Credit Corporation, representing a subsidy to the American merchant marine.

The country receiving PL 480 aid is also obliged to ensure that it does not curtail its normal trade purchases of wheat flour, rice, or any other agricultural product. Each PL 480 agreement has included a statement that adequate measures should be taken "to safeguard the usual marketing of the United States and to assure that sales under this will not unduly disrupt world prices of agricultural commodities." In September, 1958, the words "or normal patterns of commercial trade with friendly countries," were added to the above clause in the act. From 1959, Ceylon agreed to purchase 100,000 tons of Australian wheat flour annually despite the fact that the price of Australian flour was sterling £26 per ton compared with the average European price of £20 per ton.

Under the five PL 480 agreements entered into from 1958 to 1966, Ceylon was committed to purchase some 75,000 tons of rice and 230,000 tons of flour at a total cost of $27.9 million. The actual quantities purchased were 88,474 tons of rice at a cost of $9.2 million and 231,345 tons of flour at $14.3 million. In addition, $1.7 million was credited to the rupee counterpart fund as freight payable on cargo transported in U.S. vessels, and $1.8 million in foreign exchange was paid for freight in respect of cargo transported in non-U.S. vessels. The total cost of rice and flour imported under the five commodity agreements inclusive of freight amounted to $27.0 million. Of this, rice imports had cost $10.2 million. According to the Food Commissioner's estimates, the same quantity of rice could have been obtained from Burma, Ceylon's traditional supplier, at a cost of $7.2 million. On this basis, rice imports under PL 480 had resulted in an extra cost of $3.0 million over usual commercial supplies. Similarly, 231,345 tons of flour imported under PL 480 cost Ceylon some $16.8 million, whereas the same quantity was available from Australia at $15.2 million. In this earlier period, especially in 1958 and 1959, there are fairly significant differences between the price of Australian and Continental wheat flour. But, as years passed, the price of Continental wheat flour leveled off with Australian prices and by 1960-61 there was hardly any difference in price.

In computing real cost differences between PL 480 imports, where payment is made in local currency, and open market imports for which payment is made in foreign exchange, an allowance should be made for the shadow price of foreign exchange. After 1958, because of the very sharp fall in reserves and the increase in the restrictions on imports, the open market price or the free market price of foreign exchange was considerably higher than the official rate. According to estimates in Pick's Currency Year Book, the open market price of an American dollar was Rs 6.15 in 1958 and Rs 11.60 in 1966, representing premiums of 29 per cent and 144 per cent respectively. Since the premium on foreign exchange was relatively low in the period up to 1960, from the point of view of costs alone the earlier PL 480 agreements were disadvantageous to Ceylon. However, imports after 1960-61 were advantageous to Ceylon mainly because the shadow price of foreign exchange was substantially higher than the official rate. The latter would be material only on the assumption that the shadow price for foreign exchange is a relevant factor in the examination of cost benefit where payment is made in local currency.

Another important aspect of PL 480 transactions is whether imports of wheat flour under these agreements would be very much higher than they would otherwise be and whether it has encouraged the population to maintain consumption of these commodities at a level higher than they are normally accustomed to. Although there is no such evidence, it is theoretically possible that the import of rice and flour under PL 480 may have also marginally discouraged the local production of rice through a change in relative prices of off-ration rice. This would have been so especially if increasing supplies of wheat flour tended to depress the price of locally grown rice in the free market that would have acted as a fairly severe disincentive to the producer.

SUPPLIERS' CREDITS

Apart from government to government aid, a fair amount of the assistance has been received by the government and the private sector since 1965 as suppliers' credits. There is official evidence of suppliers' credits only after 1965, although this form of credit was probably availed of by Ceylon importers in the 1950's primarily to finance imports of consumer goods and capital equipment. Suppliers' credits are similar to commodity aid because they are relatively short-term and are given for the import of specific goods and services. They are different to the extent that commodity loans are made on a government to government basis while suppliers' credits are essentially given directly to an importer by the producer of goods involved in the transaction. Table 29 gives suppliers' credits negotiated since 1958.

Accurate records were available from 1965 and the amount of credit contracted was only $1.6 million. In 1967, the quantum had increased to $50.4 million. Thus, in the three-year period 1966 to 1968 the total suppliers' credit negotiated was $78.4 million, which works out to an average of $25.2 million per year. To a large extent, these suppliers' credits have helped to supplement the external finance made

TABLE 29

Suppliers' Credits Negotiated by Ceylon contrasted with Certain Economic Indicators (In millions of dollars)

	1958	1959	1960	1961	1962	1963	1964	1965	1966	1967	1968
1. Value of Suppliers' Credits Negotiated (annual totals)	2.1	-	-	-	0.5	0.8	2.5	1.6	22.2	20.8	33.8[a]
2. Value of Suppliers' Credits Negotiated (cumulative Totals)	2.1	2.1	2.1	2.1	2.5	3.3	5.8	7.4	29.6	50.4	84.2
3. Total value of imports	287.9	329.1	337.1	301.5	320.3	314.1	329.4	323.0	339.2	333.6	393.4[b]
4. Total value of exports	272.9	298.0	301.8	286.9	296.3	287.1	297.0	320.8	281.3	277.3	331.9[b]
5. Trade balance	-15.0	-31.1	-35.3	-14.6	24.0	-27.1	-32.4	- 2.2	-57.8	-56.3	-16.5[b]
6. Project loans (net) obtained	-	5.4	2.7	1.3	5.6	11.1	6.9	12.4	8.0	13.2	2.3[c]
7. Commodity loans (net) obtained	-	-	-	-	-	-	-	-	13.7	37.2	24.7
8. Total of (6) and (7)	-	5.4	2.7	1.3	5.6	11.2	6.9	12.4	21.6	50.4	27.0

[a]As of December 15, 1968.
[b]Provisional.
[c]Including sterling loans.

Sources: Ministry of Planning and Economic Affairs; Central Bank of Ceylon.

available in the form of project aid and commodity loans and have eased pressure on the country's external assets to finance current imports. They have also been instrumental in helping to maintain supplies of capital and intermediate goods at a very high level. These credits have been released to three economic categories, public corporations, government departments, and private firms. Between 1958 and 1968, public corporations have obtained $60.9 million or 65.1 per cent of suppliers' credit, government departments $28.1 million or 33.4 per cent, and private firms $1.3 million or 1.5 per cent.

Among the government corporations, the major recipients have been the Ceylon Petroleum Corporation, the Ceylon Government Railway, and the Department of Government Electrical Undertakings. Up to 1968, nineteen countries had extended suppliers' credits to Ceylon. Of these, credits contracted with the Federal Republic of Germany and the United Kingdom were quite substantial, being 18.7 per cent and 15.8 per cent, respectively. The interest on suppliers' credits have varied from 1½ to 6 4/5 per cent. About 76 per cent carried interest rates of 5½ to 6 per cent, and credits free of interest were negligible being 2.6 per cent. About 5 per cent of the credits were subject to relatively high rates of interest ranging from 6 to 8 per cent. The effect of this was to increase the cost of merchandise and services that were imported. Periods for which these credits have been obtained have varied from one year to ten years. About 30 per cent of them matured in one year, 5 per cent in five years, 14 per cent in six years, and 28 per cent in ten years. In contrast to these, most project aid and commodity loans had a maturity of ten to twenty-five years. The bulk of the suppliers' credit so far negotiated have been mainly for the import of capital goods to develop the infrastructure of the ecomony and to increase the productive capacity of the industrial sector. A significant item in this category has been the credit for the refinery of the Ceylon Petroleum Corporation, where the foreign exchange component of about $16.8 million was financed entirely out of suppliers' credits. This suppliers' credit is repayable over a period of ten years. With a foreign exchange saving estimated to be in the region of $5.0 million per year; the refinery will be in a position to liquidate this credit in a relatively short time. Similarly, plant, machinery, and equipment to the value of $8.1 million for the Puttalam Cement Works were also financed by suppliers' credits repayable in ten years. The purchase of a Trident aircraft for Air Ceylon at $5.2 million and the new equipment for the Piliyandala Ceramics factory were obtained on suppliers' credits.

COMMODITY AID

The extent to which the country has depended on commodity aid since 1965 has been outlined earlier. There are certain aspects of commodity aid which deserve attention. A good part of the commodity aid has been tied to the donor country, and very few agreements have provided for negotiations on price and on the range of commodities supplied. Under most agreements, only commodities that have been specifically mentioned could be procured. Very often the prices quoted for particular items were competitively not the lowest in the international markets. Several donor countries presumably have had the liberty to determine prices quite independently. There have been instances where items such as tires, motor vehicles, spare parts, and equipment have been imported from countries where prices are relatively high whereas the identical products could have been obtained from other sources at considerably lower prices. Since fairly high rates of interest have been applied to commodity aid, the final prices paid by the receiving country are very much higher, and it tends to push up the real rate of interest. In a market where there is a scarcity of essential consumer and capital goods, the fact that supplies of goods under commodity aid have been available at high prices has had little or no effect on demand.

Another aspect of commodity aid is that substandard articles have been supplied. Ceylon, which has been accustomed to goods mostly from Britain, has found that those goods obtained under suppliers' credit from countries such as Germany and France often do not meet the requirements of the consumer. Problems of this nature arise because most of the commodity aid is tied. If aid can be used multilaterally, then there would be no disadvantage either from the point of view of prices or from the specific requirements of the country.

Despite the criticisms that might be leveled against various forms of aid, it is an unquestionable fact that aid has greatly helped to ease the strain on the economy resulting from a shortage of foreign exchange. The high rate of growth, particularly in 1968 and 1969, has been due entirely to the contribution of aid in providing a wide variety of essential inputs to both agriculture and industry. Industrial growth, in particular, has been due largely to the availability of foreign exchange for imports of industrial raw materials and also capital equipment for the private and public sector industries. Since 1965, the change in the composition of external assistance from project aid to commodity aid has had a more immediate impact on growth. The consortium of countries that pledged aid was convinced that constraints in the economy were due mainly to the lack of sufficient inputs to sustain industrial and agricultural activity at a very high level and that this gap could have been bridged only with the assistance of commodity aid. Had the pattern of aid not changed, growth would have been considerably retarded resulting in domestic inflation and continunig severe shortages of consumer goods at a time when there was a general tendency for wage and salary increases to take place.

With the continuing strain on the balance of payments, it is very likely that the country will have to depend on aid, particularly commodity aid, for a long while more because the industrial sector in Ceylon is heavily dependent on imported raw materials. Very little has been done up to now to shift the emphasis in industrial development policy to the utilization of domestic raw material substitutes wherever possible. More attention must be paid

TABLE 30

Modes of Financing the External Resources Gap, 1968 and 1969
(In millions of dollars and per cent shares)

	1968		1969	
	millions of dollars	per cent share	millions of dollars	per cent share
Resources Gap	109.1		201.3	
Financing:	109.1	100	201.3	100
1. External Assets	-2.4	2.1	14.5	7.1
2. Foreign Bank borrowings	-	-	38.2	18.9
3. IMF Drawings	35.8	32.8	12.9	6.4
4. Bilateral trade balances	7.1	6.5	3.0	1.5
5. Short-term trade credits	14.1	12.9	31.1	15.4
6. Suppliers' credits	n.a.	n.a.	29.6	14.7
7. Commodity Aid	42.9	39.3	45.7	22.7
8. Project Aid	6.7	6.2	15.0	7.4
9. Grants	4.1	4.3	7.7	3.8
10. Private capital	1.3	1.2	1.5	0.8
11. Other	1.5	1.4	3.0	1.5
12. Errors and Omissions	-2.7	-2.5	-0.8	-0.4

Source: Central Bank of Ceylon.

immediately to this aspect of industrial policy because the balance of payments prospects do not provide sufficient leeway to maintain industrial imports at a very high level, especially at the levels obtaining during the last three years. Commodity aid could be reduced if local raw materials and equipment could be used on a considerably wider scale. This, of course, will involve the emergence of a group of secondary industries that will be primarily concerned with the manufacturing and processing of inputs and intermediate goods for the major industries. The continuance of aid will depend on the goodwill of the consortium and the general political situation in the country. Any radical change would severely curtail the potential for securing more aid in the future.

NOTES

1. Economic Division of the General Treasury, Foreign Economic Aid. A Review from 1950 to 1962 (Colombo: Ministry of Finance), p. 20.

2. Economic Division of the General Treasury, Foreign Economic Aid. A Review from 1960-62, (Colombo: Ministry of Finance), p. 8.

3. Ibid.

4. Theodore W. Schultz, "Impact and Implications of Foreign Surplus Disposal on Underdeveloped Economics," Journal of Far Economics, Vol., XLII (December, 1960), p. 1021.

CHAPTER 12

THE EMPHASIS ON AGRICULTURE—POLICY AFTER 1965

A striking feature in the agricultural sector in recent years has been the rapid expansion in output of products intended for domestic consumption, mainly rice and subsidiary foodstuffs, while the output of export crops has not shown equally significant advances. This divergence of production trends between domestic and export agriculture has been due to the much greater emphasis placed by policy makers on domestic agriculture owing to the sense of uncertainty in the export industries with prices continually falling.

By the end of 1964, with the worsening of the balance of payments situation, exchange reverses were depleted, and it was clear that exchange earnings were no longer sufficient to meet basic consumption requirements and to provide the inputs for long-term economic growth. As external assets continued to decline, the government reoriented its earlier policy of emphasizing production of industrial goods and extended import substitution to cover even the more essential items such as rice and subsidiary foodstuffs. It will be remembered that import substitution came first in the industrial consumer goods sector as a result of import restriction and bans.

In 1965 with another government (the United National Party) in power came a change in emphasis. A shortage of rice occurred in the world market, with prices skyrocketing and a resultant higher subsidy on rice. In this context, the capacity to maintain imports was seriously impaired, especially with a further reduction in export earnings from the traditional plantation crops. With declining tea prices, much of the mid and low grown tea areas became uneconomic. For mid grown companies, the sale price of 28 cents in 1967 almost equalled the production costs of 27.5 cents, and for low grown companies the sale price of 24 cents was only slightly higher than the cost of production of 23 cents. Rubber prices also fell, the average price being 13 cents a lb., and the competition from synthetics stiffened considerably. At the same time, population was rapidly increasing, although the birth rate had fallen recently to 2.3 per cent from 2.8 per cent. The trend towards import substitution reached its climax in December, 1966, when, consequent to the difficulties in obtaining adequate rice supplies from abroad, the government reduced the rice ration and increased the guaranteed price of paddy. If agricultural productivity does not increase, existing levels of food consumption can be maintained only by increasing food imports, which could result in valuable foreign exchange being diverted to consumption. Table 31 shows the outlays on food imports over the period 1964 to 1969.

INCREASE IN RICE PRODUCTION

The encouraging record of increased production of rice has been due to the existence of a positive and comprehensive government policy on domestic agriculture. The rationale of this policy has been primarily economic and relates mainly to the balance of payments. High priority has been given to reach self-sufficiency in rice at the earliest possible date. As for the production of rice, there is no technical or economic constraint that is likely to stand in the way of Ceylon achieving this objective in the early 1970's. The success of this program up to now could be measured in terms of the fall in the imports of rice and other subsidiary foodstuffs from 1966 onwards. In 1966, imports of rice were 549,173 tons, in 1967 imports had fallen to 372,000 tons, and to 248,625 tons in 1969.

TABLE 31

Imports of Food Products, 1964-69

Commodities	Value in Millions of Dollars					
	1964	1965	1966	1967	1968	1969
Rice	54.8	24.2	61.7	35.5	57.3	43.2
Flour	23.0	16.5	19.0	38.5	42.0	42.9
Sugar refined	31.1	11.9	17.3	12.4	16.3	19.3
Others	0.3	0.2	0.3	-	-	-
Milk and Milk products	15.8	12.9	12.9	11.1	12.4	8.7
Meat, fish, and eggs	12.4	10.3	17.0	9.4	11.8	14.6
Other foods:	27.6	20.8	28.6	21.2	21.0	24.4
Potatoes	4.2	3.0	4.0	1.2	-	-
Grams and Pulses	8.6	6.6	10.8	8.9	9.4	13.1
Onions	4.4	3.5	3.4	3.2	2.9	2.9
Chillies	7.7	5.0	7.2	4.9	5.7	4.4
Drink and manufactures of tobacco	0.5	0.3	0.3	0.3	0.3	0.7

Source: Central Bank Annual Reports 1968 and 1969.

This was due largely to the progressive increase in yields per acre resulting from the use of superior techniques and inputs. Moreover, after 1967, supplies of agricultural inputs such as fertilizers, tractors, agro-chemicals, barbed wire, and agricultural implements were freely available on open general license. The output of paddy reached the peak level of 65.9 million bushels in 1969, which is equivalent to 900,000 long tons as against 55.1 million bushels or 769,000 long tons in 1967.

The quantum of output in domestic agriculture is determined mainly by changes in productivity in paddy cultivation because paddy constitutes more than 50 per cent of the output from nonplantation agriculture. It is Ceylon's second largest crop and in 1969 provided about 22 per cent of the value of agricultural production. In 1962, out of a total area under cultivation of 4.02 million acres, 1.25 million acres were cultivated with paddy; by 1968, the extent of land under paddy had risen by approximately 150,000 acres to 1.40 million acres. The crop is grown in some one million holdings, and rice at present provides 75 per cent of the total cereal consumption. It is the direct livelihood of possibly three to four million people.

Improving the production of rice arises from the fact that rice is the staple diet of more than 95 per cent of the country's population. In 1964, the population of Ceylon was estimated to be 10,971,000, and the Central Bank in the same year provisionally estimated rice consumption at 1,138,944 tons. On the assumption that per capita consumption will remain unchanged and that population will increase at a rate of 2.5 per cent per annum, the net addition to the population each year would be 275,000, which will mean that an additional 28,000 tons will have to be produced each year to sustain the increase in population. On this basis, the total consumption of rice in 1965 would be 1,167,182 tons and in 1970, 1,307,182 tons. The present requirements would be equivalent to about 95 million bushels of paddy and a further 3.5 million bushels of paddy will be required annually for seed paddy requirements. This would raise the figure to almost 100 million bushels of paddy.

The total extent of paddy land under cultivation in 1965 has been estimated at 1,249,160 acres, but

TABLE 32

Rice: Imports and Domestic Production, 1964-69

	1964 tons	Per cent	1965 tons	Per cent	1966 tons	Per cent	1967 tons	Per cent	1968 tons	Per cent	1969 tons	Per cent
Rice Imports[a]	549,300	43.2	574,838	52.6	547,173	45.6	372,462	32.1	387,566	29.5	248,625	20.9
Domestic Production[b]	721,500	56.7	517,900	47.4	654,100	54.3	785,714	67.8	922,857	70.4	940,871	79.1
Total	1,270,800		1,092,738		1,203,273		1,158,176		1,310,423		1,189,496	

[a]Rice imports are for financial years
[b]Domestic production figures are for calendar years

Source: Central Bank of Ceylon

the actual extents sown in Yala and Maha were 1,505,198 acres, showing that in each season all the available paddy lands have not been cultivated. A considerable proportion of lands are brought under cultivation in the Maha season, but in the Yala season, lands in the dry zone, unless they are fed by irrigation, cannot be brought under cultivation. Assuming that 85 per cent of the sown extent is harvested, the estimated current requirements of approximately 95 million bushels of paddy could be produced on the harvested acreage if the average yield was approximately 67 bushels per acre. The requirements of the additions to the population every year can be produced on the present harvested acreage by an increase in the average yield of about 1.5 bushels per acre per annum. During the last ten years, the increase in the national average acre yield has been only about 0.9 bushels per year.

Both area and yield increases have contributed to the increase in paddy production in Ceylon. From 1957 to 1965 the increase in net area harvested was 29 per cent and in yields 14 per cent. In the four year period 1966 to 1969 the situation was reversed, with the area increasing by 6 per cent and yields by 13 per cent. Between 1957 and 1969, Maha production increased by 87 per cent and Yala by 57 per cent. The divergence is due mainly to the much larger increases, proportionately as well as absolutely, in the area harvested in the Maha than in the Yala seasons. The absence of reliable irrigation water in the Yala season accounts for the reluctance of farmers to cultivate in that season.

Rice policy has several aspects. The paddy producer is entitled to a highly subsidized ration, thus making it possible for him to sell his crop of paddy at a higher price. The high prices realized in open market sales by farmers have also been supported by a guaranteed price. The guaranteed price of rice was raised from $2.02 to $2.35 per bushel in December, 1967. Since the guaranteed price is the price at which the government purchases paddy, to supplement imports for distribution to consumers under the rationing scheme, that price is both a market price as well as a floor price. The weighted average producer price in 1967 was $2.19 per bushel as compared with $1.95 in the previous year. The higher prices after 1967 reflect the cut in the rice ration in December, 1966, when the ration was halved and the consumers had to buy a substantial part of their requirements at the open market price. As the producer price has changed only once over a long period of time, it has not provided a very significant spur to accelerated production. The guaranteed price has had to be supplemented by other measures. One of these is the rice seed improvement program that has operated for at least 30 to 40 years.

TABLE 33

Paddy Production Inputs, 1961-68

	Area under ('000 acres)	Improved Seeds Per cent of Net Harvested Area	Fertilizer Usage ('000 tons)
1961	n.a.	-	25
1962	n.a.	-	38
1963	88	7	47
1964	104	8	60
1965	607	58	42
1966	672	49	42
1967	943	71	53
1968	1065	75	89

Source: Ministry of Agriculture and Food.

More recently a breeding program, using both local and imported varieties, has produced several varieties of high yielding seed material. The government has paid a subsidy of $0.34 per bushel on seed paddy and carried the cost of handling and storage. In the preceding five-year period, the area under high yielding varieties of paddy, such as H^4 and IR^8, has increased tenfold and covered 75 per cent of the acreage harvested. Fertilizer has been available to farmers with a subsidy of 50 per cent on cash sales and 33 per cent on credit sales. In effect from October, 1968, a subsidy of 50 per cent was introduced uniformly on all fertilizer sales; as a result, fertilizer usage has nearly doubled. Fertilizer imports have been made at the official rate of exchange and not at the FEEC rate. The Department of Agriculture also hires out tractors to farmers at lower rates than do private firms. The availability of tractors has trebled. The frequent use of these various inputs has been encouraged by a liberal supply of institutional credit. In the period 1962 to 1964, the volume of credit for agricultural purposes from government was about $1.7 to 3.4 million per year; under the new agricultural credit scheme in 1967 this exceeded $11.8 million. On the assumption that this credit was used for paddy production, the average credit per acre of net area harvested was $8.2. The production gains achieved in the period 1966 to 1969 cannot be interpreted in terms of a single factor; they have been the result of several factors operating simultaneously, such as production inputs, credit, organizational matters, and incentives and attitudes.

The complex of government and cooperative services available to farmers has been improved in many vital respects. The central problem of the lack of coordination of the various services has been overcome by the establishment of a continuing ministerial committee and by vesting the responsibilities for all aspects of food production in twenty-two government agents.*

---

*The government agents' districts are subdivided

An additional government agent has been appointed so that he can devote his time exclusively to domestic agricultural matters. Previously, responsibility for the food production program had been so widely dispersed between ministries and other administrative bodies that, in practice, effective coordination had become almost impossible. For instance, the Department of Agriculture was responsible for the supply of seed paddy, the Department of Agrarian Services for credit, and the Cooperative Department for the cooperative societies, which was responsible for administering services such as the Guaranteed Price Scheme and the fertilizer subsidy. At the village level there were the cooperative societies and the cultivation committees also carrying out overlapping functions. A singular achievement over the past three to four years has been the greater coordination among these various agencies.

The policy of the government in the period 1966 to 1968 in regard to irrigation has been to concentrate on works already in hand rather than to undertake new schemes. The food production drive has not required heavy investments in new irrigation facilities and land clearance. For the supply of water, farmers have been charged considerably less than actual cost; this represents a significant element of subsidy. In paddy production, increases of 26, 21, and 15 per cent have been recorded in 1966, 1967, and 1968 respectively. The value of present production exceeds production costs even after all inputs are valued at real costs rather than at subsidized prices. Available estimates suggest that the adjusted cost of production of paddy would not exceed $67.2 per acre as compared

---

into 137 revenue divisions, each under a district revenue officer. The senior agricultural policy-making body under the previous government was the Cabinet Sub-Committee on Food Production, which included the Prime Minister, the ministers of Agriculture, of Land, Irrigation and Power. This committee decided on the broad targets for the food production drive and the means to achieve them.

with production valued at $110.9 per acre.

THE IMPLEMENTATION OF AGRICULTURAL POLICY

Since the publication of its five year-development program 1966-70,[1] the Ministry of Agriculture and Food has issued annual reports on the progress made. These progress reports have been a valuable source of information on agricultural development since 1966 and have provided a direct link between the agricultural development proposals and the annual programs and budgets. They have also covered export crops, domestic agriculture, subsidiary food crops, animal husbandry, and vegetable production; in other words, they have dealt with the entire supply of essential foodstuffs for the population.

After a period of relative stagnation up to 1961, the production of paddy rose appreciably; but real gains were achieved only after 1967.

After a very good harvest in 1964, paddy production declined to 36.3 million bushels in 1965, rising to 45.7 million bushels in 1966 and to 64.6 million bushels in 1968, an increase in output of more than 50 per cent in three years. In 1969, 65.9 million bushels were harvested as against a target of 70 million in the agricultural development proposals.

This increase in output could, to a large extent, be attributed to the efforts made by the Ministry of Agriculture to carry out effectively the program of work outlined in agricultural development proposals 1966-70 within the time schedules laid down. When launching this program, the Minister emphasized, "The drawing of plans and their implementation are entirely different propositions. The best plans can be nullified unless a detailed strategy of implementation is worked out and imaginatively carried through. Having this in mind, the Ministry of Agriculture and Food with the assistance of other government departments and nongovernmental organizations is working out ways and means of implementing these proposals

TABLE 34

Rice Production, 1957-70
(In millions of bushels)

Year	Paddy
1957	31.3
1958	36.6
1959	36.4
1960	43.0
1961	43.1
1962	48.0
1963	49.2
1964	50.5
1965	36.3
1966	45.7
1967	55.1
1968	64.6
1969	65.9
1970	70.0

Source: Ministry of Agriculture and Food.

in the areas of the island. In this respect, field officers engaged in agriculture and particularly the government agents have a crucial role to play. The recent decision of the government to appoint senior and experienced officers as government agents will considerably strengthen the organization for implementing these programs at district and village levels. Government agents and public officers responsible for implementing these programs are being given a clear idea of the implications of these programs as broken up into their specific components in relation to their districts and areas of authority".[2] This statement shows the new strategy adopted by the ministry to achieve objectives in the development proposals.

The first in the series "Implementation Programs and Targets" was brought out in 1966 and was meant to acquaint those who were directly responsible for the agricultural productivity drive with the broad targets of production and the facilities necessary for the improvement of agriculture. A detailed breakdown of annual targets for each of the agricultural areas was given, and the most feasible lines of implementing the program in each region were also indicated.

The Implementation Program and Targets, 1966, indicated that the production of paddy over the five years commencing in 1966 and ending in 1970 would increase from 50 million bushels to approximately 70 million bushels, or by about 45 per cent. This target was to be achieved by raising the yields of land already under cultivation and by expanding the acreage through the normal programs of irrigation and colonization, which would bring in an area of approximately 100,000 acres under cultivation. The increase in average yields was also to be secured by more fertilizer application and pure line seed. The use of fertilizer for paddy was to be increased from 60,000 tons in 1966 to 150,000 tons by 1970. To procure and supply additional quantities of fertilizer, facilities were to be provided for its storage at the district and village levels. The Ceylon Fertilizer Corporation was expected to construct a series of district stores, each capable of storing 1,000 to 3,000 tons of fertilizer. Arrangements were also made to increase the quantity of high-yielding pure line seed paddy. To control pests and weeds, agrochemicals were to be used on an extensive scale, and $0.5 million in foreign exchange was set apart for this purpose. The shortage of agricultural tractors was to be met by the importation of 1,500 four-wheeled tractors and 500 two-wheeled tractors in 1966. Steps were also taken to implement the Paddy Lands Act effectively by strengthening cultivation committees so that they would be in a position to function effectively and to clear up the backlog of cases where tenant cultivators had appealed against eviction from their holdings. Increased funds were also to be diverted for the purposes of developing minor irrigation works.

Details of output of the major crop, paddy, and

subsidiary crops were given in the report. Targets for paddy were laid down from 1966 to 1970 as follows:

1966-67	53.87 million bushels
1967-68	56.58 "
1968-69	60.01 "
1969-70	69.75 "

These totals were broken down again into respective targets for the seasons, Maha and Yala, in each year. The Maha season crop is always larger than the Yala because of the greater extent of paddy land that comes under cultivation. Targets were also fixed by districts, and estimates were made of anticipated production in each area on the basis of the area already under cultivation. Target yields, moreover, were laid down for each of the districts and the projections provided for a progressive increase in yields from 1965 onwards. In these targets, the district-wide variation in the yields for the Maha 1969-70 was from a low of 34.4 for the Jaffna district to a high of 71.3 bushels per acre for the Polonnaruwa district. The corresponding yields for 1965-66 were 29.3 and 57.6 bushels. Similar targets were specified for fertilizer consumption. These computations were based mainly on the extents of paddy land already under cultivation in each area and also on the respective yields in these districts. The regional fertilizer consumption for land already under cultivation was to vary from 2,000 tons in the Nuwara Eliya district to 18,000 tons in the Kurunegala district.

The strategy laid down for the implementation of these proposals was reviewed in successive issues of the "Implementation Program and Targets." The government agents in each of the areas were to convene meetings of the Standing Committee on Agriculture to discuss the program. Arrangements were made to review the targets for each district and distribute them within the various district revenue officer divisions. Thereafter, the district revenue officers with the help of the agricultural committees would take further steps to break down these programs between the cultivating areas. The cooperation of the village organizations such as cultivation committees and cooperative societies was to be sought to ensure that the targets proposed for fertilizer consumption, distribution of seed paddy, agricultural credit, and guaranteed price scheme purchases were realized.

The government agents, district staff officers, divisional level field officers and village level field officers were to play a vital role in this food production drive by mobilizing their institutions to carry out the program effectively. With this end in view, the government organizations were to undertake a widespread propaganda campaign. In the final stages, the assistance of government agents and district level officers was to be utilized to organize a district-wide mechanism to check the performance of the various programs ranging from credit and fertilizer to the intake of agro-chemicals and the availability of tractors. Their task was to bring to light various shortfalls in performance so that remedial action could be taken without delay.

The Implementation Program for 1967 covered a much wider field than the first program, because for the first time it included targets of performance for nonplantation agriculture as well. Specific targets were assigned for subsidiary crops and for the export crops, tea, rubber, and coconut. With regard to actual performance, the program stated that the production target set for paddy in 1966 could not be achieved because of adverse weather conditions. Despite this, production of paddy was within 95 per cent of the projected targets, and there was a reasonable chance of securing the target of 53.3 million bushels for the two seasons of 1967, provided weather conditions were not unfavorable. With a view to achieving this target, the program mentioned that an expanded scheme of certified seed paddy production was to be undertaken in 1967. The new program also provided for the extension of area not only under high yielding seed paddy H^4, but also, for the extension of areas under H^7, a further improved hybrid. With regard to consumption of fertilizer, the succession of bad seasons had resulted in the fertilizer consumption falling short of targets, and in the future it was proposed to ensure that these targets were reached by an intensive and vigorous propaganda campaign by means such as demonstration plots, publicity meetings, posters, and film shows. The report stated that in view of the changed circumstances arising from the rice ration cut, the targets for agricultural credit and purchases under the Guaranteed Price Scheme were not reached. The same was true of the paddy storage program for 1965-66, and it was hoped to make good the poor performance in that year by completing all storage facilities in 1966.

The subsequent implementation programs were prepared on a slightly different basis. Commencing in 1967, each government agent, not the Development Division of the Ministry of Agriculture and Food, prepared the implementation program for his district. This was meant primarily to identify a planning body at the village level. For most purposes the cultivation committee was thought to be the most suitable. But since the Paddy Lands Act limited the scope of the cultivation committees, and since village-level planning included crops other than paddy, there had to be some level of expansion and diversification of the membership of cultivation committees. Furthermore, most cultivation committees did not function at uniform levels of efficiency. To overcome this difficulty, the cultivation committees were strengthened.

As a first exercise, village-level institutions assembled data in a questionnaire covering basic agricultural information in the area such as the extent sown, inputs used, the availability of man or machine power, and so on. These questions were intended to identify the strength of the village agricultural organizations, their levels of performance, and to work out appropriate targets. The village level planning institutions were to be assisted in their tasks by officials from other government departments. Thereafter, the individual implementation programs for cultivation committee areas were combined into divisional level programs at meetings of the divisional committees. These divisional level programs were in turn combined by the government agents into district level programs at meetings of the district agricultural committees. And the Development Division of the Ministry prepared a statement of indicative targets for each district. At meetings of the District Agricultural Coordinating Committee, at which representatives and several other important government departments connected with agricultural development were present, district targets that had emerged from the earlier consultation with cultivation committees, and divisional and district level committees were compared with the indicative targets furnished by the ministry; and after considerable discussion, a final schedule of targets for each district was decided upon. On the basis of these final targets, each government agent was expected to issue an agricultural implementation program for the year for his district.

The Implementation Program for 1968 differed from that of the previous year in the magnitude of the targets laid out. The implementation program for 1967 set a production target of 55 million bushels of paddy and an average yield of 40 bushels per acre for the island. The actual production figures were slightly in excess of this; total production was 55.1 million bushels while the average yield was 40.8 bushels per acre; the latter was an all-time record for the island.

When the rice ration was halved in 1966,* it was estimated that purchases under the Guaranteed Price Scheme in 1967 would amount to a total of 100,000 tons of locally produced rice. But even before the year (1968) was out, 140,000 tons were collected, and the prospect of collecting even more

---

*The cut in the subsidy was effected by reducing the ration from 4 lbs. per person per week at a price of 9 cents per pound to a free weekly ration of 2 lbs. The immediate reaction to this was a sharp rise in the price of unrationed rice from 9 cents a lb. to about 13 to 15 cents.

was very good. The outstanding performance of rice production was the result of increasing utilization of new inputs. Fertilizer consumption during the Maha 1967-68 season of 37,980 tons was the highest on record, while in the previous season, Maha 1966-67, 34,701 tons were used. The issue of certified seed paddy also exceeded the target. As against a target of 100,000 bushels, the actual quantity sold was 103,948 bushels, the previous highest being 69,000 bushels.

A new technique, which was not reflected in the overall implementation program but which had appeared in the individual implementation programs of the government agents, was the intensive area development projects, modeled on the package program scheme adopted extensively in India. This is based on the principle that impressive increases in production can be secured only if all required inputs and improved cultural practices recommended are applied at the same time. Up to 1968, the program was limited to paddy cultivation. It involved the provision of adequate credit facilities, sufficient power for tillage, supplies of improved seed and recommended fertilizer and agro-chemicals, and ensuring that transplanting and row seeding and harvesting are all done at the proper time. In 1967, there were two such projects in the North Central Province, and yields increased from 25 to 75 bushels of paddy per acre. The program proposed to establish such projects in selected areas, each covering approximately 300 to 500 acres of paddy.

The Ministry of Agriculture and Food issued its fourth Implementation Program and Targets for 1969. The program reviewed the progress made and gave some indication of the immediate prospects for further improvement. It stated that conditions in Maha 1967-68 were exceptionally favorable for paddy production because cultivators were able to obtain premium prices after the cut in the rice ration in 1966. Along with this the new scheme of agricultural credit, increased storage facilities for paddy, the availability of high quality seed paddy, and other inputs had helped to boost production. At the same time, there was a steady improvement in the provision and maintenance of irrigation facilities and drainage by the programs carried out between 1966 and 1968 by the Ministry of Lands, Irrigation, and Power.

For the sale of certified seed paddy, the target for Maha 1967-68 was 201,766 bushels while actual use of seed paddy was 228,663 bushels; the areas using superior varieties of paddy exceeded the targets by 36.1 per cent. The use of fertilizer was almost equal to the target of 78,836 tons; the actual use was 78,166 tons. This represented an increase of 42.1 per cent over the figure for 1966-67. The use of inputs such as superior seed, fertilizer, and paddy and almost doubled in the Maha 1967-68 season as against Maha 1966-67. Production in Maha 1967-68 was 43.5 million bushels, which is 3 million bushels more than the target of 40.5 million bushels. Similarly, the average yield per acre in 1967-68 of 46.1 bushels exceeded the target of 42.5 bushels. These higher yields were also confirmed by increased purchases of paddy under the Guaranteed Price Scheme.

Between January, 1967, and June, 1967, total paddy purchased under the GPS was 125,820 tons. In the same period in 1968, the collection amounted to 170,339 tons of rice. Increased levels of production in the Maha 1968-69 season were reflected in the open market price of rice in Colombo, which is the largest center of consumption, where rice continued to be available at 15 cents to 19 cents per measure during the major part of the year. Rice imports were 370,068 tons in 1967 but did not exceed 300,000 tons in 1968 because of increased purchases under the Guaranteed Price Scheme.

In Maha 1968-69 there was a fairly sharp fall in the use of short term credit from $10.3 million in 1967-68 to $7.5 million in 1968-69. The shortfall in credit was largely because farmers who had defaulted in the repayment of loans in the previous years were ineligible for credit; but there was no restriction on the availability of credit. Fertilizer consumption had increased despite unfavorable weather conditions primarily because more land came under improved varieties of seed paddy. The high open market prices which prevailed after the cut in rice subsidy continued up to 1969. Essential inputs such as fertilizer, tractors, agro-chemicals, and agricultural implements continued to be freely available especially after the liberalization of imports under the OGL and FEEC schemes.

Paddy production in Maha 1968-69 was 47 million bushels, which is the highest crop ever obtained and had exceeded the previous Maha crop by about 3.6 million bushels. Even more significant was that about 17 districts exceeded the high targets fixed in regard to average yields per acre. Five areas, Polonnaruwa, Nuwara Eliya, Badulla, Kandy, and Hambantota recorded harvests of over 70 bushels per acre, while three others exceeded 60 bushels. The average yield for the island was 51.17 bushels per acre, as against 47.49 bushels in the previous year. Higher levels of output were also evident from the record purchase of paddy under the Guaranteed Price Scheme. These purchases between January and July, 1968, were 12.5 million bushels. The corresponding figure for the previous year was 12.1 million bushels. Rice imports in 1968 amounted to 334,000 tons, and estimated imports for 1969 were under 300,000 tons.

SUBSIDIARY FOOD CROPS

Apart from rice, the diet of the local population includes a substantial amount of subsidiary foodstuffs such as chillies, onions, and potatoes that are equally important as rice. In fact, chillies, potatoes, Bombay onions, red onions, and pulses constitute 90 per cent of the country's imports of subsidiary food crops. With the increase in population and the rise in per capita income, these imports have been going up steadily every year. Today, the country produces about 90 per cent of Ceylon's requirements of potatoes and red onions while most of the Bombay onions and dried chillies are imported. The unrestricted flow of imports from abroad with lower costs of production, until the middle 1960's, frustrated earlier attempts to grow these crops on a scale sufficient to meet

TABLE 35

Imports, 1964 and 1967

	1964		1967	
	Quantities ('000 cwts.)	Value (Millions of dollars)	Quantities ('000 cwts.)	Value (Millions of dollars
Chillies, dried	425	7.8	290	4.9
Red Onions	140	0.5	37	0.1
Bombay Onions	1,244	3.9	1,111	3.0
Potatoes	1,471	4.3	362	1.1
Pulses	1,750	8.8	1,398	8.8

Source: Customs Returns

the country's requirements. With the deterioration in the balance of payments situation and the urgency to conserve foreign exchange, restrictions were imposed in 1963 on imports of red onions and chillies. A total ban on imports of potatoes was introduced in 1967.

A major breakthrough was achieved in the production of subsidiary foodstuffs with the effective operation of the Guaranteed Price Scheme and its increased efficiency brought about by close supervision at the district level. Furthermore, guaranteed prices paid by government were increased for some subsidiary food crops. Two other factors have contributed to substantial increases in the production of major subsidiary food crops. There has been a steady reduction in foreign exchange allocations for their imports, and domestic prices have risen.

Furthermore, the popularization of the use of agro-chemicals and fertilizer in cultivation has also contributed to their increased production. The total cultivated acreage under subsidiary food crops has increased steadily each year and was 110,231 acres in 1968. Of this total, 11,354 acres were under red onions, 40,070 acres under chillies, 136 acres under Bombay onions, and 2,506 acres under potatoes.

Research on subsidiary food crops has been concerned mainly with developing new varieties, improved management, and fertilizer practices. To promote the cultivation of subsidiary foodcrops, the government introduced a loan scheme to finance cultivators in 1963-64 under the Extended Credit Schemes. Short-term credit was given for the cultivation of chillies, red onions, Bombay onions, and potatoes. In September, 1967, the old scheme was revised and the New Agricultural Credit Scheme was introduced. Under this scheme, the provision of short-term credit for subsidiary food crops was continued, thus enabling farmers to undertake cultivation on a much larger scale. Since credit limits were determined on a national basis rather than regionally, the amount of credit given was insufficient, especially for cultivation in the dry zone where labor costs tend to be very high; this was especially true in the cultivation of chillies and onions. When fertilizer, insecticides, and other inputs were not available at the required time in the cooperative stores, the cultivators had to depend on other sources. The private trader and boutique keeper are always ready to accomodate cultivators with their credit requirements at exhorbitant prices that are determined by the trader himself. Very often crops are seized by the trader who has been habitually obtaining his income from the produce of the indebted farmer, although the cooperatives provide the cultivator with an organization to obtain loans at lower rates of interest.

The Short-Term Implementation Program, 1961, estimated that 150,000 acres of land should be devoted to the sustained and exclusive production of subsidiary food crops to reach self sufficiency. According to the Agricultural Development Proposals, 1966-70, dried chillies, red onions, potatoes, and Bombay onions have been selected for immediate development. The 1966-70 proposals seek to achieve the target of 7,701 acres of potatoes, 52,586 acres of dried chillies, 13,779 acres of red onions, and 404 acres of Bombay onions by 1970. The aim was to bring under cultivation 40,000 acres of irrigated land in addition to the land already under cultivation and to rotate cultivation between chillies, onions, and pulses during five-year period. It was expected that this additional acreage would be sufficient to produce a major part of the island's requirements of chillies, to ensure self-sufficiency in the production of red onions, and to make a substantial reduction in imports of pulses. This new land was to be made available for cultivation by providing lift irrigation for approximately 15,000 acres; 10,000 acres were to be the high land allotments of major colonization schemes, while approximately 20,000 acres were to come under gravity irrigation schemes. A further proposal was to grow these crops in rotation on paddy lands and to develop large irrigated holdings under the Special Leases Scheme.

Reliable figures of chillie production have always been difficult to obtain largely because it is grown as a mixed crop and also because a good part of it is sold as green chillies. But increased consumption and relatively stable prices are sufficient evidence of increased production. The output figures given here are based on a survey that was conducted by the Ministry of Agriculture and Food for the specific purpose of obtaining data. It covered 10,286 acres and was confined to the Maha 1968-69 season. The average yield per acre was 4.35 cwts., giving an estimated production of 44,774 cwts. of dried chillies. The target set for the production of chillies in Maha 1967-68 was 74,000 cwts. and the provisional production figure works out to 96,260 cwts. for 1968-69. The guaranteed price for chillies of Grade I quality was raised from $28.2 per cwt. to $42.4 per cwt. in 1965.

According to provisional estimates, the production of red onions has increased from 335,023 cwts. in 1965 to 680,308 cwts. in 1968. This increase is reflected in a fall in imports from 130,286 cwts. in 1965-66 to 20,000 cwts. in 1969. The red onion scarcity from June to December is being eased by encouraging cultivation during December-January in regions of relatively low rainfall and light textured, well-drained soils in Trincomalee, Mannar, Puttalam, Ratnapura, and Hambantota districts. While there has been a bigger yield of red onions in recent years, increase in production in areas outside the traditional regions has been significant. For Bombay onions, although allocations for imports have been minimized, production has remained at 5,000 cwts. per year. However, cultivation continues to expand in the North Central and North Eastern provinces. Although the production of Bombay onions in the dry zone has increased, there are still problems to be overcome because this is a new crop in Ceylon and its popularization among cultivators is bound to take much effort and time.

Remarkable progress has been achieved in the production of potatoes; whereas output in 1965-66 in both Maha and Yala was 2,133 tons, in 1967-68, output rose to 14,445 tons, an increase of more than 400 to 500 per cent. The target set for the cultivation of potatoes was 4,462 acres, with an output target of 18,120 tons for Maha 1968-69 and 3,500 acres with an output of 17,000 tons for Yala 1969. The actual extent cultivated in Maha 1968-69 was 4,160 acres with a production of 17,900 tons, which shows a shortfall in relation to the target figure. Progressive increase in production in the last three years has been reflected in a fall in prices in the open market. The guaranteed price of potatoes was increased from $4.70 per cwt. to $5.60 per cwt. in 1965, and to $7.50 per cwt. in 1968.

Pulses not only are an essential item of diet but also represent a considerable drain on foreign exchange resources. In 1966, 1,813,043 cwt. of pulses--lentils, chickpeas, dhal, green gram, edible peas, black gram, and other pulses--to the value of $10.9 million were imported. In 1967, the aggregate value of imports of pulses amounted to about $15.1 million, which was about 5 per cent of total imports.

It has been estimated that if Ceylon's total requirements of pulses are to be produced, 150,000 to 170,000 acres would be needed.

Though attempts have been made to grow pulses locally, they have not met with much success. Some varieties, however, have recently been produced on a small scale. Since they represent a considerable drain on foreign exchange resources, more research will have to be done; but it is difficult to say how long Ceylon will take to reach self-sufficiency. Table 36 reveals the extent to which pulses have been cultivated and the corresponding yields, many of which are low.

Apart from the subsidiary crops already mentioned, there is a wide range of crops that have been successfully grown--for example, manioc, groundnuts, yams, sorghum, maize, and kenaf. These come primarily from chena cultivation, where there has been an increase in the extent under cultivation. Maize and groundnuts are two crops that have fared exceedingly well in the Badulla and Moneragala districts. Progress in regard to subsidiary food crops has been unsatisfactory during the past few years. This is due possibly to lack of physical facilities such as irrigable highland, the inadequacy of individual farm-oriented agricultural extension services, and the lack of regional specialization. Despite this, the prospects seem to be favorable; over a period of about ten years it will be possible to supply a large part of the country's requirements of subsidiary crops from domestic production.

Some indication could be given of the total import savings from the production of subsidiary food crops. In 1968, total imports of chillies, red onions, and potatoes amounted to \$8.6 million. In terms of weight it was 1.3 million cwts., or roughly 300,000 cwts. more than the total domestic production. Total domestic production in 1968 amounted to a little over 1 million cwts., or 78 per cent of the total imports for that year. On this basis a rough estimate of the value of local production of subsidiary food crops could be made and a figure of \$6.7 million

TABLE 36

Production of Pulses, 1960-67
(In Bushels)

Year	Green Gram			Cow Peas			Dhal		
	Acre-age	Produc-tion	Yields per acre	Acre-age	Produc-tion	Yields per acre	Acre-age	Produc-tion	Yields per acre
1960	11,610	401,211	3.45	8,057	133,259	16.59	140	761	5.94
1961	9,016	66,841	7.41	7,250	44,437	6.12	46	120	3.61
1962	7,469	95,036	12.72	5,427	54,578	10.06	109	764	25.72
1963	13,156	97,887	7.44	10,783	85,240	7.91	4	10	2.50
1964	9,582	86,663	9.04	9,097	80,509	8.85	22	137	6.24
1965	17,460	158,701	9.09	9,374	86,050	9.17	54	347	6.43
1966	12,621	88,434	7.01	10,287	91,755	8.92	6	42	7.00
1967	14,992	89,615	5.98	14,495	103,068	-	-	-	-

Source: Department of Census and Statistics.

could be arrived at. To what extent is Ceylon self-sufficient in subsidiary food crops? It is difficult to make an estimate because after the restrictions on imports there has been artificial suppression of consumption because of high prices. In the case of potatoes, for instance, there has been a considerable substitution of other yams.

OTHER PRODUCTS

For the first time, targets were laid down for animal husbandry, and attempts were made to draw up an implementation program for vegetable cultivation in areas where large scale cultivation was being done. Considerable progress was made in achieving the targets laid down in the development plan for animal husbandry. The program for milk production in the agricultural development proposals had two objectives: to increase local milk production and to manufacture milk products in Ceylon with a progressive reduction of imports. The first objective has been achieved through higher prices for milk and better collection procedures. In terms of the second objective, a condensary and milk-packing plant have been set up with foreign technical assistance. The capacity of the condensed milk factory at Polonnaruwa is sufficient to meet the country's entire demand. The condensary needs 120,000 pints of milk to meet the country's requirements, and projections have been made to meet these requirements over a period of time. The target was to supply the condensary with 12,000 pints in the first year. By the end of December, 1968, the target was exceeded, as it was receiving 25,000 pints of milk, or approximately 20 per cent of its raw material. The annual foreign exchange saving from the output of the condensary has been estimated to be about $3.0 million.

Several other major projects, including the sterilized milk project at Pallekelle and the first phase of the powdered milk project, were carried out according to targets laid down in the agricultural plan. The increase in the output of milk production was reflected in the increase in the daily intake by

TABLE 37

Production of Minor Food Crops, 1960-67

Year	Kurakkan		Maize		Groundnuts		Manioc		Sorghum	
	Acreage	Production (bushels)	Acreage	Production (bushels)	Acreage	production (bushels)	Acreage	Production (cwt.)	Acreage	Production (bushels)
1960	88,811	732,518	35,827	332,132	2,325	48,429	192,337	2,864,529	3,745	27,951
1961	70,982	726,066	32,470	363,535	2,716	52,534	95,668	5,194,738	4,069	41,174
1962	57,326	630,163	28,380	358,030	2,271	39,878	85,050	5,147,963	2,786	47,949
1963	71,053	777,699	36,866	417,053	4,908	86,427	166,183	6,131,717	4,598	62,658
1964	55,741	606,182	27,464	352,932	7,340	197,712	111,249	7,269,253	2,806	29,705
1965	64,635	684,791	29,408	377,900	8,008	117,987	130,592	6,460,994	4,008	50,766
1966	55,084	700,665	30,433	363,977	10,840	149,617	121,261	5,692,668	3,435	47,586
1967	55,186	583,720	35,322	637,117	8,678	172,888	176,138	7,554,372	2,813	40,119

Source: Department of Census and Statistics.

the Milk Board from 65,000 pints in 1967 to 84,000 pints a day in 1968. The present daily production of milk in Ceylon is estimated to be about 700,000 pints. The Milk Board has stepped up its collection from 40,000 pints in 1965 to 100,000 pints per day in 1968. This was due partly to the increase in the price by 2 cents per pint for milk purchased by the Board.

Figures relating to the production of vegetables have not been given because of the difficulties connected with the collection of data on a continuing basis. Moreover, the agricultural development proposals did not lay down targets in respect of fruits and vegetables. However, the program covers the extent to be cultivated with various vegetables in the Maha and Yala seasons for each year and broadly sets out the requirements of imported and local certified vegetable seed. Although there is definite evidence of a greater area of land having been brought into cultivation over the years, fruit and vegetable prices have fluctuated from time to time due to shortages arising from adverse weather conditions and other factors.

The administration report of the Commissioner of Marketing for 1962-63 indicated that there were more than 53 varieties of vegetables that find their way into the wholesale markets every year. Although Ceylon has all the natural advantages to produce more than its requirements of vegetables, the consumer has not been assured of a steady supply of good quality and cheap vegetables because of shortcomings in organization of the vegetable trade. It is estimated that in the up-country alone about 21,000 acres of vegetables are cropped every year. Additional intensive vegetable cultivation is found in the Jaffna district and in the vicinity of the big towns. Ceylon's main problem is not one of overproduction or underproduction of vegetables but maladjustments in the production and distribution mechanism. The Agricultural Development Program has highlighted some of these issues. The program places primary emphasis on the need to even out present surpluses and shortages and to ensure that these crops are cultivated throughout the year in suitable zones; emphasis has also been placed on improving the present channels of wholesale and retail distribution.

AIDS TO AGRICULTURAL IMPROVEMENT--IRRIGATION AND LAND DEVELOPMENT

In 1966, the Ministry of Land, Irrigation, and Power released a development program covering the period 1966/70. Of the ministries, the two main systematic development programs came from the Ministry of Agriculture and Food, and the Ministry of Land, Irrigation, and Power. The proposals of the Ministry of Agriculture and Food placed emphasis on raising the level of production and on the attainment of higher levels of efficiency in agriculture, while the investment proposals of the Ministry of Land, Irrigation, and Power concentrated on new settlements, the development of land and irrigation, and the extension of production. This was indeed the first time when this ministry presented proposals for development separately. On previous occasions, the development schemes under the ministry were incorporated in the general plans for the development of the economy as a whole. The proposals of the ministry stressed the need to provide irrigation facilities for new lands under paddy and to extend and improve irrigation facilities to existing paddy lands.

The plan estimated that roughly 736,000 acres of paddy would be brought under major or minor irrigation schemes. Requirements of irrigation were confined not only to the dry zone but also to the wet zone where rainfall is adequate but sometimes fairly unevenly distributed.

The five-year program of irrigation outlined in the plan included the provision of irrigation facilities to 182,625 acres of new crown land and 143,500 acres of private lands under multi-purposes, major, and minor irrigation schemes. It was also proposed to provide 13,500 acres with irrigation under village schemes, which was likely to benefit 36,500 acres of existing paddy lands. The plan also envisaged irrigation for about 18,000 acres in Gal Oya and the Uda Walawe for sugar and other crops. The total outlay on irrigation works in the villages was to be $60.5 million, and the net increase in production has been estimated at $16.5 million. Irrigation facilities for 140,000 acres of paddy were estimated to result in the value of output of paddy increasing by about $8.4 million, while subsidiary food crops, mainly chillies and Bombay onions, were to bring in an income of $8.1 million.

The irrigation works outlined in the plan were classified into four types--multi-purpose schemes, major irrigation works (those that provide irrigation for 2,000 acres and above), medium scale works (those costing over $12,605), village works (those costing over $1,680 but under $12,605). In the multi-purpose schemes, development was to be handled by the River Valleys Development Board, and irrigation facilities for 3,660 acres of paddy and 4,000 acres of sugar under the Gal Oya Resevoir Scheme were to be provided. It was also proposed to develop 12,000 acres of highland for the cultivation of other crops in the Gal Oya Valley. Furthermore, it was intended to develop 28,500 acres in the Uda Walawe, of which 14,000 acres were to be devoted to food crops and 12,000 acres of highland crops. Under the major schemes, efforts were to be concentrated on the provision of irrigation facilities for ten projects that would bring into production 68,388 acres of new land and 3,869 acres of existing land. This program of development also provided for 28,425 acres of highland to be brought under cultivation.

A project associated with the provision of irrigation and of bringing more land under cultivation was the scheme for the drainage and reclamation of low-lying areas along the south and southwest coast of Ceylon. Its purpose was to reclaim for paddy cultivation abandoned marshy land that is periodically subject to floods and to check or reduce the increased salinity of soils in this area. In this way it proposed to rehabilitate 20,000 acres of land over a five-year period at an average rate of 4,000 acres per year. The overall cost of the project was estimated at over $1.7 million spread over a period of five years ending in 1970.

During this period, monies were also to be set apart for investigation and designs of new projects.

Fifteen projects were itemized, most of them connected with the major rivers in the island. Nine of them consisted of construction of fairly large reservoirs on some of the major rivers or their tributaries. Included in these proposals were the development schemes under the Samanala Wewa project, the Kelani Ganga basin, and the Mahaweli basin. The Samanala Wewa project is based on the Walawe Gana, one of the five largest perennial rivers in the island. The development of river basins includes the construction of several reservoirs both for the purpose of irrigation and power generation. Of these, the most important reservoir is the Samanala Wewa, which would cover an area of 3,240 acres at maximum capacity. Associated with the resevoir would be a power plant capable of generating 30 megawatts. Also included in these proposals for the investigation and design of new projects was the Mahaweli Ganga Basin project, the largest development project ever to be undertaken in the country.

For the first time, the report stressed the importance of lift irrigation because of the nondevelopment of the highland areas in the colonization schemes. Hitherto, development had been confirmed to the low-lying areas with adequate supplies of water throughout. This resulted in the total neglect of highlands, which could be profitable used to cultivate a very wide range of crops. The first consideration was that the development of highland would be possible only in colonization schemes where there was no shortage of water for the cultivation of existing lands. It was pointed out that under present conditions, these lands could be best developed by lift irrigation, while emphasizing that no work had hitherto been done by the Department of Irrigation in this regard. The proposals outlined in the plan were for the development by lift irrigation of 10,000 acres of land in existing colonization schemes for subsidiary food crops. An additional 5,000 acres were selected for development for the cultivation of subsidiary food crops under lift irrigation from rivers and channels. In this connection, studies of ground water resources were made in areas where lift could be profitably used. A separate division was established in the Irrigation

Department to deal with lift irrigation from surface sources and from ground water sources. The total cost of the lift irrigation scheme has been estimated at $1.5 million. It is still too premature to evaluate the impact of lift irrigation, but present indications are that it has been a too costly in relation to the returns.

EXPORT AGRICULTURE

Tea

The acreage under cultivation, production and yield per acre are given below:

Year	Acreage	Production (million lbs.)	Yield per acre (pounds)
1965	594,308	503	848
1966	596,446	490	823
1967	598,814	487	829
1968	597,490	496	848
1969	596,514	484	845

Source: Annual Reports, Central Bank of Ceylon.

These figures illustrate that tea production has been more or less stagnant throughout the period. After having reached a peak of 503 million pounds in 1965, tea output declined by nearly 3 per cent to 490 million pounds in 1966. In 1967, output showed a further fractional decline which was due mainly to adverse weather conditions and to the adoption of finer plucking in order to improve quality and thereby realize better prices for the high-and medium-grown categories. In 1969 there was a decline in both output and yield per acre. During the ten-year period up to 1965, Ceylon's tea production rose at an annual average rate of 2.8 per cent, which compares favorably with India's 1.8 per cent but lagged far behind the 7.6 per cent growth rate of the five major tea producing countries in Africa--Kenya, Uganda, Tanzania, Malawi, and Mozambique. In quality, Ceylon tea surpasses the Indian and African counterparts, although in absolute terms the yield per acre is still much lower in Ceylon than in India.

Adverse trends in world tea prices have prevailed for a long time, but in the last five years they have been accentuated. Sharp price declines occurred in September, 1966, and May, 1969. This has been attributed to an unsatisfactory supply and demand relationship. While supplies have increased by 3 per cent, consumption has increased only by 1 per cent. Measures to improve the competitive position of the tea industry, such as the replanting subsidy, were taken even before the price decline appeared in the 1960's. Latterly, the government has taken further steps, both at the national and international level, to deal with the problem of declining prices.

In an earlier chapter, the tea replanting subsidy scheme was discussed. A review of replanting in the 1960's shows that the progress under the scheme has been much lower than was anticipated. The area replanted up to the end of 1967 was less than 4 per cent, or about 27,000 acres; of this, 17,310 acres were replanted in the period 1965 to 1968. The yield obtained from areas replanted by means of vegetative propagation has been twice that of plants raised from seedlings.

With regard to overall coverage of the tea replanting subsidy scheme, over 38,000 acres of tea were participating in the scheme in 1967; this represented approximately 6 per cent of the total registered tea acreage of 596,292 acres. From the standpoint of ownership of estates, the best response has come from sterling companies. Of the 38,000 acres under the scheme at present, sterling companies have been authorized to replant 14,000 acres. In 1967, of this area, over 12,000 acres had been cleared for replanting while over 8,000 acres had already been replanted. Next in importance were the rupee companies that have been authorized to replant approximately 12,000 acres; of this, almost 9,000 acres had been cleared and 6,000 acres had been replanted in 1967. From the point of view of the size of the estate, the largest group of beneficiaries has been the owners of estates over 500 acres, where 58 per cent of the permits have been issued to estates in favor of groups where the size of the estate ranged from 100 to 500 acres.

The tea fertilizer subsidy scheme was introduced in 1967 with a view to providing greater incentives to smallholders to increase productivity. Under this scheme smallholders of tea lands below 100 acres in extent are given a subsidy amounting to one-half the cost of fertilizer applied, up to a maximum of $16.80 per acre. In 1969, 12,200 tons of fertilizers had been issued at a cost of $0.5 million for 56,200 acres.

Another scheme of importance has been the tea factory development subsidy introduced in 1966. The object of the scheme was to improve the quality of tea and to effect economies in production costs. One-half of the interest on loans availed of by estate owners for improvements to existing tea factories and for the construction of new factories was paid as a subsidy. The subsidy on interest was limited to a period of five years, for improvements to existing factories, five years; and for the construction of new factories, ten years. In the period 1966 to 1968, a total of $3.3 million was approved as loans, and the actual amount utilized was $1.0 million. The government also now pays an outright grant to factory owners of one-third of the cost of approved items of machinery, appliances, and equipment installed in tea factories. In 1969, the period of subsidy under these arrangements was extended from five to ten years for improvements to existing factories and from ten to twenty years in the case of new factories.

TABLE 38

Tea Acreage Replanted, 1965-69.

	Registered acreage	Acreage permits issued	Acreage up rooted	Acreage planted	Percentage replanted in relation to registered acreage
Based on elevation					
High	195,932	11,133	9,039	5,369	2.74
Medium	241,506	13,855	10,764	7,165	2.97
Low	158,292	13,112	9,661	6,509	4.09
Total	596,292	38,100	29,464	19,043	3.19
Based on Ownership					
Sterling companies	181,477	14,219	12,293	8,266	4.55
Rupee companies	153,053	11,979	8,953	5,997	3.92
Ceylonese individuals	243,426	11,045	7,715	4,416	1.81
Non-Ceylonese	16,125	459	266	180	1.12
State	2,211	398	237	184	8.32
Total	596,292	38,100	29,464	19,043	3.19
Based on acreage					
Over 500 acres	288,460	21,869	17,791	12,167	4.22
100-500 acres	145,789	12,069	9,090	5,958	4.09
10-100 acres	62,864	2,806	1,803	700	1.11
Below 10 acres	99,179	1,356	780	218	0.22
Total	596,292	38,100	29,464	19,043	3.19

Sources: Central Bank of Ceylon, and Administration Reports of Tea Controller.

The replanting scheme has been in operation for a long time; there is also the factory development scheme and the fertilizer subsidy scheme for smallholders. These, however, are only attempts to deal with specific problems but do not constitute a comprehensive policy towards the problems of the industry as a whole. It is this factor that presumably compelled the government to appoint a commission in 1967 to report on the condition and future prospects of the tea industry in Ceylon. The more important recommendations in the report of the Commission, which was submitted in May, 1968, were (1) the establishment of a Central Tea Board,(2) raising the rate of replanting to 12,000 acres per year in order to bring under clonal tea 200,000 acres by 1984,(3) lightening the tax burden on the tea industry,(4) providing government assistance for the establishment of new distribution channels for packaged tea. Soon after the report was issued, the government promised to give active consideration to these matters. As a result, legislation was prepared to set up a Central Tea Board. The Government has offered incentives in the form of a loan scheme to step up the rate of replanting from an average of 5,000 acres per year to 12,000 acres. The loan scheme came into operation in May, 1969. Under this, the State Mortgage Bank gives loans for replanting at $336 per acre on low rates of interest and relatively easy terms of repayment. These loans are in addition to the payment of a subsidy of $630 per acre. Steps have also been taken to change marketing methods, and the Government has authorized the extension of private sales of tea, which had earlier been confined to the U.S.A. and the Common Market countries.

Rubber

Rubber production, which provides about 16 to 18 per cent of Ceylon's foreign exchange earnings, has been increasing continuously since 1961; the average annual rate of increase during the period 1961-66 was about 6 per cent, in contrast to the virtual stagnation during the period 1956-61. The rate of increase during 1961-66 compares favorably with that of Malaysia at 4 per cent, Indonesia at 1 per cent, and Thailand at 2 per cent. The average yield per acre, however, is still far lower than that of Malaysia. In 1967, production amounted to 316 million pounds, an increase of more than 9 per cent over the previous year compared with 11 per cent in 1966. In 1968, rubber production rose by 13 million pounds, reaching a total output of 328 million pounds. This was higher than the estimated target of 320 million pounds for the year. The recent rise in output is attributable to favorable weather conditions and the higher yields obtained from the replanted acreage. Rubber output has increased despite very low prices in 1966-68. Prices improved only in the latter half of 1968 after having reached the lowest point in twenty years in February, 1968. This production record is largely a reflection of the success of the rubber replanting scheme.* However, the present rate of replanting has fallen below 3 per cent of the total acreage per year and on the basis of Malaysian experience is lower than the economically desirable rate.

The contribution in 1968 to total production from the replanted acreage was nearly 60 per cent, and the overall average yield per acre from tapped areas was 671 pounds in 1968 as compared with 400 to 500 pounds per acre in the early 1950's. In 1966, a total of 11,582 acres was replanted with approved varieties of high-yielding clones, while in 1967 and 1968 it amounted to 10,086 and 12,734 acres respectively. The position at the end of 1968 is that about one half of the island's acreage of rubber, or almost 264,000 acres, has been replanted under the scheme, which works out to an annual average of about 20,000 acres. This is slightly lower than the theoretically ideal way of replanting on the basis that

---

*Subsidies paid under the replanting scheme have increased as the replanting cost rose, and the present replanting subsidy of $235 for estates and $252 for smallholdings was introduced in October, 1966.

the economic life of a rubber tree is about 30 to 35 years. This average, to some extent, also conceals the fact that there has been a marked fall in the replanting scheme in the last few years, which is due presumable to the very sharp price declines in 1965, 1966, 1967, and 1968. The largest shortfall in applications for the subsidy has been from estates over 100 acres in extent and those between 10 and 100 acres. Smallholders have continued to take advantage of the inducement offered under the replanting subsidy scheme, though not to the same extent as in the earlier period.

Because vigorous replanting and rehabilitation schemes have been undertaken by other rubber-producing countries, the view has been expressed that unless Ceylon can keep pace with these developments, she will soon be pushed out of world markets by competitors. In this context, it has been the policy of the government to accelerate the rate of replanting. For some years, the natural rubber industry has been given a breathing space to prepare itself for increasing competition from synthetics and gradual erosion of the premium that natural rubber commands over synthetic. Planting interests have expressed the view that to accelerate the current rate of replanting it would require incentives in the form of higher rates of subsidy. Proposals have been put forward that the replanting subsidy should be increased to $252 per acre for estates over 100 acres and to $285 an acre for estates under 100 acres in extent. Despite these, doubts have been expressed whether the past average replanting rate of 20,000 acres per annum could be exceeded.

The current expenditure on the subsidy scheme is met by an annual advance not exceeding $3.4 million from the consolidated fund. The limitation is a statutory one in terms of the Rubber Replanting Subsidy Act No.5 of 1968. The accelerated program will involve commitments in excess of $3.4 million. The projections for the period ending 1972 are that the replanting program would have covered a total of 330,000 acres while about 40,000 acres of the acreage planted outside the rubber replanting scheme can also be classified as high-yielding plantations. According to an agricultural survey conducted in 1962, the actual acreage under rubber has been estimated at 580,000. On this basis, by 1970 there would be a balance of some 200,000 acres that will need rehabilitation. The total expenditure would amount to $50.4 million and should result in a minimum net addition to the output of about 30,000 tons per annum. On the basis of prices at about 18 cents in 1969, the replanting of the additional 200,000 acres should bring in foreign exchange to the value of about $11.8 million a year. On the assumption that only 100,000 of the 200,000 acres are replanted, in effect, then, in less than 2½ years the increased production from 100,000 acres would pay for the entire expenditure incurred by government on the replanting scheme.

The major short-term problem in the rubber industry is the production of new standardized and technically graded forms of natural rubber such as dynat and hevea crumb. None of the new forms of crumb rubber are yet in production on a commercial scale in Ceylon, despite the fact that Malaysia has made considerable advances in this direction. Sustained efforts now seem to be necessary both in financial and technical assistance to enlarge the possibilities of producing sufficient quantities of the new rubber.

Coconut

The output of coconut products has fluctuated markedly from year to year; after having reached a peak in 1964, it has shown a falling trend. In 1967, output fell by about 2 per cent following declines of 11 per cent and 8 per cent in 1965 and 1966 respectively. In 1969, output rose to 2,601 million nuts from 2,421 million nuts in 1967. The fall in output in 1965-67 is attributed partly to drought experienced in those years and partly to the difficulty of maintaining the output of old trees. The government is making efforts to improve yields by means of a rehabilitation subsidy scheme with the main purpose of increasing the use of fertilizer.

Fertilizer used on estates and small holdings under the subsidy scheme since 1965 are given below:

Year	Quantity (tons)
1965	52,000
1966	54,000
1967	52,000
1968	62,000
1969	70,000

About 50 per cent of the total subsidized fertilizer issued went to estates where the estimated yield per acre is twice that of the small holding. At present, the government subsidizes 50 per cent of the costs of fertilizer used by smallholders. Before October, 1968, only 30 per cent of the costs was subsidized. Fertilizer use has increased considerably since the introduction of the subsudy scheme in 1956 whereas in 1950-56 fertilizer consumption has been more or less static at approximately 50,000 tons, which is very much lower than the amounts recommended by the Coconut Research Institute. The immediate problem is how to increase the rate of fertilizer application, particularly by smallholders who own more than 70 per cent of the total area under cultivation. Estimates show that if fertilizer application is doubled by 1973, nut production should rise by approximately 23 per cent over the 1968 figure.

A scheme to grant credit facilities through commercial banks to coconut land owners to purchase fertilizer was put into operation. The banks participating in the scheme are the People's Bank and the Bank of Ceylon, and loans are granted to those who own lands over 20 acres in extent. The second major issue is to rehabilitate the industry by replacing a high proportion of the palms that are old and are considered uneconomical. The replanting program in coconut has been much slower than in all other export crops. Incentives have been afforded in the form of the supply of subsidized seedlings through the Coconut Research Institute to the smallholders, but here again, the incentives have not been sufficient to make a significant impact. In 1965, the number of seedlings distributed was 1.2 million, in 1967 it was 1.4 million, and in 1968 1.5 million.

NOTES

1. *Agricultural Development Proposals, 1966-70* (Colombo: Ministry of Agriculture and Food, 1966).

2. *Implementation Program and Targets, 1966* (Colombo: Ministry of Agriculture and Food).

CHAPTER

13

THE ECONOMIC POLICY OF THE NEW GOVERNMENT

At the General Election held on May 27, 1970, the United Front secured an overwhelming victory by winning more than 116 seats in a legislature of 157.* The party's election manifesto consisted of a number of proposals designed to effect substantial changes in economic policy. Major aspects of these proposals were subsequently elaborated in the Throne Speech of June, 1970, which is the official statement of economic and social policy.

For a more comprehensive statement, however, the budget speech had to be awaited. The budget, which is normally presented in late July or early August, was postponed until October, 1970, presumably to enable the government to formulate its economic policies in more precise terms. From a practical standpoint, the budget for 1970-71 has been the most

---

*The previous government was the United National Party. The United Front is a coalition of the Sri Lanka Freedom Party, the Lanka Sama Samaja Party and, the Communist Party. The United Front is under the leadership of Mrs. Sirimavo Bandaranaike of the Sri Lanka Freedom Party, which has over 90 seats, giving the latter an absolute majority. Of the 21 ministries the Sri Lanka Freedom Party has 17 ministries, the Lanka Sama Samaja Party three, and the Communist Party one.

important policy statement so far (December, 1970) because it included not only the fiscal policy of the government but also dwelt with a large number of economic issues.

CHANGES IN THE ADMINISTRATION

Within a month of assuming office, far-reaching changes were effected in the administration and many of these were consistent with the pronouncements in the joint election manifesto as well as speeches made during the election campaign. Several new ministries were created. Among these was the Ministry of Public Administration, Local Government, and Home Affairs, which was assigned the task of overhauling the administration to gear it to the more urgent needs of development. The entire public service, which previously came under the Ministry of Finance, is now under the purview of this ministry.

For the first time, a Ministry for Plantation Industry was established. This Ministry is concerned primarily with the private sector, since nearly all plantations are privately owned. Its function is to determine economic policy for the plantations and regulate agency houses and management firms that have been intimately connected with the successful running of estates over a long period of time. In view of the growing importance of tourism as a foreign exchange earner, shipping and tourism were specifically assigned to a new ministry. This ministry is also expected to develop a national shipping line so that the country would be less dependent on foreign shipping monopolies.

The most important ministry entrusted with economic policy, the former Ministry of Planning and Economic Affairs, was renamed Ministry of Planning and Employment because employment policy featured very prominently in the United Front manifesto and in the election campaign. In fact, it can be assumed that the large number of educated unemployed youth voted the government into power; they had considerable influence over the rest of the voting population.

The problem of the educated unemployed has already been referred to in Chapter 7. The new Ministry of Planning and Employment basically has retained the organizational framework of the previous Ministry of Planning and Economic Affairs, except that an employment division has been created along with a Bureau of Graduate Employment. At the apex of the planning organization is the Cabinet Committee on Planning and Economic Affairs presided over by the Prime Minister. The Plan Implementation Division and the External Resources Division remain, but some of the senior officers have been replaced by others. A reconstituted Foreign Exchange Budget Committee continues to determine allocations for imports on the basis of priorities and the total amount of foreign exchange available each year.*

The government is re-examining the entire organization of planning, and under the new set-up contemplated, each local authority will be the focus for development and plan implementation. Popular participation will be ensured by the establishment of divisional development councils in which the most important organizations at the village level will participate. The plan implementation procedures are being strengthened with the object of maintaining a regular review of progress on all government expenditure and ensuring that each implementing agency is in a position to achieve the quarterly targets. Performance would be reviewed periodically from the village level upwards to the principal departments responsible for plan implementation.

Administrative changes have taken place in most ministries and important government departments. Permanent secretaries, most of whom happened to be

---

*This Committee consists of the Permanent Secretary, Ministry of Planning and Employment, who is the chairman, the permanent secretaries to the ministries of Foreign and Internal Trade, Finance, and Industries and Scientific Affairs, and a representative of the Central Bank of Ceylon.

members of the old Civil Service, a relict of British administration, were replaced, with one or two exceptions, by younger men from outside the service. The average age of permanent secretaries was reduced from about 55 to 42 years. The criteria applied in the choice of persons for these posts was not seniority but experience, with the accent on specialized knowledge of the subject area of each ministry. For the first time, engineers were appointed permanent secretaries to the ministries of Housing and Construction, and Irrigation, Power, and Highways. Economists were appointed permanent secretaries to the ministries of Planning and Employment, Foreign and Internal Trade, Shipping and Tourism, and Industries and Scientific Affairs. Similarly, a practicing doctor became permanent secretary to the Ministry of Health. Previously there was much agitation against the practice of appointing civil servants to posts that required technical skill and knowledge.* Moreover, those appointed had little or no understanding of the problems involved in economic development.

Furthermore, with a view to improving the economic viability of the public sector corporations, particularly the industrial corporations, directorates were reconstituted. This was intended to eliminate administrative bottlenecks, corruption, and other deficiencies that had impeded progress earlier. In several corporations, technical men were appointed as chairman or directors.

Election of employees' councils and advisory committees in government offices was encouraged to

---

*For instance, in the last quarter of 1969, engineers carried out a campaign of protest against the appointment of a civil servant as chairman of the Mahaweli Development Board, which was entrusted with the task of undertaking the biggest river valley development scheme in Ceylon with assistance from the IBRD. The new government has modified the original proposals for the development of the Mahaweli River basin.

ensure greater participation by employees in administration.* At the national level, peoples' committees are being set up on a territorial basis with a view to making "administration more responsive to the needs of the country and wishes of the people." A complete reorientation of the earlier Kachcheri and divisional revenue systems is contemplated with the object of expediting government business at the district and divisional level and to make officials participate more effectively in economic development.

FOOD AND AGRICULTURE

The major policy decision on subsidized food related to the rice ration. With effect from September 26, 1970, the United Front government restored the weekly rice ration to two measures from the previous level of one measure.** As before, the first measure was issued free, but the second measure was available to the consumer at 12.5 cents. At the same time, the government decided to recognize the Guaranteed Price Scheme to achieve the following objectives:

1. To ensure that the guaranteed price of $2.35 per bushel reaches the actual producer and not the middleman

2. To maximize the quantity of rice purchased by government under the Guaranteed Price Scheme in order to reduce imports and to meet the heavy commitments of the increased ration

---

*It will be the duty of the management to investigate any complaint brought up by an advisory committee in regard to neglect of duty, waste, attendance, and frauds. The members of an advisory committee will be elected, and the number in each committee will vary from five to twenty-five depending on the size of the institution.

**Before 1966, the ration was two measures (four pounds) per person per week.

> 3. To improve the quality of rice turned out by millers and ultimately issued under the rice ration scheme and to reduce the waste that occurs in storage, milling, and transport.

Up to now, less than 33 per cent of the local paddy has been bought by the government under the Guaranteed Price Scheme. The present objective is to step up purchases to about 65 to 70 per cent. Unless this is achieved, the bulk of the rice given on the ration will have to be imported.

On agricultural policy, the emphasis has continued to be on increasing yields and improving methods of cultivation. Plans have been completed to establish an Agrarian Research and Training Institute with United Nations assistance. About 75 per cent of the acreage under paddy is already planted with H 4 and H 8 varieties and about 5 per cent with IR 8. Experiments have been also carried out with B.G. 111, which is a new variety said to be superior to the IR 8. All these are likely to further increase output and yields. For instance, in the Maha 1970, yields have risen to 51.5 bushels per acre while total production in Maha and Yala was estimated at 72 million bushels, which is in excess of the target of 70 million bushels projected earlier.

With the provision of the second measure on the ration in September, 1970, the open market price of rice has tended to fall, although the effective guaranteed price to the farmer is $2.35 per bushel. The government has already indicated that it hopes to make paddy procuring a government monopoly. The paddy purchasing scheme would be operated under the Paddy Marketing Board Bill, which is expected to become law in the course of 1971.* This would ensure

---

*The functions of the Paddy Marketing Board would be to carry on the business of purchasing, selling, supplying, and distributing paddy and rice and also undertake the milling, hulling, and processing of paddy and rice.

that the farmer would receive the guaranteed price and not the lower market price that is caused by cheating on weights and distress during harvesting season when the farmer is forced to sell to the middlemen. Plans are in the process of implementation to double the purchasing points by 1972 when there would be approximately 4,000 purchasing centres in operation.* Increased capacity would be provided for storage and milling to correspond with the increasing intake. The government has indicated that the 4,500 cultivation committees set up under the Paddy Lands Act would be reorganized, and efforts would be made to restore tenancy to cultivators who had been evicted earlier. The Ceylon Fertilizer Corporation would be made the sole importer of the major nutrients for fertilizer, which will enable the country to obtain fertilier at a lower cost, thus saving considerable foreign exchange.

Subsidiary foodstuffs have always been a heavy drain on the country's foreign exchange resources, and plans to stimulate production locally have been given high priority. Items singled out for immediate development are chillies and Bombay onions. Self-sufficiency in these two items alone is likely to result in a foreign exchange saving of over $10.5 million. The success of self-sufficiency strategy has been demonstrated in the case of potatoes and red onions. Before 1960, the entire requirements of these two items had to be imported. The government has plans to extend import substitution to other subsidiary foodstuffs such as cereals and pulses as soon as possible. But as emphasized in the preceding chapter, there are certain physical factors which stand in the way of rapid development.

Plantation agriculture comes directly under the new Ministry of Plantations. For the first time, the government would be intervening in an area which

---

*The proposal is to have a purchasing center within a radius of three miles of each other in the principal paddy-growing areas.

is predominantly in the private sector. To clarify any doubts about the future of the plantations, an assurance has been given that intervention would largely be with regard to the country's export earnings. With the cooperation of other countries, the new Ministry of Plantations is expected to take steps to protect the tea industry and secure higher prices from purchasing countries. Proposals for a long-term tea agreement, the tea auction systems in Colombo and London, the commissions and charges of agency houses and freight rates would be matters on which the government intends to intervene.

With regard to the tea replanting subsidy scheme, estates have been required to formulate and submit their programs for the next five years. The government has stated that legislation will be introduced, wherever necessary, to ensure that the development of properties would be undertaken and that "Tea estates which do not evince interest in developing their holdings will be liable to be taken over by the state." Maximum assistance would be forthcoming in the selection of areas for replanting, and subsidies would continue to be offered under the Tea Factory Development scheme. The rubber replanting program would be accelerated with a view to completing rehabilitation of old rubber within a period of about six years.

INDUSTRY

Broadly, the policy of the new administration on industry* has been concerned with (1) the reorganization of the existing industrial framework to achieve

---

*The government has stated that major changes in industrial policy have been necessary in order to eliminate some of the social and economic consequences of earlier industrial policy. In particular these relate to the concentration of industries in the hands of a few investors and lack of diffused ownership, the heavy reliance on imported raw materials,

the social and political objectives of the government, (2) the determination of priorities for mapping out the future course of industrial development vis-à-vis the economic, social, and political context, (3) the determination of priorities for the allocation of resources for industrial production, at least in the short-run, and (4) marketing, quality control and supply of industrial raw materials.[1]

The above criteria are based on the premise that the state should adopt a socialist oriented approach in the development and regulation of industry. This means that heavy, basic, and essential industries will be under state management, if not under direct state ownership. Industries, which for reasons of technology, scale, and policy do not make state ownership vital in the national interest, are to be left to private enterprise, but subject, of course, to regulation by the state. The government proposes to carry out its industrial policy by establishing a number of industrial development corporations, each responsible for a particular sector of industry. These sectoral development corporations will be responsible for planning all development in particular areas of industry and coordinating production programs. They will allocate resources to various units and organize research devoted to the utilization of local raw materials. The corporations will be responsible not only for the management of industries in the public sector but also will regulate and direct investment in private sector units.

All existing public sector corporations will come under the purview of one of these sectoral development corporations, which will manage each factory unit through a board of directors it appoints at the factory level. The sectoral development corporations are intended to be the principal instruments through which the state will direct the activities

---

the highly capital intensive nature of industry, which has reduced employment opportunities, and the high price structure of local products.

of the industrial sector. Where necessary, they will participate in the management of private sector industries through representation on the boards of management and will regulate their activities in the field of production, quality control, and prices. Development corporations will promote and coordinate research activity within their respective areas and function as consultants for projects under their control.

The Ministry of Industries and Scientific Affairs proposes to reorganize and expand the Ceylon Institute for Scientific and Industrial Research so as to participate activity in industrial development. The Institute will engage in research on the utilization of indigenous raw materials, industrial waste, and by-products and the development of appropriate technologies. It would give special emphasis to the problems of small industries. A team of scientists from the Soviet Union has already examined the work and the facilities at the CISIR, and it is expected that their recommendations would help in the reorganization of this institution. The National Science Council will also be required to play a more active role in development by organizing a survey of natural resources and by giving assistance to utilize the resources for industrial purposes. In addition, reorganization of the Bureau of Ceylon Standards is being contemplated. In future, the bureau will not only lay down standards but also undertake certification, marketing, and provide a quality control advisory service. Highest priority in the current program for industrial development will be given to small industries based primarily on local raw materials and established under regional development programs in rural areas.

The Industrial Development Board and the Small Industries Department have been reorganized. The powers that were vested in the Industrial Development Board by the act of December, 1969, have been considerably curtailed, and the board is required to concentrate on small industries rather than on the regulation of the industrial system as a whole. The Industrial Development Board and the Department of Small Industries are expected to pay special attention to labor intensive technologies and select for promotion industries that are most suited to the rural areas. In this context, the immediate resuscitation of the handloom textile industry and the promotion of handicrafts, particularly those with export possibilities, will be given priority.

With regard to large-scale industry in the public sector, the present proposals are to revitalize and expand them to provide an effective infrastructure for cooperative, private, and small-scale industry in Ceylon. These industries will be required not only to engage in the production of essential consumer goods but also will be responsible for generating growth in the economy and providing the necessary multiplier factor for the expansion of the industrial sector as a whole. They are expected to provide the basis for technology on raw material for most of the industries in the private sector. Furthermore, the ministry has indicated that the development of heavy mineral resources will be the exclusive responsibility of public sector industry.

The present proposals on industrial reorganization are directed to ease the unemployment and underemployment problem and toward the utilization of indigenous raw materials. The ministry has stated that in 1971 new industries in the private sector will be approved only if they are based wholly on the use of local raw materials, or where at least a fixed percentage of the raw materials used are of local origin, and provided the goods produced are of an essential nature. In the alternative, industries should provide goods primarily for export, or they should be located in underdeveloped or nonindustrialized parts of the country, if the location costs are not unduly unfavorable. Units will also be approved if they are small-scale, labor intensive, and are located outside the Colombo district. Furthermore, consideration will be given to industries where performance, quality, price, output, and marketing arrangements are superior to those of existing units, provided the products are basic essential consumer goods. The same criteria will be applied in the allocation of resources, particularly foreign exchange, in 1971 and thereafter.

With the abolition of imports under Open General License in June, 1970, the basis of allocation of raw materials to industries has been revised. All locally manufactured goods have been put into three categories, A, B, and C. Items under category A are essential items, B semi-essential items, and C luxury items.* The largest allocation of 70 per cent of the 1969 allocation has been made to industries in category A, while those in category B will receive 60 per cent, and C 40 per cent. The policy is to discourage prestige industries and to promote industries of economic relevance that will contribute directly to a substantial saving of foreign exchange.

In view of the limitations of the local market, the ministry has stated that industrial development in Ceylon should be based on an external dynamics. This demands that imported goods, including raw materials, should be purchased against exports to the supplier countries concerned; barter trade arrangements would also be used to achieve this objective. Wherever possible, the state would import industrial raw materials in bulk, thereby reducing production costs, standardizing quality, and preventing exchange malpractices that, under the present system of exchange allocations, have largely gone undetected.

Already about fifteen essential items have been subject to price control. The Ministry of

---

*Included in category A are food, spinning, weaving, and finishing of textiles, leather and rubber goods industries. Category B includes tobacco, arrack, liquor, beer, and base metals. Air conditioners and deep freezers are in category C. Most of the items earmarked for price control will be in the A category. There is no restriction on the allocation of foreign exchange for the manufacture of export goods.

Industries has indicated that more locally manufactured products that are essential to the life of the community would be brought under price control. Unnecessary and extravagant expenditure on factory and administrative overheads, publicity, advertising, distribution, and marketing will be progressively eliminated. To ensure that no shortages occur in the production of essential consumer goods, priority will be given in the allocation of resources to achieve planned production targets, and steps will be taken to ensure that such targets are realized. Manufacturers will be required to deliver a fixed percentage of their output to state trading organizations in order to ensure equal distribution. The government has taken over the wholesale distribution of synthetic textiles so that the profits made on the sale of synthetics could be used to subsidize cotton textiles. The policy is to reduce progressively the volume of imports of cotton textiles and increasingly include local materials, particularly handloom products in the textiles ration.*

In December, the Business Undertakings (Acquisition) Bill to take over private business firms was passed. The original proposal was to restrict the provisions of this bill to all business concerns employing more than 100 persons. To prevent the fragmentation of business, the bill was amended to apply to all business. The bill provides for the government to take over bona fide liabilities with the business, and the Prime Minister has the power to appoint a committee of three persons to hear appeals against vesting orders.

---

*Textiles are available on and off the ration. The present ration is eight yards per person per year. Textiles on ration are available at a lower price. Textiles outside the ration are available freely but at higher prices. The most popular printed materials are distributed through the ration.

EMPLOYMENT

In the budget speech, the Finance Minister stressed that the most urgent problem was unemployment. He stated that "along with the problem of the high cost of living, unemployment demanded very urgent solutions to fulfill the aspiration of young men and women for whom life will lose all meaning unless they can find a useful place in our society."[2] The Prime Minister pointed out that the present statistics on unemployment were unsatisfactory and that detailed data should be made available before a satisfactory solution could be found. For this purpose, the government would set up an information bureau in each electorate to collect data on unemployed persons and their family circumstances. This task would be undertaken along with the implementation of a short-term program designed to relieve immediate pressure on unemployment.

The most recent estimates of unemployment show that about 480,000 to 500,000 persons, or about 12 per cent of the labor force, is unemployed.[3] If underemployment is also taken into consideration, the estimate goes up to 700,000. The present employment plan is intended to double the existing rate of new job placements from 100,000 to 200,000 per year by creating 100,000 additional jobs each year for different categories of unemployed including graduates as well as unskilled persons seeking employment.* The total estimated cost of the program over a three-year period is about $77.5 million. In the first year, a sum of $33.8 million is likely to be spent. Of the total allocation, $25.3 million has been earmarked for employment programs in agriculture and industry while $8.5 million is to be used in economic and social overheads programs. The

---

*The proposal is to create a pool of about 5000 graduates who could be entrusted with work in the public or private sector after a one-year period of training.

bulk of the expenditure would be on activities that would yield direct economic benefits with relatively limited amounts going to employment creation in cultural and recreational activities.

A part of the employment plan seeks to revitalize the rural economy, set up the necessary institutions, and initiate programs that will expand the resource base in the village, provide for better use of existing resources, and generate new employment. The complex of new institutions that will carry out this program will consist of a new government administrative center for the local authority area, a local development council drawn from personnel in the elected institutions in the village, a rural bank, probably attached to the multi-purpose cooperative, a cultivation committee, a cultural center, and a productivity and management extension center. The second part of the program consists of projects that would have to be organized and administered at the national level to cover apprenticeship schemes, development projects in selected crops, in construction, fisheries, and other fields. For the implementation of these projects, a number of organizations that will operate as development enterprises, each being regarded as a specific project with a given employment objective, will be set up.

There is some hope that foreign aid would be available to finance a part of the program. Assistance, under the World Food Program and also under bilateral agreements, notably from the People's Republic of China, is expected. Under the proposed program, the capital cost of each job would be $330 whereas in recent years the capital cost of creating a new job has been in the region of $2,500, while costs in industry have been very much higher. In the present program, the cost per job has been kept low by avoiding capital intensive activities and expanding existing investment and infrastructure. An example in this category is the intercropping of existing coconut lands.

With a view to drawing up a long-term employment

program, the government has invited an International Labour Organization team to prepare a report. The team is expected to commence work in Ceylon in early 1971. Ceylon is one of the first countries to be selected in the Asian region for a study of this kind. Previously, the ILO had undertaken a similar study in Colombia, and in view of the significance attached to the report on Colombia, the proposals that the team would make are likely to result in a fundamental breakthrough to solve the long-term unemployment problem.

FOREIGN TRADE AND THE BALANCE OF PAYMENTS

The immediate change effected in balance of payments policy by the new administration was the modification of the import program under the Foreign Exchange Entitlement Certificate scheme through the discontinuance of a large volume of imports on Open General License.* This was necessary to check the heavy drain on foreign exchange in the preceding two-year period when a wide variety of essential and nonessential imports were allowed to come in freely.**

---

*The Finance Minister in the budget speech commented on the FEEC system as follows: "There can be no gainsaying that the FEEC system can benefit to some extent in the sphere of exports. The position is quite different when FEECs are applied to imports. They must necessarily increase prices of all commodities to which FEECs apply. In an economy such as ours it is not possible to compartmentalize the effect of rise in prices. There is a tendency for price rises to permeate throughout the economy."

**Liberalization of imports was one of several conditions on which the IMF agreed to give standby credits in 1968 and 1969. A large amount of nonessential items was allowed to be imported; freely these included old woollen clothes, trinkets, and fancy oil lamps.

Furthermore, in anticipation that foreign aid would be considerably reduced in the immediate future, the import program had to be pruned so that outlays would not exceed expected receipts.

The new Ministry of Foreign and Internal Trade has been entrusted with matters relating to foreign trade. Several important government departments and corporations, particularly the Food Commissioner's Department, the Commerce Department, and the Cooperative Wholesale Establishment, are under this ministry. The policy of the Ministry has been to take over progressively the importation of items of foodstuffs and other consumer goods that have been in private hands and have not been hitherto carried out in a satisfactory manner.* As a first step, the ministry, through the cooperative Wholesale Establishment, has taken over from the private trade the import of Bombay onions and chillies. The cooperative Wholesale Establishment also took over the import of beedi leaves from India, which has cost about $1 million annually.

Economies are expected in the expenditure of foreign exchange by state trading. A bill providing for a State Trading Corporation has been passed.**

---

*This does not mean that private business and industry has no place. The government has stated that the public and the private enterprise would be partners in development. This implies that certain fields would be reserved for private business and industry, or a system of proportionate sharing will be worked out.

**The State Trading Corporation has been given wide powers. It could take over the internal retail or wholesale trade of any item, import any items, or be the sole exporter of any product. It would also have the power to take over the marketing of any product now made by the government, by any corporation, or private manufacturer. The Minister for Foreign and Internal Trade stated that the object of the bill

The State Trading Corporation is expected to progressively take over the importation of essential consumer goods from the private sector. In 1971, most of the food items will be handled by the state while the export trade would continue to be primarily in the hands of the private sector.

The government also proposes to establish a Gem Corporation. The proposed corporation will come under the Ministry of Finance, and all aspects of the gem industry are expected to be covered by it. Mining rights will be given to the unemployed, and training facilities for cutting, testing, and valuing gems will be provided. The government will buy directly from miners rather than from intermediaries and will be the sole exporter of gems. At present, gem exports are given an incentive in the form of licenses up to 25 per cent of the export earnings to import gems and equipment necessary for the industry and they are exportable free of duty, but the use of these facilities have been negligible. The significance of a state export trade in gems arises from its importance as a very large source of foreign exchange. Most of the gems mined today are not legally exported but smuggled out of the country. Losses in foreign exchange have been estimated at a minimum of $16.8 million, going up to $66.8 million. Even if a conservative estimate is made, the loss is about $25.3 million annually; the budget speech for 1970-71 indicated that the loss of foreign exchange was over $16.8 million. If the proposed Gem Corporation is able to control effectively the export market, it is likely to result in an substantial change in the current balance of payments situations.*

"is to revolutionize the country's trading structure, eliminate trade malpractices, and to save foreign exchange".

*Legislation has been passed to compel Ceylonese who hold movable or immovable property outside Ceylon in contravention of exchange control laws to declare such assets to the Controller of Exchange. The

FOREIGN AID

It will be seen that foreign aid figured prominently in the economic policies of the previous government. It is yet too early to comment on the prospects of foreign aid in the immediate future. It is anticipated that the aid consortium would meet again in April, 1971, to discuss the program for Ceylon, and a World Bank team has prepared a report on Ceylon for this purpose. In the meantime, some aid offers have been forthcoming. For instance, Canada, the United Kingdom, and Australia have signed new agreements, while offers have been received for commodity aid from Germany, Japan, and France. The U.S. government has also indicated that aid would be forthcoming under PL 480. On the other hand, aid prospects from the Eastern bloc countries have increased significantly. Aid is expected to increase from China, U.S.S.R., East Germany, Yugoslavia, Hungary, and North Korea.

All negotiations for aid and suppliers' credits are conducted by the External Resources Division of the Ministry of Planning and Employment. Ministries have been instructed that ceilings placed in the foreign exchange budget on imports and invisible payments should be complied with and that no commitments should be made without covering exchange allocations. Where specific credit terms have been stipulated, at the time when exchange is released no alternative terms should be negotiated without the prior approval of the Ministry of Planning and

---

object of this Foreign Exchange Amnesty bill is to compel repatriation of foreign assets held abroad by Ceylonese. The Finance Minister has also indicated that the Exchange Control Act would be amended to cover, *inter alia*, the over-invoicing of imports, under-invoicing of exports, the control of assets held by Ceylonese abroad, the control of tourist business, and the possession and acceptance of foreign currency by residents of Ceylon.

Employment. New bilateral trade agreements should be negotiated only in consultation with the Ministry of Planning.

The government has discouraged agreements for suppliers' credits with maturities of less than three-to-five years and, as far as possible, credits at longer terms have been negotiated. On the other hand, trade credits of at least six month's duration for imports exceeding $8,350 are still in effect; because of the shortage of foreign exchange, the government has asked industrialists to procure raw materials on deferred payments. In practice, industrialists have encountered difficulty in obtaining credits, and up to about November, 1970, only $8.4 million had been licensed by the Ministry of Industries under these arrangements.

The most important issue is servicing the outstanding foreign debt. Debt service payments now exceed $50 million per year and have impaired import capacity considerably. Foreign exchange that would have been available for imports for development have to be diverted to repay outstanding debt. The immediate cause for this has been the tendency in the last five years for credits to be negotiated with very short maturities of less than three years. The cumulative impact of this has been a bunching of repayments in the period 1970 to 1972, imposing a severe strain on the economy.

In the preceding five years, the International Monetary Fund has provided assistance under four standby arrangements. Each line of credit has been conditional on Ceylon following a stabilization program approved by the Fund. In 1968, for instance, Ceylon agreed to allow a considerable volume of imports at a devalued rate (the FEEC scheme) and to liberalize imports by placing a large number of items on Open General License. In addition, a ceiling on commercial bank credit and net domestic assets of the Central Bank was introduced. The position taken by the IMF throughout has been that Ceylon should adopt a more realistic exchange rate policy. Accordingly, the FEEC rate, which was 44 per cent in 1968, was increased to 55 per cent in 1969. Again in 1970, the Fund has argued that more imports should be covered by an enhanced rate on Foreign Exchange Entitlement Certificates. This is not acceptable, and the Finance Minister has announced that he will not agree to a further devaluation of the Ceylon rupee. The Minister stated, "The IMF is firmly of opinion that the present imbalance of payments can only be set right by a further devaluation. The Government has not accepted this proposition. We are still in the process of negotiations, and I hope to convince the IMF that a further devaluation is not the solution to our problem".[4]

NOTES

1. "Industrial Policy", a paper released by the Ministry of Industries and Scientific Affairs, December, 1970.

2. Budget Speech, 1970-71, Ministry of Finance, Colombo.

3. These are estimates made very recently by the Ministry of Planning and Employment and differ somewhat from the figures in Chapter 7.

4. The Finance Minister in the Budget Speech, 1970-71.

SELECTED BIBLIOGRAPHY

BOOKS

Corea, Gumani. Ceylon in Asian Economic Development. London: Weidenfeld and Nicolson, 1965.

Das Gupta, B.B. A Short Economic Survey of Ceylon. Colombo: Associated Newspapers of Ceylon, Ltd., 1949.

Farmer, B.H. Pioneer Peasant Colonization in Ceylon: A Study in Asian Agrarian Problems. London: Royal Institute of International Affairs, 1957.

Forrest, D.M. A Hundred Years of Ceylon Tea, 1867-1967. London: Chatto and Windus, 1967.

Gunasekera H.A. de S. From Dependent Currency to Central Banking in Ceylon: An Analysis of Monetary Experience 1825-1957. London: G. Bell and Sons, Ltd., 1962.

Gunawardena, Elaine. External Trade and the Economic Structure of Ceylon 1900-1955. Colombo: Central Bank of Ceylon, 1965.

Jennings, Ivor. The Economy of Ceylon. 2nd ed. London: Oxford University Press, 1951.

Karunatilake, H.N.S. Banking & Financial Institutions in Ceylon. Colombo: Central Bank of Ceylon, 1968.

Obeysekera, G. Land Tenure in Ceylon. London: Cambridge University Press, 1967.

Oliver, Henry, M. Economic Opinion and Policy in Ceylon. Durham, North Carolina: Duke University Press, 1957.

Ramachandran, N. Foreign Plantation Investment in

Ceylon, 1889-1958. Colombo: Central Bank of Ceylon, 1963.

Rasaputram, Wamasena. Influence of Foreign Trade on the Level and Growth of National Income of Ceylon, 1926-57. Colombo: Central Bank of Ceylon, 1964.

Richards, Peter and Stoutjesdijk, E. Agriculture in Ceylon Until 1975. Paris: O.E.C.D., Development Centre, 1970.

Smith, Howard Frank. "An Analysis of Ceylon's Ten Year Plan of Economic Development." Ann Arbor, Michigan: University Microfilms Inc., 1963.

Snodgrass, Donald. Ceylon: An Export Economy in Transition. Homewood, Ill.: Richard D. Irwin, Inc., 1966.

Tilakaratna, W.M. Agricultural Credit in a Developing Economy--Ceylon. Colombo: Central Bank of Ceylon, 1963.

Wriggins, W. Howard. Ceylon, Dilemmas of a New Nation. Princeton, New Jersey: Princeton University Press, 1960.

OFFICIAL PUBLICATIONS

Central Bank of Ceylon. Annual Reports. Colombo, 1950-69.

________. Consumer Finance Survey Reports. Colombo, 1953, 1963.

________. Survey of Cost of Production of Paddy. Colombo, 1969.

________. Survey of Private Investment. Colombo, 1970.

Colombo Plan. A Canada-Ceylon Colombo Plan Project. Colombo: Ceylon Government Press, 1960.

________. A Report on a Reconnaissance Survey of

the Resources of the Walawe Ganga Basin. Colombo: Ceylon Government Press, 1965.

________. Seminar on Manpower Assessment and Educational Planning, July, 1966. Summary of Proceedings. Colombo: Colombo Plan Bureau, 1966.

Ceylon, Department of Census and Statistics. Census Reports 1946, 1951, 1953, 1957.

________. Report of the Committee on National Income Estimates. Colombo, 1959.

Ceylon, Department of National Planning. The Budget and Economic Development. Colombo: Ministry of Finance, 1961.

________. The Development Program, 1964-65. Colombo: Ministry of Finance, 1964.

________. Draft Short-Term Implementation Program. Colombo: Ministry of Finance, 1962.

Ceylon, Department of Information. Budget Speeches 1947/48 to 1969/1970.

________. A Six-Year Plan for Ceylon. Colombo, 1950.

Industrial Development Board. Research and Industry. Colombo, 1970

International Bank for Reconstruction and Development. Economic Development of Ceylon. Parts I and II. Colombo: Ceylon Government Press, 1952.

________. Draft Report of the Agricultural Project Identification Mission to Ceylon. Colombo: Ministry of Planning and Economic Affairs, 1967.

________. Draft Report of the Fisheries Project Preparation Mission to Ceylon. Colombo: Ministry of Planning and Economic Affairs, 1967.

________. The Foreign Exchange Problem of Ceylon. Colombo: Ministry of Planning and Ecomonic Affairs, 1965.

________. Note on Recent Developments and the Exchange and Growth Outlook 1967-71 of Ceylon. Colombo: Ministry of Planning and Economic Affairs, 1967.

________. Recommendations on Economic Planning in Ceylon (Albert Waterston). Colombo: Ministry of Planning and Economic Affairs, 1966.

________. Report of the Bank Transportation Mission. Colombo: Ministry of Planning and Economic Affairs, 1966.

________. Report of the Irrigation Program Review. Colombo: Ministry of Planning and Economic Affairs, 1968.

________. Review of the Economic Situation and Foreign Exchange Problems of Ceylon. Colombo: Ministry of Planning and Economic Affairs, 1968.

________. Report of the Planning Committee on Education, Health, Housing, and Manpower. Colombo: Ministry of Planning and Economic Affairs, 1966.

________. Report on a Preliminary Reconnaissance Survey of Education in Ceylon. Colombo: Ministry of Planning and Economic Affairs, 1967.

________. Report on the Needs of the Power Supply Industry of Ceylon as of October 1, 1965 (G.E. Wyatt). Colombo: Ministry of Planning and Economic Affairs, 1966.

________. Report on the Prospects for Tourism Development in Ceylon. Colombo: Ministry of Planning and Economic Affairs, 1968.

Ministry of Agriculture and Food. Agricultural Plan: First Report of the Ministry of Planning Committee. 1958.

________. Implementation Program and Trends. Issues for 1967-70.

Ministry of Land, Irrigation, and Power. Plan of Development, 1966-1970. Colombo, 1966.

________. Implementation Program and Targets. Issues for 1967-68, 1968-69.

Ministry of Planning and Economic Affairs. Agricultural Development Proposals, 1966-70. Colombo, 1966.

________. The Development Program, 1966-67. Colombo, 1966.

________. Economic Development, 1966-68: Review and Trends. Colombo, 1967.

________. Government Policy on Private Foreign Investment. Colombo, 1966.

________. Foreign Aid. Issues for 1966-69.

________. Foreign Exchange Budget. Issues for 1966-69.

SESSIONAL PAPERS

Government of Ceylon. Report on Industrial Development and Policy. No. 15, 1946.

________. Report on the Rubber Industry, (E. W. Whitelaw and S.F.H. Perera). No. 18, 1947.

________. New State-Owned Factories. No. 23, 1947.

________. Report on the Development of Cattle Farms. No. 11, 1949.

________. Report of the Coconut Commission. No. 12, 1949.

________. Report on the Establishment of a Central Bank for Ceylon. No. 14, 1949.

________. Agricultural Wages and Earnings of Primary Producers in Ceylon. No. 2, 1950.

________. Report of the Director of Census and

Statistics on the Middle-Class Family Budget Inquiry. No. 16, 1950.

________. Report on the Ceylon Fishing Industry. No. 6, 1951.

________. Economic Survey of Rural Ceylon, Preliminary Report of Census and Statistics Department, 1950. No. 11, 1951.

________. Inland Fisheries of Ceylon. Report by W. H. Schuster, Chairman, Committee of Fish Culture, Indo-Pacific Fisheries Council. No. 24, 1951.

________. Report on the Re-organization of the Tobacco Industry in Ceylon. No. 17, 1952.

________. Report of the Committee on Crown Lands Utilization. No. 3, 1953.

________. Consumers (New) Price Index. No. 6, 1953.

________. Report of the Commission on Government Commercial Undertakings. No. 19, 1953.

________. Agricultural Production Estimation, Development of Sample Surveys. Report by R. S. Koshal. No. 19, 1954.

________. Economic Survey of Rural Ceylon 1950-51, Final Report. No. 9, 1954.

________. Rice Production in Ceylon. Report of Joint U.K. and Australian Mission, 1954. No. 2, 1955.

________. Taxation Commission Report. No. 17, 1955.

________. Report on the Establishment of Rice Research Organization in Ceylon. No. 19, 1955.

________. Fiber Industries in Ceylon. Report by R. H. Kirby. No. 13, 1956.

________. *Nationalization of Omnibus Transport in Ceylon*. No. 13, 1956.

________. *Land Surveys, Report of Committee*. No. 18, 1956.

________. *Report on Paddy and Soil Problem in Ceylon*. No. 19, 1956.

________. *Crop (Paddy) Insurance*. Report by Dr. P. K. Ray. No. 14, 1957.

________. *Electricity Supply Industry, Report of Inquiry*. No. 17, 1957.

________. *Report to the Government of Ceylon on a Pilot Crop (Paddy) Insurance Scheme*, (Dr. P. K. Ray). No. 1, Vol. I, 1959.

________. *Report for a Comprehensive Reform of Direct Taxation*, (Nicholas Kaldor), No. 4, 1960.

________. *Report of the National Wage Policy Commission*. No. 8, 1961.

________. *Report of the Committee on Agriculture Farms*. No. 14, 1964.

________. *Report of the People's Bank Commission*. No. 7, 1966.

________. *Report of the Committee on Power Requirements for Industries*. No. 23, 1966.

________. *Report of the Committee on Power Cost and Power Development in Ceylon*. No. 20, 1967.

________. *Report of the Commission on Profit Sharing*. No. 22, 1967.

________. *Report of the Taxation Inquiry Commission*. No. 10, 1968.

________. *Report of the Land Utilization Committee*. No. 11, 1968.

________. *Power Cost and Power Development in Ceylon*. No. 12, 1968.

________. *Report of the Bank of Ceylon Commission*. No. 27, 1968.

________. *Report of the Tea Commission*. No. 28, 1968.

________. *Report of the Gal Oya Project Evaluation Committee*. No. 1, 1970.

________. *Report of the Royal Commission on the* Cooperative Movement. No. 2, 1970.

ABOUT THE AUTHOR

Neville Sepala Karunatilake is the Director of Economic Research at the Central Bank of Ceylon. He is also Visiting Lecturer in Economics at two Ceylonese universities.

Mr. Karunatilake has written on a wide range of subjects on the Ceylon economy. His more important publications include The Variable Reserve Ratio as an Instrument of Central Bank Policy and Banking and Financial Institutions in Ceylon. He has also contributed to two symposiums: "Economic Interdependence in South East Asia," edited by Theodore Morgan and Nyle Spoelstra, and "Central Banking in South and East Asia," edited by Gethyn Davies.

Mr. Karunatilake has higher degrees from the London School of Economics and Political Science and from Harvard University. He was a Research Fellow in Economics at Harvard University and was awarded scholarships to study abroad under the Colombo Plan and the Fulbright program.